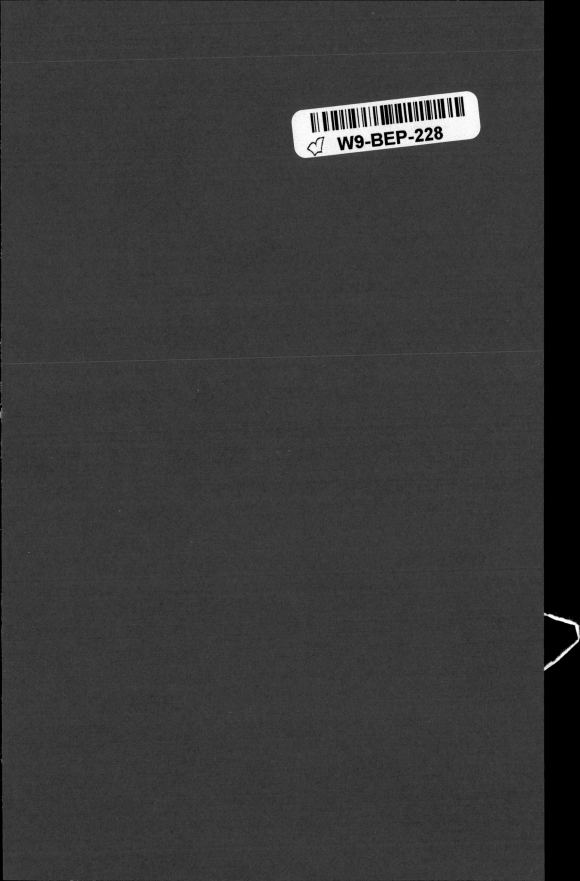

W9-BEP-228

LOVE, MADNESS, AND SCANDAL

JOHANNA LUTHMAN

LOVE, MADNESS, AND SCANDAL

the life of frances coke villiers,
viscountess purbeck

OXFORD
UNIVERSITY PRESS

OXFORD
UNIVERSITY PRESS

Great Clarendon Street, Oxford, OX2 6DP,
United Kingdom

Oxford University Press is a department of the University of Oxford.
It furthers the University's objective of excellence in research, scholarship,
and education by publishing worldwide. Oxford is a registered trade mark of
Oxford University Press in the UK and in certain other countries

First Edition published in 2017

Impression: 1

Published in the United States of America by Oxford University Press
198 Madison Avenue, New York, NY 10016, United States of America

British Library Cataloguing in Publication Data
Data available

Library of Congress Control Number: 2016948391

ISBN 978–0–19–875465–7

Printed in Great Britain by
Clays Ltd, St Ives plc

To Marko, with love

ACKNOWLEDGEMENTS

Throughout the several years that I have worked on this project, I have received invaluable assistance from many quarters. It is a great pleasure to acknowledge that help here. My colleagues at the University of North Georgia have supported me in numerous ways. Receiving the UNG Presidential Summer Scholar Award allowed me extra time to devote to research and writing. Many thanks are due to Jeff Pardue, chair of the UNG History, Anthropology and Philosophy Department, for ensuring that I received a very timely course-release, and for providing the funds to cover the cost of the permissions to reproduce the portraits that appear in the book. My department colleagues in the Works in Progress writing group commented on drafts of two chapters, which helped me restructure and fine-tune the organization of both the chapters and the book for the better. Thanks also to Amye Sokadjo for assistance with a French translation. Furthermore, the group of historians, and honorary historians, at the El Sombrero Thursday 'meetings' is the best support-group any academic can have.

I also want to thank the anonymous readers of two manuscript chapters, who made very useful and astute suggestions for clarifications and improvements. Audience members at conferences (Georgia Association of Historians, Southern Conference of British Studies, and Renaissance Society of America) where I have presented parts of the work have also given me good feedback, helping me to further fine-tune my interpretations. Big thanks are due to Alok Nath, who helped me create the two maps, cheerfully, expertly, and with short notice. The editing team at Oxford has been immensely helpful in sorting out my prose and catching mistakes. I especially want to thank Luciana O'Flaherty and Joanna North. All errors that remain are my own, of course.

Finally, I want to acknowledge my family (the members of the extensive Luthman clan are too numerous to name individually here) for providing unending moral support and cheers. My husband, Marko Maunula, deserves special thanks. An accomplished historian, he always believes in my abilities, even when I doubt myself. He is the one who has put up with my obsessing about sections slow to come together, elusive sources, and difficult interpretations, and he has done so without complaining. (Much.) Most significantly, he has read the entire manuscript multiple times in all its various stages of completion, making invaluable suggestions for improvements of my prose and the clarity of the organization. He has gone above and beyond what anyone could reasonably expect of a spouse, reading and editing my text even while in his sickbed. He is my true partner in every way and therefore I dedicate the book to him.

CONTENTS

LIST OF ILLUSTRATIONS

LIST OF ABBREVIATIONS

APC	*Acts of the Privy Council*
C	Chancery
CJ	*Journal of the House of Commons*
CPCC	*Calendar for Proceedings of the Committee of Compounding*
CSP	*Calendar of State Papers*
HMC	Historical Manuscript Commission
LJ	*Journal of the House of Lords*
LMA	London Metropolitan Archives
ODNB	*Oxford Dictionary of National Biography* (2004)
PROB	Probate
SP	State Papers

NOTE ON DATES AND SPELLING

The book refers to sources based on the New Style dating, with the year beginning on 1 January. The Old Style dating, in use in England until 1752, began the New Year on 25 March (Lady Day).

Spelling and grammar had not yet been standardized in the early seventeenth century. When quoting from original sources, I have retained the original spelling in most cases. When the original source lacked punctuation, or when the spelling made the meaning unclear, I have modernized the text. I have noted any modifications I have made.

LIST OF PERSONS

Frances Coke Villiers, Viscountess Purbeck (1602–1645). The subject of this biography. She was born Frances Coke, and received the last name Villiers when she married Sir John Villiers in 1617. King James created John Viscount Purbeck in 1619, making Frances Viscountess Purbeck.

Sir John Villiers, Viscount Purbeck (1591?–1658). Frances's husband and elder brother of George Villiers, the Earl/Marquis/Duke of Buckingham. He received a position in Prince Charles's household, but suffered from bouts of mental illness.

Sir Robert Howard (c.1598–1653). Frances's lover. He was the fifth son of Thomas Howard, Earl of Suffolk, and served as a Member of Parliament in the Commons in the 1620s and 1640s. I refer to him as 'Howard' throughout the book, in order to distinguish from his son, Robert.

Robert Wright/Howard/Villiers/Danvers (1624–1674). Frances and Robert Howard's son. In order to conceal his parentage, he was first called Robert Wright. Later on, he used the name Howard, and then Villiers. After his marriage in 1648, he took his wife's last name, Danvers.

Elizabeth Cecil, Lady Hatton (1578–1646). Frances's mother. She was married first to Sir William Hatton and would keep that name and title throughout the rest of her life, even after her marriage to Frances's father, Sir Edward Coke.

Sir Edward Coke (1552–1634). Frances's father, married to Lady Hatton. A prominent lawyer and justice, served as the Chief Justice of the King's Bench and a member of the King's Privy Council, although he often angered both King James and King Charles by insisting that their royal powers were limited.

Sir George Villiers, Earl/Marquis/Duke of Buckingham (1592–1628). King James's great favourite from around 1616, and, when James died in 1625, King Charles's most trusted friend and adviser until Buckingham's death. Younger brother to John Villiers, and thus Frances's brother-in-law. He married Katherine Manners in 1620. King James gave George more and more exalted titles, until finally, he became a duke. I refer to him as Buckingham throughout most of the text.

Mary Beaumont Villiers Rayner Compton, Lady Compton and Countess of Buckingham (*c.*1570–1632). George and John Villiers's mother. She married three times. Her children George, John, Christopher, and Susan Villiers were born during her first marriage to Sir George Villiers. Between the years 1606 and 1618, she was known as Lady Compton. King James created her Countess of Buckingham in 1618, mostly to please his favourite George, Mary's son.

King James I of England (1566–1625). King of Scotland from 1567, and King of England and Scotland from 1603 until 1625. Married Anna of Denmark, and had children with her, although he preferred male company to female, and had several male favourites. Buckingham was the last and the most powerful of all of James's favourites.

King Charles I of England (1600–1649). King James's son. King of England and Scotland from 1625–1649. Buckingham remained a close adviser to Charles until his assassination in 1628. Charles was king during the English Civil Wars of the 1640s, and he was tried and executed for treason by Parliament in 1649.

William Laud, Archbishop of Canterbury (1573–1645). He first became a bishop in 1621 (St David's), but after he became a close confidant to the Duke of Buckingham in 1625, he quickly rose in positions, becoming Bishop of Bath and Wells in 1626, Bishop of London in 1628, and finally Bishop of Canterbury in 1633. He was instrumental in the prosecution of Frances and Howard for adultery.

PROLOGUE

In early June of 1645, the town of Oxford was under siege. The Parliamentarian New Model Army had arrived three weeks prior, rapidly blockading all entrances and exits and trapping the nervous inhabitants inside. Normally a centre for learning, Oxford had been transformed into royal headquarters during the English Civil Wars, and King Charles's courtiers and supporters crowded into the small town until it was bursting at the seams. Lords and ladies, used to the luxury of palaces and large staffs of servants to tend to their every need, now had to suffer meagre and plain dishes in cramped quarters. The town streets soon overflowed with trash and filth. By now used to hearing the constant stream of news of other towns and areas falling to Parliamentarian forces, their citizens sometimes robbed, beaten, and killed, the inhabitants of Oxford worried that they would be next. News of recent royalist atrocities during the taking of the city of Leicester might ignite a desire for revenge among the Parliamentarian troops just outside the gates. At the time, the town was only protected by a small garrison, making matters even more precarious: the king and the majority of his forces were campaigning elsewhere.

The overcrowded and unsanitary conditions in Oxford made its population vulnerable to infectious diseases. A severe plague epidemic had ravaged the town the previous summer. Outbreaks of smallpox, typhus, and other diseases also kept the gravediggers busy. Before the siege, the sick had sometimes been forced into quarantine in the outskirts of the city, but with an enemy army guarding the gates, that method was not available. One of the many who fell ill during this siege was a noblewoman who had arrived in the city a few months earlier. Her name was Frances Coke Villiers, the Viscountess Purbeck. On 4 June, just one day before General Thomas Fairfax received orders to lift the siege of Oxford and join other Parliamentarian troops poised to engage the king's forces to the north, Frances died.[1]

If Frances had the mental energy for contemplation as she lay shivering and sweating during her final disease, she might have looked back on a life filled with countless struggles. As an adolescent and young woman, she had been forced to bow to the authority of her parents, in-laws, and sovereign. She grew into a very strong-willed person, increasingly insistent on being treated according to her noble status. As an adult, her head would tilt for no person, but her own choices also created increasingly difficult challenges. Those who loved and admired her believed she was a beautiful, brave, witty, and romantic, albeit tragic, heroine. Those who disliked her thought she was an annoyingly stubborn, haughty, greedy, and scandalous woman. Either way, most people found her very difficult to ignore.

Young Frances's marriage to Sir John Villiers in 1617 significantly changed the trajectory of her life. Frances's parents, Sir Edward Coke and Elizabeth Cecil (known as Lady Hatton) clashed over the issue of her marriage, sending huge waves and ripples through the courtly society of King James I. Frances, like so many other daughters of the seventeenth-century elite, did not choose her own husband, but conceded that her parents would bestow her in marriage. Her marriage to John Villiers, her father's candidate, initially afforded her many privileges, including membership in the highly favoured and influential Villiers family with even closer connections with the royal court.

Frances's in-laws, the Villiers family, owed their power to the fact that John's younger brother, George Villiers, was King James's beloved, the last and greatest of his royal favourites. Like his predecessor Queen Elizabeth, King James I (ruled 1603–25) enjoyed having handsome, flattering men close at hand, who could provide company, adoration, and entertainment. While Elizabeth had been sparing in gifts, wealth, and positions to her favourites, James seemingly could not lavish enough rewards on those he loved. They rose to great positions of political power, collected a variety of influential offices, became enormously wealthy, and also made influential and rich marriages. This was true of George Villiers, who eventually became Duke of Buckingham, arguably the most powerful man in England next to the king. When Frances came of age, Buckingham reigned supreme in the heart of the king, and all attempts to lessen James's attachment to him had failed.

Despite its apparent benefits, Frances's marriage turned out to be a disaster. Frances's own responses to her marital difficulties in turn created endless problems in her life. First, her husband succumbed to an intermittent and debilitating mental illness. Separated from him, Frances then struggled with her resistant in-laws to receive financial support. At this juncture, she took a lover, became pregnant, and gave birth to an illegitimate son. Her actions turned her in-laws even more firmly against her, and their great powers now became a burden instead of a boon, as they had both the political and economic capital to pursue her relentlessly. Frances had to fight the consequences of her illicit love for the rest of her life. As the years passed, she became even more tenacious than her pursuers, and no matter how much they fought her, she never gave up.

The historical Frances has remained rather elusive. The biographer's main challenge is her silence. She was neither a political person, nor a literary one, and thus no one thought it important to preserve most of the papers an upper-class life necessarily produced. Only a precious few of her letters and petitions have survived, giving us a glimpse of Frances's own interpretations of her life and actions. Instead, we learn about her mostly because of others' reactions to her deeds, movements, and decisions. Because her parents, husband, and in-laws were influential people at court, people who cared about court politics and wanted to keep abreast of the news often wrote about Frances's contentious marriage and the scandals that followed when she had an affair. For example, the letters courtiers, politicians, and other influential friends wrote to Sir Dudley Carleton (1573–1632), English ambassador in The Hague and personal friend of Frances's mother, make up an invaluable source for the earlier parts of Frances's life. Other sources include administrative and legal records, like those of the High Commission court, both houses of Parliament, Acts of the Privy Council, and the extensive State Papers, a rich collection of letters, petitions, royal orders, warrants, and investigations. Frances's life is like a puzzle, where many pieces unfortunately are irretrievably lost. Nevertheless, the picture that emerges of this seventeenth-century woman from the pieces that we do have is both intriguing and compelling, and more than worth the telling.

CHAPTER 1

CONTENTIOUS ORIGINS

In late August 1598, a magnificent funeral procession slowly snaked its way through London, from Burghley House in the Strand towards the stately Westminster Abbey. Dressed in fine black mourning clothes ordered especially for the occasion, high officers of state, members of the nobility, and numerous servants and attendants, carefully arranged according to social and political prominence, slowly followed the carriage with the coffin, also draped in reams of black cloth. The body in the coffin belonged to William Cecil, 1st Lord Burghley, Queen Elizabeth's most trusted and longest serving minister. His remains would eventually be interred at his country home in Stamford, but first were to be revered in Westminster, the place where only the most significant people in the realm were buried. On this solemn occasion, the story of Frances Coke Villiers begins: Lord Burghley was Frances's great-grandfather, and although the two never met, his death provided the impetus for her parents' marriage and thus her birth.

During Burghley's funeral procession, the queen's ambitious Attorney General, Edward Coke, approached two of the main mourners, Thomas and Robert Cecil, sons of the dead man. Coke, whose first wife had just died, took the opportunity to ask for the hand in marriage of the recently widowed daughter and niece of the two men: the young, beautiful, and very rich Elizabeth Cecil, Lady Hatton. In the shadow of the coffin, the men came to a preliminary agreement. Just some two months later, Edward Coke and Lady Hatton, Frances's parents, were married. The sad and sombre setting of the early marriage discussions presaged the misery to come. The marriage was not a happy one and the disagreements of Frances's parents created a difficult life for their youngest daughter.[1]

In theory, the marriage between Coke and Lady Hatton was a good political and financial arrangement, but in practice, it was a disaster. Frances's mother and father had incompatible personalities and different expectations regarding the proper roles of wives and husbands. The only trait they had in common was that they were both fighters, headstrong and stubborn, and since they were public figures in the upper echelons of late Elizabethan and Jacobean societies, their battles over money, political influences, and marital matches for their children, were fought very much in public as well, giving fodder for the news writers and gossips of the day.

Frances's mother, Elizabeth Cecil, was born in 1578, the daughter of Dorothy Neville and Thomas Cecil. Thomas Cecil inherited the title Lord Burghley after his father's death, and later King James raised him to become Earl of Exeter. Thomas's brother, Robert Cecil, later Earl of Salisbury, was Queen Elizabeth's Secretary of State and Lord Privy Seal, and he continued his career in high state offices under King James's reign. Thus, Elizabeth was a desirable young bride, since marriage to her would bring inclusion in the powerful and increasingly extensive Cecil network. In the mid-1590s, while Elizabeth was still a teenager, she married the widower Sir William Hatton. Hatton was nephew and sole heir to Sir Christopher Hatton, who had been made wealthy by being Queen Elizabeth's favourite. It was a short marriage, as Hatton died on 12 March 1597. When Elizabeth was left a young widow, she was even more attractive on the marriage market: in addition to her Cecil connections, she was now also rich, having received a sizeable chunk of her dead husband's estate. Among other properties, such as Corfe Castle in Dorset, Lady Hatton also received the stately London residence called Hatton House in Holborn. Hatton House would be Frances's London home for most of her youth, and her escape during times of troubles in her own marriage.[2]

Edward Coke was born to a solid middling Norfolk family in 1552. Coke himself was fond of telling the story of his birth, as he 'came into the world unexpectedly, at the parlor fireside, before his mother could be carried up to her bed'.[3] As the speedy boy grew up, he decided to make his way in the world through the practice of law. He went to Trinity College in Cambridge, and then studied law at the Inns of Court in London. By 1578, he was admitted to the bar. By the time he was thirty, he began looking for a wife. He wanted a woman who could help him further his career ambitions, give him wealth, and children to inherit his legacy. He found the perfect candidate in the eighteen-year-old Norfolk heiress Bridget Paston. The couple married in 1582. Her very large dowry of £30,000 gave him a big push both in his legal career and in his position as an ever more substantial landowner. He continued to purchase land and manors, thus increasing his holdings and the annual income they brought from rents and production. In 1592, he became Queen Elizabeth's Solicitor General, and two years after that, Attorney General. One year after Hatton died leaving Lady Hatton a widow, Edward Coke also found himself without a spouse, as Bridget Paston passed away on 27 June 1598, just short of thirty-four years old. Coke quickly set about finding another wife, opening marriage negotiations with the Cecils at Burghley's funeral only weeks after having buried Bridget.[4]

Both Coke and Lady Hatton had successful and happy first marriages, which they looked back upon with fondness. Lady Hatton was not married for very long, but she remembered her first husband as a loving, kind, and generous man, and that during their marriage she had been a 'happy wife' who 'abounded with temporal felicity'. The couple had no children of their own, but William Hatton had a daughter from a previous marriage, also named Frances. Hatton entrusted his daughter's care to his young wife before he died. Lady Hatton also received the legal wardship of Frances, which was a financial benefit. Wardships could be bought and sold, and gave the holder the right to control the property and person of the ward until he or she was of age. When Lady Hatton reflected on her life in her old age, she wistfully wrote that with the death of 'her first most faithful and dear husband' all her 'transitory happiness expired'.[5]

While Lady Hatton brought only a step-daughter to her new union, in contrast Coke had a large brood from his first marriage. During their fifteen years of marriage, Bridget gave birth to ten children, seven of whom survived to adulthood. Bridget mostly resided at Huntingfield manor in Suffolk, overseeing the running of the country estate, only occasionally making her way to London. She was a successful household manager and a beloved wife and mother. For Coke, and for many of his contemporaries, she was the picture of the ideal wife: she brought lands and money to her husband when they married, she gave him sons to inherit his fortune, daughters to forge new alliances, she cared for home and hearth, and she provided a happy family life for her husband to enjoy when he came from London in between the legal terms. Coke's biographers generally agree that the marriage to Bridget was the happiest time in the lawyer's life. When Bridget died, Coke wrote: 'My most beloved and most excellent wife—who well and happily lived—the true handmaiden of the Lord—fell asleep in the Lord—now lives and reigns in heaven.'[6]

Perhaps Bridget's experience was quite different: she spent most of the marriage either pregnant or recuperating from childbirth, one baby barely out of the womb before another began its development. Women in wealthy families did not usually breastfeed their own children, but instead hired wet-nurses. Since breastfeeding itself can inhibit conception, and people at the time believed that sex with a nursing woman should be avoided or at least limited, poorer women who nursed their own children usually did not get pregnant again as quickly as their richer sisters. Wealthier women also had access to better nutrition, which often added to their fecundity. Having many children was usually considered a divine blessing, and infertility a shame, sorrow, or curse, so Bridget was probably thankful for the plenitude, although the many pregnancies must have worn her down and perhaps aged her prematurely. In the early 1590s, an astrologer Bridget consulted cast doubt on her age (she was only twenty-seven years old). 'It must not be so', he remarked, concluding that she must be older. In January 1598, Bridget gave birth to her last child, a little boy who did not survive. The pregnancy and difficult birth proved to be hard on the mother. Six months later, she was dead.[7]

The fact that Coke remarried so quickly after Bridget's death does not necessarily imply a lack of grief: rapid remarriages, especially for men, were not uncommon. The practicality of having a spouse, and the necessity of forming new alliances, sometimes outweighed personal feelings. Moreover, in letters of condolences, writers often exhorted the bereaved to temper their outpouring of emotions, and quietly accept God's will. First and foremost, Coke was ambitious, and as the attractive Lady Hatton had many suitors, he needed to move fast in order to secure the prize. The son of the Earl of Pembroke and Sir Fulke Greville were already rumoured to be potential grooms for Lady Hatton, but most troubling for Coke was the fact that his long-time rival Francis Bacon had his eyes on her.[8] Bacon was also a lawyer by trade, as well as a courtier, and the rivalry between the two men was fierce. To Bacon's great chagrin, Coke had received the appointment as Attorney General in 1594, even though Bacon had lobbied hard to get it, and a witty observer of Bacon's legal skills had remarked that 'the Bacon may be too hard for the Cook'.[9] The two men were also allied with the two major opposite factions at court. While Coke was tying himself more closely to the Cecils, Bacon's political patron was Robert Devereux, the dapper and overly confident Earl of Essex, Queen Elizabeth's last favourite. When Lady Hatton was widowed, Essex wrote to Burghley on Bacon's behalf, putting his protégé forward and arguing that if he had a marriageable daughter himself, he could not imagine a more worthy bridegroom than Bacon. The Cecils were not immediately convinced by Essex's endorsement. Thus, Bridget's death gave Coke an opportunity to snatch another potential boon from his rival, and also ensure that his links to the Cecils were strengthened. He could only accomplish it if he acted swiftly.[10]

When Coke negotiated his marriage with Lady Hatton, he was forty-seven years old. Lady Hatton was only twenty. Lady Hatton's first husband is often described as a man much older than her, suggesting that she was accustomed to an old husband. In fact, Hatton was only thirteen years older than his bride, which was not unusual. But a twenty-seven-year gap was not as common, and often not recommended. Moralists and advice writers argued that 'May to December' marriages would lead to unhappiness for both parties: the young wife would be more nurse than wife, having to care for her old husband, and would not be as likely to become a mother, whereas the old husband would have to worry about his spouse looking for sexual satisfaction in the arms of a younger, more vigorous lover. For example, when the fifty-something William, Lord Knollys, fell head over heels in love with Mary Fitton, a much younger maid-of-honour, some viewed him as ridiculous and pathetic, especially since Mary clearly preferred the handsome and virile young Earl of Pembroke. (As a result of their illicit affair, Mary became pregnant and bore Pembroke a son, but Pembroke refused to marry her, even after considerable pressure from both Queen Elizabeth and Mary's family.) Knollys comforted his wounded pride and broken heart by marrying the nineteen-year-old Elizabeth Howard in 1605. The young Elizabeth, in turn, later spurned her old husband and took the younger Edward, Lord Vaux, as her lover. Social, political, and economic considerations weighed heavy in the making of marriages, but in an ideal marriage of the period, the couple also developed a mutual affection. When people insisted on making marriages between outwardly incompatible people, the political and economic reasons became even more glaring, since in those cases, they so obviously outweighed the personal happiness of the bride and groom.

We have no evidence of either Lady Hatton or Coke being sexually unfaithful throughout their long thirty-six years of marriage. While Coke was significantly older than Lady Hatton, he was no doddering grey old man in need of a young nurse. He was a healthy forty-seven, still handsome, and took pride in his exterior, as he used to say 'that the outward neatness of our bodies might be a monitor of purity to our souls'. He was a good dresser, preferring dark colours and fine tailoring, which he thought fitted the gravity of his professional persona.[11] In the case of this couple, the differences in personalities had more to do with their incompatibility than the age difference. Coke was a brilliant lawyer and very influential thinker when it came to constitutional and common law, a highly principled man fighting against the royal prerogative, often to his own detriment. But at the same time, his disposition was 'selfish, overbearing, and arrogant' and he was 'early imbued with ambition and a grasping love of riches', according to his biographer John Campbell. He was a hard worker, regularly rising at three in the morning, but did not care for entertainments and the arts. He did not attend plays, he did not like poetry, and he did not care for music.[12] He had a flaring temper and sometimes became violent when he felt he was wronged. As will become evident, Lady Hatton was radically different from her husband. She was a highly sociable person, who wanted to make a career for herself at court. She had the desired qualities of a court lady: she was beautiful, witty, a good conversationalist, and certainly had a flair for the dramatic. She cultivated the friendship of Queen Anna when James came to the throne, participated in masques and other courtly merrymaking, and she shone as a hostess for the other members of the courtly circles. She was keenly aware of her social status and position as a member of the powerful Cecil family, as well as of her wealth, and accordingly she wanted to be treated with respect. When left out in decision-making that impacted her life, this determined woman did not hesitate to make her displeasure clear. Like her husband, she was loath to bow to anyone if she felt herself in the right, and she could be very persuasive when she needed the assistance of others.[13] In her adulthood, Frances would come to share many of her mother's character traits, further complemented by her father's dogged determination.

On 6 November 1598, Coke and Lady Hatton married. It was not a grand wedding, but rather a quiet and brief affair, perhaps reflecting Coke's desire to clinch the deal. The occasion was also highly irregular. Technically, all that was needed for an early modern English marriage to be valid in the eyes of God was that the bride and the groom, both free to marry, stated their consent to marry using the present tense. Once the two said 'I take thee for my wife/husband', or some version thereof, they were married. If they used future tense, they became betrothed, and the betrothal would turn into a marriage if the relationship was consummated, as both the law and custom considered consummation as implied consent. This idea was based on medieval canonical law and teachings. However, marriage by consent alone made for potentially very messy and contested situations, so by the late sixteenth century, the English Church had come up with additional rules to regulate the making of marriages. According to these rules, a wedding ceremony should take place in the morning, between eight o'clock and noon. Morning nuptials would be less likely to be followed by night-time revelry, with too much drinking and dancing. Instead, the Church insisted that the ceremony should be solemn, to fit with the gravity of the occasion. Also, the wedding ceremony should be public, held in a church, or by the church door, as was sometimes the case, and not in a private home. A properly ordained priest should officiate, and take great care that the couple had the banns called three times, or had a licence to dispense with the banns. These last steps ensured that the marriage was not secret, that the bride and groom both were who they said they were, that they were not too closely related, and that neither of them were betrothed or married to anyone else.[14] For reasons not entirely clear, Coke and Lady Hatton broke the rules: they married at night, in the privacy of Hatton House in London, with neither banns read nor licence procured. Lady Hatton's parents were present, as was her elder brother William Cecil and his wife. Sir Anthony Ashley, Clerk of the queen's Privy Council, rounded out the very small group of witnesses. Other writers have suggested that it was Lady Hatton who insisted on the private marriage, either because she thought Coke was so old that she was embarrassed to be seen in church with him, or because Lady Hatton wanted to 'test' Coke, insisting on the private marriage in order to see if he would break the rules for her, that is, bend to her will. In another, much more plausible theory, Coke's nineteenth-century biographer Humphrey Woolrych suggests that it might have been Coke's sense of his own importance, as well as Lady Hatton's high status, which made them think that they could dispense with the rules and go for convenience.[15]

They were not alone, as it was a constant struggle for the Church to enforce the marriage regulations. Around the time of the Coke–Hatton marriage, John Whitgift, the zealous Archbishop of Canterbury, wrote to other bishops about the importance of enforcing the proper forms for marriage. Whitgift had also been Coke's academic mentor at university, so the two knew each other well, which made Whitgift even more disappointed at Coke's flagrant flouting of the rules. In a fit of theological and bureaucratic anger, Whitgift declared that Coke was certainly not above the ecclesiastical law and should be dealt with accordingly. He instigated a suit in the Canterbury church court against Coke, Lady Hatton, the witnesses, as well as Henry Bathwell, the priest who had performed the offending ceremony. The archbishop threatened all with excommunication. Through a proxy, Coke submitted and begged for forgiveness from the court. The archbishop relented and granted them all a dispensation, as long as they admitted that they had acted out of ignorance rather than wilful negligence. So, the great lawyer Coke, who prided himself on his vast knowledge of the law, had to humble himself and admit that he was ignorant of the church laws governing marriage. It was not a great start for the marriage.[16]

Once knowledge of Coke and Lady Hatton's marriage spread, many in London's high society reacted with a mix of indignation and surprise, thinking that Lady Hatton surely could have done better than the cranky and grasping Attorney General. He might serve the queen and he might be comfortably rich, but he was a social upstart without a title or even knighthood. (He was knighted in 1603.) In addition, he already had many sons and daughters to support and settle in life. John Chamberlain, a leisured gentleman living in London with friends at court and steady access to the major news-hub that was St Paul's Cathedral, wrote to his absent friend Sir Dudley Carleton and reported about the marriage. He pointed out that people were amazed that 'after so many large and likely offers she shold decline to a man of his qualitie' and that 'the world will not believe that it was without a misterie'.[17] The 'world', as Chamberlain termed it, suspected that the quick and private marriage was a necessity, in order to cover up the fact that Lady Hatton was already pregnant. In April the following year, an affidavit in the State Papers collection shows an investigation into rumours that Lady Hatton had given birth to a son only ten weeks after the wedding, that 'the child was by one of her servants, who was sent away with a piece of money', and that 'it was no marvel Mr. Attorney wept sitting with the Judges, for he has gone up and down ever since his marriage like a dead man discomforted'. Apparently, the rumours were widespread enough that the seventeenth-century writer John Aubrey later baked them into a clever joke in his short biography on Edward Coke:

> His second wife, Elizabeth, the relickt of Sir William Hatton, was with Child when he maried her: laying his hand on her belly (when he came to bed) and finding a Child to stirre, What, sayd he, Flesh in the Pott. Yea, quoth she, or else I would not have married a Cooke.[18]

The rumours about Lady Hatton's premarital pregnancy were in fact false. The proof arrived almost exactly nine months after the wedding. On 6 August 1599, Lady Hatton gave birth to a daughter, Frances's elder sister Elizabeth. The baby was baptized shortly thereafter and Queen Elizabeth herself was godmother. No doubt the child was named after her, rather than after her mother. The queen sometimes rewarded people who served her well by acting as godmother for their children, so the decision serves as an indicator of Coke's standing. Queen Elizabeth did not attend the christening ceremony herself—she rarely did—but sent the Countess of Oxford as her stand-in, along with a handsome gilt bowl with a cover as a christening gift. The Countess of Oxford, Anne Cecil de Vere, was also Lady Hatton's aunt. Usually, parents selected three godparents—two women and one man—for their girls, so Alice Spencer Stanley, Dowager Countess of Derby, and Thomas Sackville, Lord Buckhurst and the queen's Lord Treasurer, also joined the queen in this role.[19]

Three years later, in late August 1602, Frances made her entrance into the world, without fanfare. Lady Hatton gave birth to her second daughter at Hatton House, and her christening was recorded in St Andrew parish at Holborn as having taken place on 2 September. The clerk of the parish spelled her name 'Francis', but she is further identified with the last name Cook, and the addition 'daughter of Mr Cook the Quenes Maygesties Atorney general' leaves no questions about her identity.[20] Frances's life began in great obscurity: the parish record is the only evidence of her birth. Unlike in the case of her sister Elizabeth, neither her family and relatives, nor the newsmongers or letter-writers, noted her birth or described her baptism, at least no such descriptions survive. Of course, Elizabeth's birth may have been more newsworthy, as it stopped the 'old slander' and rumours about Lady Hatton's need for a hasty marriage. What is more notable, perhaps, is that Frances's father, who had dutifully recorded the birth of every single one of his other eleven children in his papers, including his first daughter with Lady Hatton, did not make note of this, his youngest child. While she was thus quite anonymous in her younger years, the circumstances of her life would ensure that she would become the most famous of all of Coke's children.[21]

After the births of their two little girls, Coke and Lady Hatton would have no other children. Clearly, the couple did not have issues with fertility. Had the two newlyweds liked each other and agreed together, Lady Hatton may have repeated Bridget Paston's experience of a new baby every year or two. That would not be the case. The war between husband and wife began early, and even during periods of temporary truces, the marriage never prospered.

The couple's disagreements centred on control of property and wifely economic maintenance and allowances. In his first marriage to Bridget Paston, Coke had made decisions about the purchase and management of the growing number of properties, bought with the Paston dowry and inheritance, without much interference from his wife. She mostly dealt with the management of the main family home and the care of the children. Coke expected a similar arrangement during his second marriage, but Lady Hatton had other ideas. She felt entitled to some control over the extensive property she had brought into the marriage and she accused Coke of first forcing her to give in to his demands, and then not carrying out agreements and promises made between them. In addition, she argued that he did not give her and their girls enough money for their upkeep and that he made changes in the agreements about the girls' dowries and inheritances to their detriment. English property law was not in Lady Hatton's favour: in theory at least, the husband controlled all the property. Wives could not buy or sell property, or even will it to others, without their husbands' approval. In reality, the legal landscape was much more complex. People created financial agreements, trusts, and a variety of other legal instruments in order to be able to ensure property for wives and daughters.[22] While Coke strictly had the law on his side in many of their disputes, Lady Hatton appealed to principles of equity and fairness. She turned expectations of wifely obedience around by accusing Coke of being a bad husband who abused his power. When Coke complained that his wife was not obedient, respectful, and loving in later petitions to the king, Lady Hatton responded by accusing her husband of being greedy and selfish, and of not properly caring for his wife and their children. 'I presume it will not be thought fit', she argued at one point, that her husband should 'take away all maintenance from her and make her lyve of these poor gatherings that shee in her younger yeares had spared from her pleasures for the good of her children'.[23]

One of the earliest disagreements between the two had to do with Coke refusing to satisfy some as yet unfulfilled legacies to friends and servants from William Hatton's estate. Apparently, these were payments that Hatton had detailed in his will, but which at the time of Coke and Lady Hatton's marriage had not yet been paid out. While Lady Hatton called the legacies 'smale', and estimated them to 'not aboue 7 or 900 l [£700–900]', it was not an insignificant sum. We only have Lady Hatton's version of this particular disagreement, but Coke might have argued that the legacies should come out of the estate inherited by Hatton's nephew, rather than from Lady Hatton's jointure. (A 'jointure' was the widow's share of her husband's estate. The families usually negotiated and decided on the jointure at the same time as they decided on the dowry, although couples could also make jointure agreements after their marriage.) In either case, when Coke refused, Lady Hatton determined not to take her new husband's name, but rather keep Hatton's. If Coke would change his mind and 'bury [her] first husband according to his directions', then she would 'willingly stile [herself] by his name'. Whenever others, including her own father and brother, asked why she refused to take Coke's name as convention required, she told them the same reason for her decision. Coke did not change his mind about the legacies, and neither did she about her name, especially not after their fights grew worse and more complicated. She remained Lady Hatton for the rest of her life, a clear marker of her desire for independence from a husband who displeased her. Others obliged her, always addressing and referring to her as Hatton rather than Coke. Clearly, Lady Hatton's refusal to use his name was something that irked Coke, because he brought it up in one of his official complaints against his wife in 1617, after they had been married for a full nineteen years.[24]

Lady Hatton said that Coke had, from the very beginning of the marriage, made it clear that he was going to take over the control of the Hatton property. According to Lady Hatton, Coke had initially promised that he would leave any property that he purchased after their marriage to Lady Hatton and their children, rather than to the Coke–Paston children. Once married, he had regretted this deal, and he hounded her and threatened her until she gave in and returned the written agreement to him, although she said it was against the advice of her father and brother. After many other vicissitudes, with Lady Hatton accusing Coke of maliciously tricking her out of rents she believed she was due from Hatton properties prior to their marriage, as well as ownership of several manors, and Coke arguing that he had the right to make all the decisions regarding the monies and the properties, Lady Hatton's father and uncle stepped in to mediate. They made Coke promise to give Lady Hatton an annual allowance of £2,000, which she was free to control. This agreement seemed to have ended the fighting about money, since it ceded control of marital property to Coke, and at the same time assured some financial independence for his wife. However, the peace would prove temporary. The couple's disagreements flared up again during the negotiations about Frances's marriage in 1616 and 1617, causing

Coke to stop his annual payments, and Lady Hatton to struggle mightily against him yet again to regain some semblance of financial control.

The couple's arguments were not always about finances. In the year 1600, they also had a disagreement about the marriage of Anne Barnes, one of Lady Hatton's gentlewomen, to Coke's ward, Walter Aston. The marriage between the two took place without Coke's knowledge. Coke was furious that his ward married without his permission. He was also convinced that his wife had promoted and encouraged the marriage of her gentlewoman behind his back. Once he found out that the deed was done, he entered Lady Hatton's chamber in a fury, giving her 'unworthy blows' and violently pulled the ruff from her neck before he even asked her any questions. He promptly ensured that the marriage was annulled, although Lady Hatton believed that the couple were 'lawfully marryed' with 'sufficient witnesses' and that Anne was a suitable bride, a 'gentlewoman of a good house and well allyed'. (Aston later married another woman, with Coke's approval, in 1607.) Lady Hatton retold this story of Coke's violent behaviour much later, in a petition to the king shortly after Coke's death. Considering that Coke displayed violent behaviour at other times, the story is credible, but Lady Hatton was of course also ensuring that Coke was painted in the worst possible light in order to argue her cause to the king. In her petition, Lady Hatton declared herself entirely innocent of having anything to do with the problematic marriage of Barnes and Aston, vowing 'before God and whosoever shall read this paper I am no more guiltye of then the Child new borne'. Coke clearly thought differently.[25]

At around the same time as the fight about the marriage, Coke also 'brake open [Lady Hatton's] Closett and Cabinette' and removed a note he had written to her, promising her the £4,000 in profit he had received after selling the wardship of Frances Hatton, Lady Hatton's step-daughter. Lady Hatton was already upset that he had sold away the wardship and the control of her step-daughter, presumably without her consent—and that he 'most tyrannously broke open my doores and took her [Frances Hatton] away'—but she had had enough when he also stole away what she claimed was the evidence that he had at least promised her the money from the wardship sale. In a great passion, Lady Hatton called her husband a 'base treacherous fellow'. Coke would not forget her outburst, as he considered it a slanderous insult. At this juncture, Lady Hatton had had enough. She left Coke and went to live with her father for a whole year, determined never to go back. But separated and fighting spouses, especially when they were members of the elite and servants of the sovereigns, were a problem for the whole society. According to ideas of the time, both the public and the private lives of monarchs as well as of the elite should serve as role models for commoners, as royal and noble power was often discussed in paternalistic terms. Harmonious marriages where husbands ruled with a firm but fair hand, and wives were loving and subservient, were the ideal. If wives were too rebellious, they upset what was considered the 'natural order', possibly inviting others lower down the social ladder to also rebel against their 'betters'. Conversely, husbands should not be abusive tyrants, but should love their wives and use their great powers for the benefit of all the members of their households, for which they were responsible. As a result, monarchs sometimes stepped in to mediate between upper-class spouses in conflict. Queen Elizabeth ordered Lady Hatton's father and her uncle (Robert Cecil, Secretary of State) to contrive a way to reconcile the couple. They were successful, at least for the time being. Lady Hatton moved back in with Coke.[26] Since the falling out about the marriage and the selling of Frances Hatton's wardship occurred in 1600, and Lady Hatton lived with her father for a full year afterwards, Frances, born in August 1602, must have been the result of the royally ordained reconciliation between her parents.

Frances and her sister Elizabeth initially grew up with parents in a temporary, but uneasy, truce, and as members of a large, blended family. We tend to think of blended families as a modern phenomenon, but considering the short lifespans of many men and women due to the dangers of disease, childbirth, accidents, and war, multiple marriages and families with children from various combinations of parents were not uncommon in the sixteenth and seventeenth centuries. That does not mean that families necessarily blended in the sense of becoming one household: oftentimes, children of different marriages were raised apart from each other, in the households of relatives. It is not clear if the two sets of children in the Coke and Hatton union lived in the same household, or if they even spent any time together at all as children. The fighting between the parents might have kept them apart: it definitely created a rift by the time of Frances's marriage in 1617, when many of the Coke–Paston children were firmly in their father's camp, actively assisting him and openly disapproving of Lady Hatton and her actions. Coke's children with Bridget were older than Frances, of course, ranging in ages from eighteen to six when she was born. As a result, they were sent to be educated, married off, and otherwise settled in life during Elizabeth and Frances's early childhood, so even if they had been living together, it would have only been for a period of a few years at most. Anne, Coke's eldest daughter, married Sir Ralph Sadler in 1601, a year before Frances was born.[27] Frances Hatton, Frances's step-sister, may not have lived with the family after the selling of the wardship, but in either case, she was married to Sir Robert Rich, later Earl of Warwick, in 1605. Coke prepared his sons for adulthood in the early 1600s. Robert, the eldest boy, was knighted in 1607 and married in 1613. Arthur was probably married by 1608, as he and his wife had a daughter born in

1609. Henry and Clement, the youngest boys, were off to school, first to Westminster, and then to university. They both attended Cambridge, Henry arriving at Queen's College in 1607, and Clement at Trinity College in 1608. In 1610, both boys studied law at the Inner Temple in London, following in their father's footsteps. Clement married in 1613, Henry in 1619.[28] Little Bridget was the baby of the Coke–Paston progeny, only two years old when she lost her mother and Coke and Hatton married. It would be pleasant to imagine that the little girl found her younger half-sisters to be fun and entertaining playmates, as they were the closest in age, but we cannot know. While Frances socialized with her step-sister and namesake Frances Hatton as an adult, nothing suggests that Bridget and Frances were close later on in their lives.

At the beginning of the reign of King James, both of Frances's parents worked to establish themselves at the new royal courts. After the death of the unmarried and childless Queen Elizabeth in March 1603, her relative, James VI of Scotland, inherited the English throne and became James I. Ambitious women who wanted to establish careers at the new court hurried to meet James's wife, Queen Anna, as she travelled south through England towards the capital. Lady Hatton was among those competing for the attentions of the new queen. Anna and her large entourage travelled slowly, stopping at the country estates of her new subjects for refreshment, rest, and entertainments. In June, Anne Clifford, a young diarist, recorded witnessing Lady Hatton in favour with the new queen at Althorpe in Northamptonshire. Lady Hatton desired a position as a lady-in-waiting, and also aimed for the prestigious appointment as the queen's Keeper of the Jewels. She asked her uncle Sir Robert Cecil, the king's new Secretary of State, to intercede for her, but in the end, the positions went to others. Although a permanent position eluded her, Lady Hatton did manage to land a coveted role in Queen Anna's first Christmas entertainment, the masque called *A Vision of Twelve Goddesses*. A masque was a highly symbolic form of play that included fanciful, rich dress, elaborate stage sets, poetry, and carefully choreographed dances, in which select members of the audience also participated at the very end of the performance. It was not performed by professional actors, but rather by important people at court for an audience of equally important people, such as the king, princes, high officers of state, courtiers, as well as foreign ambassadors. Preparing and rehearsing for the masque must have kept Lady Hatton at court for most of the long Christmas season. While she never quite managed to get into the closest circle of ladies around the queen, she was invited back for another role in *The Masque of Queens* during the 1608–9 Christmas season (the queen had skipped putting on entertainments during the two previous years). Lady Hatton thus seems to have been an occasional courtier during the first thirteen years of the

Jacobean reign. Ironically, it was Frances's later marriage, which Lady Hatton initially vehemently opposed, which established the closer courtly connections she had desired for a long time.[29]

While Lady Hatton was struggling for greater access to queenly royal favour, her husband was succeeding in getting King James's attention. On 22 May 1603, the new king knighted Coke. He also reconfirmed the lawyer's position as Attorney General. In 1606, he was appointed Chief Justice of the Common Pleas, and by 1613, he became Chief Justice of the King's Bench, one of the highest legal offices in the realm. Coke's position as Chief Justice was the pinnacle of his legal career. Along with his advancing career, Coke's personal fortune also increased significantly and he continued to purchase more land and estates.[30]

Frances's experiences as a child are mostly hidden from our view. She was the youngest daughter of a second marriage, and was not really interesting to news writers or others who would later comment on the more public aspects of her life, like her marriage, her adultery, and her ensuing legal troubles. While correspondence between parents or family members has given us precious, if brief, glimpses into the lives of a few sixteenth- and seventeenth-century children, they do not include Frances. No surviving letters between Coke and Lady Hatton mention the everyday life or upbringing of their two little girls. However, in order to understand what life might have been like for a girl like Frances, we can turn to what historians of children and childhood have learned about the Tudor and Stuart period from the available sources for other families.

While Frances was a little girl, her parents were busily trying to establish themselves at courts, both royal and legal. As a rule, young children were not brought to the royal courts. While her parents were thus preoccupied, Frances would have stayed at home, at the homes of relatives, or perhaps with a wet-nurse while an infant. It was not uncommon for children of the nobility and gentry to spend their first months or even years mostly separated from their parents. Frances was not even a year old when Lady Hatton travelled north to meet the queen, and only a little over a year old when her mother was at court rehearsing her role in Queen Anna's first court masque. As a result, she probably did not see her mother much during that time. Doctors and religious writers argued that mothers should breastfeed their own children, because they believed the mother's milk was healthier and that mothers would take more care with their children than a paid nurse would. However, elite women and their families in England did not really listen to this advice for another century and a half or so, continuing to employ wet-nurses. When Lady Anne Newdigate insisted on breastfeeding her own children in the late 1590s, many viewed her behaviour as strange, and a male friend of the family even told her that if he were her husband, he would not allow it.[31]

Wealthier women did not breastfeed for several reasons. First, the activity would hinder their responsibilities as household managers, as well as their social obligations as hostesses and guests, which were supposed to continue as soon as they had recovered physically from giving birth and gone through the churching ceremony. (Churching took place forty days after birth: it welcomed the woman back into the religious community after her confinement and enabled her to fully participate in all religious rites again.) Second, wives were supposed to be sexually available to their husbands, and nursing women should avoid sexual activity, as it was believed it would negatively affect their milk. As a result, husbands of wet-nurses had to agree to their wives' employment, not only because they were supposed to rule over their wives and control their labour, but also because it would affect their ability to have sex with—and impregnate—their wives. In short, wealthier families could pay someone else to care for infants, so that the couple could continue on with their lives with fewer disruptions and quickly conceive again. Sometimes, babies were sent away to the residence of the wet-nurse, and sometimes the nurse came to live with the family of the newborn. Girls were slightly more likely to be sent out to nurse than boys: generally speaking, boys were more favoured than girls throughout childhood, since in a society ruled by men, boys would inherit the family estates and carry on the lineage. Wet-nurses were selected with great care, as doctors taught that the personal qualities and characteristics as well as the physical constitution of the nurse were transmitted through the milk to the baby.[32]

If Frances was sent out to nurse, she would have returned to her parents by the time she was fully weaned. While their parents were busy with their duties at court, servants—such as nurses and governesses—would have continued to care for Frances and her sister Elizabeth mostly in Hatton House in London or at Coke's new spacious manor in Stoke Poges in Buckinghamshire, which served as the two main residences for Coke and Lady Hatton (see Figs. 6.1 and 7.2). Hatton House was a stately mansion in Holborn, London, to the north of the church of St Andrew, where Frances and her sister Elizabeth were baptized (the church has been rebuilt several times since then, most significantly after the Great Fire of London in the 1660s). Unfortunately, Hatton House no longer exists, but it probably stood somewhere between the modern-day streets of Hatton Garden and Ely Place. Originally, Hatton House was known as Ely House, and belonged to the bishop of Ely, but Queen Elizabeth granted portions of the estate to her favourite Sir Christopher Hatton, who in turn had left it to his nephew, Lady Hatton's first husband, and thus it came to Lady Hatton and Coke. Sir Christopher had spent large sums on rebuilding the house into a fashionable and comfortable town home, in addition to establishing lovely gardens, famed for their beautiful roses and sweet strawberries. The two young sisters certainly would have had plenty of space to play outside even while in London.[33]

Stoke, about twenty miles west of London, came to be a part of the growing Coke estates in 1599. Two years later, Coke entertained a visiting Queen Elizabeth at Stoke. While gaining royal favour could certainly be a great financial bonanza, it did not come cheaply. The Stoke manor was built in 1555 in the then fashionable Tudor style: three storeys, tall and narrow red brick chimneys, and plenty of windows, allowing both for natural light and display of expensive glass. The estate included a thousand acres of forests and fields, so its wealthy inhabitants and their guests could spend their leisure time hunting, while farmers worked the land they leased from Coke. The house itself was richly furnished. We know of some of the details of the household items because of the intermittent fighting between Lady Hatton and Coke: at one point, Lady Hatton had carried off some goods she claimed were hers, part of her Hatton inheritance, and Coke, outraged, created a list of possessions at Stoke which he argued had never been part of the Hatton estate. The walls of the great hall were covered with nine large woven tapestries, depicting Old Testament scenes of the Israelites in Egypt. A thick Persian carpet lay on a large table, and leather-upholstered chairs provided extra comfort. In the window seats rested long embroidered cushions of cloth of silver. The parlours had thick red carpets and matching velvet drapes, to keep the draughts out. The main bedroom upstairs, presumably Coke's bedroom, was swathed in gold and silver. The wooden bed itself was gilded, and hung with white taffeta and striped cloth of silver. The bedroom curtains were of 'clouded taffita, fringed with gould and silke'. In his study Coke had, among other objects, a great iron chest, a small ivory cabinet, a map of the world, and a map of his alma mater, Cambridge. Stoke was clearly a place of both comfort and luxury. Only some small bits and pieces of the original house remain today, as the original structure was mostly torn down and rebuilt over the centuries that followed.[34]

During the heat of the summers, Frances and Elizabeth in all likelihood travelled to their mother's southern coastal country estate, Corfe Castle, on the peninsula called the Isle of Purbeck in Dorset (see Figs. 1.1 and 7.2). Corfe Castle, located at the top of a hill with a clear view of the surrounding landscape, was originally built as a Norman stronghold during the eleventh century, and added to over the centuries. The castle was owned by the crown until Queen Elizabeth sold it to Sir Christopher Hatton in the 1570s, and then it came into Lady Hatton's possession. The thick stone walls and towers of what was essentially a fortress might not have made it as

Fig. 1.1. Corfe Castle ruins, Isle of Purbeck, Dorset. This castle was part of Lady Hatton's Purbeck estate, and Frances in all likelihood spent time here during her childhood, hunting and hawking with her mother in the surrounding area. King James tried to force Lady Hatton to give the estate to her son-in-law, but she refused.

comfortable a place as Hatton House or Stoke, but probably provided a great sense of adventure for Frances and her sister. Lady Hatton enjoyed hawking and hunting at Corfe Castle, and her daughters may have also participated in those pastimes.[35]

While Coke certainly worked hard to establish and make advantageous marriages for his sons and daughters, he may not have been the most expressive or loving parent. At one point, Lady Hatton complained that Coke did not really pay much attention to his youngest daughter. Lady Hatton was closer to her daughters; at least she spent more time with Frances during the ill-fated marriage negotiations and the early years of Frances's married life. Historians who pioneered the field of studying Tudor and Stuart families in the 1960s and 1970s argued that parents stayed emotionally detached from their young children, since it was so common for children to die young. Such theories have now largely been debunked. It is true that most parents did experience the loss of a young child at some point during their lives, as Coke certainly did, but more recent studies show that far from being distant and resigned to the death of infants and young children, parents often felt the sorrow of a loss keenly, although they may not have exhibited their grief in ways that we recognize now. Even if they tended to be more physically removed from their children than parents today, parents were still heavily emotionally involved in their offspring and their well-being. Conduct writers and ministers often argued that children should not be coddled, but some parents did not heed the advice and were quite indulgent towards their children. Children were often given loving nicknames—Frances was called Franck by a family friend—and parents delighted in hearing news of their little ones while they were away.[36]

According to ideas of the different 'ages of man', the first seven years of children's lives were considered the period of 'infancy'. During this 'infancy', boys and girls were usually dressed alike. Babies were tightly swaddled, carefully wrapped with strips of linen cloth to ensure that the limbs developed straight. Toddlers and young children of both genders wore long tunics, which made it easier to change soiled linens when necessary, and also gave young children ease of movement. (See the young Prince Charles in Fig. 7.5, for example.) The first major outward gender distinction in clothing occurred when boys were about six or seven years old. At that time, they were 'breeched', that is, they started to wear the masculine breeches or pants. At about the same time, young girls started to wear dresses that looked more like those designed for adult women, appropriately fancy or plain depending on both their family's social station and the occasion.

Generally, mothers oversaw and were in charge of the care of both boys and girls while they were 'infants'. When boys were breeched, fathers took over the direction of their sons' education. At this time, boys' education also began to differ from that of girls. Boys might receive a male tutor, for example, or be sent away to school, like the Coke sons who attended school at Westminster. Sixteenth- and seventeenth-century boys went to university very early, often in their early to mid-teens. For example, Frances's half-brothers Henry and Clement matriculated at Cambridge when they were sixteen and fourteen years old respectively. Neither boy left Cambridge with a degree, which was rather common: the universities functioned not only as an educational institution, but also as a place for boys and young men to create ties and connections for later in their lives. Increasingly, wealthier families also sent teenage sons on European travels as a form of final education, to learn and practise their language skills, as well as to make them more cosmopolitan and familiar with other European cultures. The Netherlands, France, Germany, and Italy were popular destinations. The young men often travelled with a servant/tutor, whose job it was to keep an eye on the youngsters, promote good habits, and to ensure that they actually learned something. Not surprisingly, sons often wrote back home asking for more money, and parents often wrote to their sons exhorting them to be frugal and mindful of their expenses, as well as to stay away from heavy drinking, gambling, and women. One of the Coke sons, young Clement, travelled to the Netherlands in 1616, where he quickly managed to get himself into trouble as well as establish his reputation as a brawler. He became involved in an argument with an English soldier, and fought a duel. The other man died as a result of his injuries. Then, Clement quarrelled with two of the dead man's friends, and actually attacked the messenger one of the men had sent him to challenge him to another duel. Both the messenger and Clement were injured in the ensuing mêlée, although neither fatally so. Luckily for the hot-headed Clement, his father knew influential people who could clean up after him and get him out of trouble. Coke's good friend Sir Ralph Winwood, then Secretary of State, managed to get the assistance of Sir Dudley Carleton, the English ambassador, to emphasize in his report that the death was the result of the bungled treatments of inept doctors, rather than the wound inflicted by Clement. After the altercation with the messenger, Carleton promptly sent Clement home, under guard, to ensure that he would not cause any further problems.[37]

Like the boys, upper-class girls were taught how to read and write, and they might perhaps also learn another language, most likely French. If Frances learned French as a girl, it turned out to be especially useful for her, as she ended up spending many years in France as an adult. However, while boys were taught Latin, history, and philosophy, those subjects were not usually a major part of girls' curriculum, as they were considered masculine. Sometimes, girls were allowed to sit in on their brothers' lessons, but both Frances and her sister were too young to share tutors with their elder half-brothers. It does not appear that Frances had an especially rigorous academic education, or that she was much interested in it later in life either. Both girls and boys received religious instruction, reading the Bible as well as other religious materials. Girls were taught the importance of obedience and of submitting to God's will and divine order, whereas boys were taught to become the religious leaders of their future families. Primarily, girls in elite families would have been prepared for their roles as future household managers, learning the art by following and helping their mothers in their tasks and gaining knowledge of the supervision of servants. In addition, producing clothes and household textiles was generally viewed as female work and were laborious processes. While poorer girls were taught to spin, weave, and sew, girls in wealthier families would, like their mothers, focus on the more luxurious forms of textile work, like fine embroidery and other, less utilitarian and more decorative, forms of stitching. They could afford to have servants and hired seamstresses to do the heavier work.[38]

In addition, Frances needed to excel in the courtly arts, like dancing, playing the lute or virginals, and conversing well. In all likelihood, she and her sister received lessons from tutors specializing in those skills. These were not just extracurricular activities, but rather central to the education of girls of Frances's status. If they were going to be successful in high social circles, they needed to learn how to entertain and delight others, as well as to exude gracefulness and seemingly effortless physical control. In his famous and popular sixteenth-century conduct manual, *The Book of the Courtier*, Baldassare Castiglione argued that the female courtier needed to be a well-practised dancer, who knew how to move with 'sweetness' and 'soft mildness', avoiding 'swift and violent tricks', which he considered too jarring, boastful, and unladylike.[39] Letter-writers who commented on successful courtiers or would-be courtiers often pointed to their skills in dancing. Frances's future brother-in-law and royal favourite George Villiers was an accomplished dancer, often entertaining James with his grace and athletic abilities. At one point during a lacklustre court performance of a masque, the bored king grew impatient and exclaimed: 'Why don't they dance? What did they make me come here for? Devil take you all!' In order to stave off a royal temper tantrum, Villiers quickly leapt into action and awed the company—and mollified the king—by extemporaneously performing a series of impressively high-cutting capers. In the late 1590s and early 1600s, Rowland Whyte regularly reported to his absent master, Sir Robert Sidney, on his children's education. He especially mentioned the daughters' improving abilities in dance and as musicians. Little Mary Sidney excelled, both on the dance-floor as well as in playing the lute. Mary and her siblings also danced for Queen Elizabeth when she briefly visited their country estate, and received royal praise, causing her parents to beam with pride.[40] Girls were also sometimes placed in other elite households under the care of a trusted noble-woman, as a sort of 'finishing-school', where they could learn proper manners and social graces. Frances would have much use for all those skills once she was married, as she was then often at court, as well as socializing with courtiers in settings outside the royal palaces.

Children of courtiers and the great noble families sometimes made a first formal appearance at court in their early to mid-teens. The children were fitted with new clothes for the occasion, in many cases the fanciest and costliest clothes they had ever worn. Their parents, or an influential relative, briefly presented them to the king or queen, who then, along with other courtiers in attendance, carefully scrutinized the youngsters' comportment and their ability to make a good impression. The oldest Sidney children were presented to Queen Elizabeth in 1600 and 1602. It is possible that Frances and Elizabeth, like the Sidney children, may have been presented at court at some point before Frances's marriage in 1617, although no one made a note of it.[41]

Let us at least hope that Frances's childhood was as happy and joyful as possible, and that she and her sister were relatively shielded from the warring of her parents.

If that was so, then that shield shattered in a spectacular manner by the time Frances entered her mid-teens. It was then time to plan for her marriage. According to an admiring observer, young Frances would be a bride 'fitt for the greatest Earle of the Land', considering 'her beautie and person'.[42] When her father began the process of finding a husband for Frances, the still simmering discontent between Coke and Lady Hatton boiled over. Frances was caught in the overflow.

CHAPTER 2

THE MARRIAGE MERRY-GO-ROUND

On the morning of 29 September 1617, servants helped Frances into a beautiful but heavy and stiff white dress, which one of the wedding guests later remarked 'did become her very well'. A maid brushed her long dark brown hair to a shiny gloss, but left it hanging loose down her back, as long, free-flowing locks symbolized the virginity of the bride. After finishing off the toilette with rich jewels, perhaps pearls similar to those Frances wore in a later portrait (see Fig. 3.2), the bride was helped into a coach. An additional eight coaches, holding Frances's family members and relatives, joined the cortège now leaving from Frances's brother's home in Kingston. A short drive later, the bride alighted at the royal palace at Hampton Court (Fig. 2.1), where her future brother-in-law and Prince Charles met her and escorted her to the chapel, supporting her on either side. Once they arrived, Sir Edward Coke took over from the younger men, leading his daughter onwards towards the waiting groom. The magnificent ceiling of the royal chapel, painted a deep, brilliant blue colour and heavily accented with intricately carved and gilded wood and golden stars, had been built during Henry VIII's reign almost a century earlier. It was under this splendid ceiling that Frances became a wife.[1]

The events that led to Frances's Michaelmas Day walk down the aisle of the royal chapel had been incredibly dramatic. Frances did not choose her own 'yoke-fellow', as her contemporaries often called spouses. Her marriage, as most marriages of the upper classes at the time, was arranged, but her parents could not agree on a candidate. As was by now their habit, Lady Hatton and Coke's disagreements quickly escalated and the marriage arrangements for Frances eventually engaged scores of family, friends, courtiers, politicians, and even King James himself.

Because of Coke's and Lady Hatton's positions, influence, and needs, Frances's marriage was a direct result of the complex politics surrounding the court of King James. By the time of the first marriage rumours in late 1616, court politics and positions were in a state of flux. Most notably, the spectacular downfall of the king's former favourite, Robert Carr, Earl of Somerset in 1615–16—who was convicted of accessory to murder—left a vacuum both in the halls of power and in the affections

Fig. 2.1. Hampton Court Palace, Hampton Court. The wedding between Frances and John was celebrated in this sprawling Tudor palace.

of the king. This shift in fortunes in turn enabled the meteoric rise of George Villiers, later Duke of Buckingham, the man who so adamantly insisted on becoming Frances's brother-in-law and who would play a huge role in Frances's life.

George Villiers was born in 1592 at Brooksby, his father's estate in Leicestershire. The family was solid regional gentry, but certainly did not mix with the upper echelons. In addition, George Villiers was a second son of a second marriage and therefore did not stand to inherit, as the estate went to his eldest half-brother when his father died. The propitious third marriage of Villiers's mother, Mary Beaumont Villiers Rayner, to Sir Thomas Compton, provided adequate funds for George and his elder brother John to travel to France and Germany to gain the requisite international experience for aspiring courtiers. Villiers also befriended crucial court contacts, which allowed him to meet King James for the first time while the latter was visiting Northamptonshire for summer hunting and entertainment in 1614. An exceptionally handsome and charming youth, Villiers made a favourable impression on James. Rumours of a budding royal infatuation worried the current favourite Somerset enough to try to block the young man's entrance to any official court appointments. But Somerset could not keep Villiers from appearing at court and with some financial backing from Somerset's enemies, he was able to enhance his natural good looks with better clothes. He also learned refined manners, vital skills for a courtier. By April 1615, the anti-Somerset faction, which at this point also included Queen Anna, finally managed to outmanoeuvre Somerset and persuaded the king not only to knight Villiers, but to appoint him Gentleman of the King's Bedchamber. The appointment meant that he would be close to King James on a regular basis and could thus hope for further favour. He was one of the very few with official access to the inner sanctum of the king's bedroom, since his new duties included helping the king to wash and dress, as well as providing him company. As a bonus, Villiers also received an annual pension of £1,000. He was on his way.[2]

As the new royal favourite, Villiers rapidly joined the peerage, receiving ever-more lofty titles. The enamoured James made him a baron and a viscount in 1616, Earl of Buckingham in 1617, Marquis of Buckingham 1618, and finally, Duke of Buckingham in 1623, although the title 'duke' was usually reserved for persons of royal blood. (For clarity's sake, I will refer to him simply as 'Buckingham' from now on, avoiding the complications of when he held which titles.) Buckingham also collected an impressive number of offices, such as an appointment to the Privy Council, Master of the Horse, Lord Lieutenant of Buckinghamshire, Kent, and Middlesex, Lord High Admiral, and Warden of the Cinque Ports, among others. He managed to secure his position as the king's last and most powerful favourite, although jealous courtiers attempted to dislodge him. Each time, James stood by him and Buckingham prevailed. When upbraiding councillors who he felt had acted against Buckingham's interests in 1617, James assured the listeners that 'he loved the Earl of Buckingham more than any other man' and that they should 'not think of this as a defect in him, for Jesus Christ had done just what he was doing', further explaining that 'just as Christ had his John, so he, James, had his George'. As a New Year's gift in 1617, James gave Buckingham a miniature portrait of himself holding his heart in his hand, a powerful symbol of his love for his 'Steenie', as he called George. The nickname was a version of St Stephen, who was supposed to have been as beautiful as an angel, just like Buckingham, in James's eyes.[3]

In King James's England, homosexuality was considered a most terrible sin, punishable by death.[4] For that reason, it might seem odd that the king (Fig. 2.2), the Supreme Head of the Anglican Church, was able to love men so openly and yet reign over both Church and country. Part of the explanation lies in the fact that James married and had children and encouraged his favourites to marry as well, ensuring both outward propriety as well as dynastic and familial continuity. In addition, James's contemporaries did not want to risk being critical of the sovereign, so they largely avoided discussing the possibility of their king being a 'sodomite' or 'buggerer', as homosexual men were called. As a result, the precise nature of the

Fig. 2.2. King James I of England and VI of Scotland. Daniel Mytens, 1621. National Portrait Gallery, London.

king's relationships with men is largely hidden from view, although some modern historians have argued that they were sexual.[5]

While we can debate what exactly went on in the king's bedroom, there is no debate about the king's intense affections for Buckingham and other favourites: those were clear for all to see and hear. In the presence of others, James kissed and embraced his favourites, walked with them arm in arm, and spoke with them and about them in a way that left no doubts that he loved them above all others. When separated, the king wrote passionate letters to his beloved Buckingham, whom he called his 'wife and child', while he signed himself off as Buckingham's 'dear dad and husband'. Whether they approved of the relationships or not, James's courtiers understood that gaining the friendship of James's favourites was a path to power. Introducing potential new male favourites constituted another path, and on occasions court factions tried to entice James with handsome young men in attempts to dislodge and replace the current favourite.[6]

Other members of the Villiers family were also ambitious and the besotted James was happy to oblige, showering the family with honours and rewards. Buckingham's two brothers were knighted and received royal appointments: John became Prince Charles's Groom of the Bedchamber and Master of Robes, and the younger brother Christopher also became a Gentleman of the King's Bedchamber. The brothers later received noble titles: John became Viscount Purbeck, and Christopher Earl of Anglesey. Since advantageous marriages were the prime method of social climbing, Buckingham worked hard to secure good— and especially rich—marriages both for himself and for his siblings and relatives. His mother, Lady Mary Compton, was also actively involved in the marriage negotiations of her children. Lady Compton certainly knew the value of a good marriage: born into lower gentry, she married three times and each time she managed to move a little higher on the socio-economic ladder. Eventually, she would also become a countess, not through marriage, but rather as a result of her son's favoured position with the king. James created Lady Compton Countess of Buckingham in 1618.[7] By 1616, George and his mother were actively looking for a wife for George's brother, John Villiers.

Rumours about a potential marriage first surfaced late in 1616, when Frances was only fourteen years old. By the time of her wedding one year later, she had just turned fifteen. While that may sound young to modern readers, Frances was legally old enough to marry. According to seventeenth-century English marriage law, based on medieval canonical law, the bride had to be at least twelve years old and the groom a minimum of fourteen years old in order to be able to give consent. Consent was crucial: without the expressed consent of both bride and groom there could be no marriage, as it was required to make the union binding. Nonetheless, as we will see in Frances's case, sometimes the idea of what constituted consent could be very flexible, as children could come under enormous pressure to agree to their parents' designs.

Historians have often pointed out that in England (as in other parts of north-western Europe), women tended to marry relatively late compared to their peers in central and southern Europe. In England, the average age for first marriages for women was in the mid-twenties, while English men generally married in their mid-to-late twenties. In light of these averages, Frances seems unusually young to be a bride. However, upper-class women (and sometimes men) often married at significantly younger ages than their poorer counterparts, so examples of noble and gentry teenage brides and grooms are plentiful. While commoner couples worked as servants or as apprentices for around a decade before having saved enough money to establish a new household, wealthy couples had greater resources and could begin their married life sooner. In addition, noble and gentry parents were often keen on getting daughters settled in marriage early, creating the most beneficial alliances.[8] In Frances's own family, young brides were the norm: Lady Hatton was in her mid-teens when she married her first husband; Frances's step-sister married at fourteen; and her half-sisters, Anne and Bridget, both married at seventeen. Her elder sister Elizabeth was the exception to the norm: she was twenty-three years old when she married. Coke and his sons married later: Coke was thirty when he married Bridget Paston, and their sons ranged in ages from nineteen to twenty-eight at the time of their weddings.

On 6 November, Sir John Throckmorton informed Sir Dudley Carleton that Coke was hoping to return to the king's favour by 'marrying a daughter of his wife to a brother of Viscount Villiers [Buckingham]'. Carleton received another report, written three days later, which mentioned a 'flien [fleeing] tale' that John Villiers should marry Coke's daughter and get land worth £900 annually from Coke, and additional land worth £2,100 from Lady Hatton.[9] Coke was seriously considering the match because Buckingham seemed very interested in it. What would be pleasing to Buckingham would be pleasing to James, and Coke badly needed to please the king at that time. Since the previous summer, Coke had found himself in disfavour. In several court cases and legal writings, Coke had essentially challenged the king's prerogative and acted against the king's expressed commands. He had also tried to hide the fact that some of the estates he had received upon the marriage to Lady Hatton had crown debts attached to them. Sir Christopher Hatton, the Elizabethan favourite, had borrowed large sums of money from his queen, and the estate he left to his nephew, Lady Hatton's first husband, was supposed to pay those debts back to

the crown. When Queen Elizabeth died, King James became the beneficiary, but as James's financial advisers initially did not know about it, Coke had enjoyed the Hatton estates without paying the crown debts ever since King James ascended to the throne.[10] Throughout the summer and autumn of 1616, Coke's situation was very tenuous. Nervous friends and gleeful enemies recorded every little sign that might indicate if James intended to forgive and forget or throw the book at Coke. In November, James finally removed him from his office as Lord Chief Justice. The suggestion of the marriage could thus potentially tip the scales back in Coke's favour. In December, rumours circulated that Coke's position at court was on the mend again because he had agreed to the marriage.[11]

But Coke still hesitated, unsure if this was the right action: he worried that the marriage, with its sizeable dowry, would be too costly and that it would not really help his standing with a king he considered rather fickle. Why should he 'buy the Kings favor too deare being so uncertain and variable', he mused? Clearly, his primary concern was political and financial: he was not really thinking about his daughter's personal preference. In Coke's view, a happy daughter was an obedient daughter, so the decision of her marriage was his, and his alone. He made a low counter-offer, which was not well received. The unsuccessful negotiations plunged him into a state of uncertainty again and the rumour mill suggested that he would be called to answer for his old offences at the Court of Star Chamber, although that threat did not materialize.[12] Coke would learn the hard way that the reasons for his initial hesitation proved both sound and true, but then it was too late, both for Coke and especially for his daughter.

The earliest marriage rumours do not name Frances specifically: they refer to 'Coke's daughter', or Coke's 'wife's daughter'. As it was usual for the eldest daughter to marry first, it is possible that the early negotiations were actually for Frances's elder sister Elizabeth's hand. In February 1617, Chamberlain mentioned that although there was still talk of a potential marriage between one of Coke's daughters and John Villiers, 'there have ben long shew to Sir W. Cavendish, and the young Lord Dacres' as husbands for the two sisters (Richard Lennard, Lord Dacre of the South).[13] Nevertheless, it became clear by the summer of 1617 that both Coke and the Villiers family intended Frances to be John's wife. In the end, Elizabeth married neither Cavendish nor Lord Dacre.

When the discussions for a potential Coke–Villiers marriage first began, Lady Hatton did not participate. She was certainly not likely to cooperate with her husband at that moment. In fact, one of the most divisive periods in the Coke–Hatton marriage was about to commence. Lady Hatton had briefly supported her husband during the beginning of his troubles with the king in July of 1616.[14]

However, she was in no mood to be supportive later that autumn. She was worried about the potential financial consequences of Coke's fall from favour and concerned that Coke's machinations regarding the old Hatton debts might get her into trouble as well. A year later, she submitted to the king that Coke had forced her to agree to the silence about the debts, saying that if she did not agree to it, he would be 'revenged double and treble of [her]' and she feared she would be 'toaren in pieces'.[15]

By the time Coke was stripped of his office as Chief Justice, Lady Hatton decided to take action in order to secure whatever valuables she could. While Coke was summoned to the king, who was hunting in Newmarket, Lady Hatton proceeded to remove furniture and plate from both Hatton House in London and the country estate at Stoke. Coke later also accused her of taking important legal papers. She was not able to take quite as much with her as she had planned, as some of the packed trunks were mistakenly held up during the removal process. She also absconded and initially refused to let her husband know where to find her. Coke was not happy about Lady Hatton's actions, but perhaps he was too worn down by the disappointment of losing his position to have the strength to deal with his wife right away. He left town and went to stay with his devoted daughter, Anne Sadler, in Hertfordshire for the time being.[16] It is also possible that Coke did not feel he was in a good position to counter Lady Hatton at the time, considering he had lost the king's favour. He had to wait for a better opportunity.

Lady Hatton did not receive the support she had hoped for, as even her friends and family believed that she had gone a bit too far when she cleaned out the houses of valuables. It was too severe a breach for a wife, who was supposed to be submissive and ruled by her husband. Ever the mediator, Lady Hatton's father, troubled at the escalation of the situation, wrote to Coke to hear his side of the story. At the behest of her father, Lady Hatton pulled back a little, pretending that Coke had simply misinterpreted her actions.[17] She would not pull back half a year later, but rather strike back at her husband with all her might.

By May of 1617, the situation between Coke and Lady Hatton had deteriorated further. They were openly and publicly airing their grievances against one another, both the issues from the previous year, as well as the old wounds from the tempestuous early years of their marriage. The situation became so bad that the Privy Council called the couple to appear before it, so that the councillors could settle the dispute. Both the king and council found that their fighting negatively affected the social harmony among the elite, as well as the workings of the state since many high officers were either friends of or related to the couple. When she appeared before the council, Lady Hatton brought as much support as she could muster among her connections and relations: her brother William Cecil, Lord

Burghley and his wife; the military hero from the Irish wars and Keeper of St James's Palace, her first cousin, Henry, Lord Danvers; her brother-in-law Edward, Lord Denny; her nephew-in-law Sir Thomas Howard and his wife, and others. Sir John Chamberlain, who always enjoyed drama, claimed that the popular actor Richard Burbage himself could not have done a better job than Lady Hatton in portraying the wrongs she had suffered at the hands of her terrible husband. Indeed, the couple 'accused each other in a grievous manner'. Lady Hatton argued that Coke was in contempt of the king when he threatened her jointure, kept her from being able to disclose the Hatton debts to the crown, and refused to pay her annuity. Coke in turn accused Lady Hatton of theft of his goods and slander, recalling her telling others that he was 'a false, treacherous villain'.[18] It is not immediately clear if he was referring to her outbursts from years earlier, or if Lady Hatton in her frustration had again repeated what Coke viewed as terrible insults. In early June, the council impressively managed the feat of reconciling the battling spouses. Coke's 'curst heart hath been forced to yield more than he ever meant' in the agreement: in addition to establishing ownership, inheritance rights, and income of various properties, Coke also had to promise that he would 'not hereafter meddle with any of the money of the sayd Elizabeth [Lady Hatton] which she now hath or hereafter shall raise of the proffitts of her landes or otherwise by her owne endeavors'. Coke may have thought that the costly agreement was worth it, as he seemed to labour under the impression that Lady Hatton would cleave to him at last. He was mistaken.[19]

Rather than working with her husband, Lady Hatton decided to undercut him. Hoping to wrest the potential benefits of a Coke–Villiers match away from Coke, she tried to reopen the negotiations with the Villiers family herself. She sent her friend John, Lord Holles, as a go-between to John Villiers's mother, Lady Compton. Holles told Lady Compton that considering how Coke had bungled the negotiations before, had mistreated his wife, and that the greatest part of Frances's dowry would come from Lady Hatton's estate, she should negotiate directly with Lady Hatton about the marriage rather than with the 'unworthy' Coke. While Lady Compton at first seemed to agree to this plan, she then renewed marriage discussions with Coke behind Lady Hatton's back. Angered and outraged at what she—somewhat ironically, considering her own tactics—considered underhanded opportunism, Lady Hatton decided to fight against the marriage with everything she could muster. For a woman with her connections, resources, and stubborn and determined personality, it constituted a formidable arsenal.[20]

In fact, while Lady Hatton had pretended friendship towards Lady Compton, the truth was she did not like the favourite's mother much. At court a year earlier, Lady

Hatton had said some 'braving and uncivill words' about Lady Compton and then intimated that she was just repeating what the queen herself had said.[21] Whether Queen Anna had actually said something disparaging about Lady Compton we do not know, but Anna, who constantly had to compete with the favourites for influence over her husband, certainly would not have wanted any such words repeated, even had she uttered them. The king and queen promptly forbade Lady Hatton from coming to court for several months. Lady Hatton's first little run-in with Lady Compton in 1616 would just be a warm-up for the marriage negotiations.

When he thought his relationship with his wife was patched up, Coke decided to return his attentions to his daughter's marriage. Oblivious that his wife had already tried to best him, he made a new overture to Buckingham and the Villiers family. The Villiers responded smoothly that John Villiers was very smitten with Frances and would have been 'well pleased to have taken her in her smock', but nonetheless, 'he should be glad, by way of curiosity, to know how much could be assured by marriage settlement upon her and her issue'.[22] Villiers was making a complimentary gesture, suggesting that he was already so in love with Frances that he would wed her even if she was poor. Obviously, considering the fact that the marriage negotiations had already been broached but not completed over the very issue of the dowry, he was not seriously considering marrying Frances without a hefty settlement. After all, procuring a wealthy bride for John was one of the main reasons for the marriage in the first place. This time around, Coke realized he needed to make a more substantial offer to get the match through. He agreed to a settlement worth around £30,000, which translates to more than seven million pounds in current value. It was a very substantial sum indeed, mirroring the amount Coke had received when he married Bridget Paston. At this point, on 10 July, he informed Lady Hatton that the negotiations were almost concluded. He had not bothered to ask her advice or opinion.[23]

Lady Hatton sprang into action: Coke should not get his way and the Villiers should not get their hands on Frances. The very same night that Coke had informed her about the impending marriage, Lady Hatton secretly took her daughter out of London and hid her away from her father and the Villiers. Knowing that Coke had a habit of going to bed early, Lady Hatton and Frances waited until he had retired, snuck out under the cover of darkness, and hurried out of the city, Frances still in her night-clothes. The fleeing pair sought refuge with a relative, Sir Edmond Withipole, who had rented a house at Oatlands, south-west of London along the River Thames, near Weybridge.[24] Lady Hatton surely could not think that she would be able to keep Frances away from her father for any longer period, as it would be illegal for her to do so. She was probably just trying to buy some time, until she could figure out another, more efficient, strategy to prevent the marriage from taking place.

Coke was furious when he realized that his daughter had disappeared. His people quickly fanned out and started investigating, trying to learn where Lady Hatton had hidden Frances. Having heard a rumour that Frances might be at Oatlands, one of Coke's servants managed to verify it by questioning Withipole's unsuspecting scullery boy, having first engaged the lad in conversation by pretending to be looking for a lost spaniel. Once he knew where Frances was, Coke gathered a posse to bring his daughter back, forcibly if need be. Being a man of law, he first visited Sir Ralph Winwood, Secretary of State, to secure a warrant to search Withipole's house.[25] Clement, Frances's half-brother, by then known by his well-deserved nickname 'Fighting Clem', joined the party, as did Robert, the eldest of the Coke sons. The men armed themselves with pistols, to ensure that they would be taken seriously. Lady Hatton, who had returned to London once Frances was safely stowed away in Oatlands, heard of Coke's plan. Desperate, she set out for Oatlands herself, trying to make sure that she would arrive there before Coke, according to one account even riding with one of Withipole's servants on the back of an unsaddled pack horse after her own coach horses had tired from the fast pace. While Lady Hatton managed to get there before her husband, Coke had sent his son Robert ahead with some of their men. Robert blocked Lady Hatton from entering the gate, having received orders from Coke not to let anyone in or out of the estate. When Coke arrived, Lady Hatton threw herself in front of the gate, trying to keep him out. As Coke impatiently pushed her aside, his wife 'cried she would lose her blood before she would suffer him to enter', telling one of the Withipole servants that he should draw his sword. The man was not willing to do so, and ignoring Lady Hatton's pleas, Coke and his men broke through the outer gate. Once by the house, Coke demanded that Withipole and his wife deliver his 'derest daughter' to him immediately. When the Withipoles refused, Coke and his men summarily broke down the door, entered, and searched the house. They found a terrified Frances hiding in a closet upstairs. Coke and his men grabbed the girl, dragged her downstairs, and left hastily. Lady Hatton, now in turn furious and outraged by her husband's rough treatment of their daughter, decided to follow. Members of the Withipole household armed themselves and went with her, fully prepared for bloodshed. Although they travelled at breakneck speed, they were not able to catch up with Coke. Lady Hatton's party eventually had to slow down and then stop altogether, the horses simply too exhausted to continue. Commentators believed Lady Hatton's interrupted journey proved fortunate, sure that a meeting of the two parties would have ended with bloodshed. Coke and Frances continued on to Robert Coke's house in Kingston.[26]

Lady Hatton was not the surrendering type. Re-supplied with rested horses and renewed determination, she continued on to London. Once in town, she went to seek out male support and help from Lord Holles, who agreed to accompany her onwards. The two then went to see the Lord Keeper, Sir Francis Bacon, the one-time suitor for Lady Hatton's hand and Coke's main rival, both at court and in the legal profession. They drove so fast that the coach turned over, and the passengers were thrown into the street. Bruised and shaken, but still determined, the pair continued on towards the Lord Keeper. Bacon, feeling ill, had taken to his bed, and Lady Hatton was told he was not receiving guests. Lady Hatton was not deterred, but rather insisted on being allowed to wait in the room right next to Bacon's bedroom so that she would be the first person to see him as soon as he was 'stirring'. She was given a chair and allowed to wait, but was frustrated with the delay. After a while, she 'rose up and bounced against my Lord Keeper's door, and waked him and affrighted him that he called his men to him; and they opening the door, she thrust in with them, and desired his [Lordship] to pardon her, but she was like a cow who had lost her calf, and so justified herself and pacified my Lord's anger'.[27]

Lady Hatton managed to make Bacon see the urgency of the matter and he promised to bring her case to the attention of the Privy Council right away, even though it was Sunday and the Lord's Day of rest. King James was away in Scotland over the summer and could therefore not immediately intervene in the matter. The Privy Council first considered Lady Hatton's written petition. According to the Privy Council's report to King James, the lady was 'complaining in somewhat a passionate and tragical a manner' that she had been 'by violence dispossessed of her child'. Lady Hatton argued that she had simply sent Frances out of the city for health reasons, since her daughter had a weak constitution. She had not done so secretly and Coke did not usually worry about where Frances was, since he was 'never asking or taking accompt what has become of her'. Then, as Lady Hatton's version continued, Coke, with his son and ten or eleven other men, all armed, had broken down the doors and violently dragged the girl out of the house to the waiting coach. The council decided to call Coke to a hearing on the following Tuesday, but Lady Hatton wanted more immediate results. Having first waited outside the Council Chamber while they deliberated, she now asked to speak to them in person. Granted access, she pleaded that Frances, whose health was in grave danger as a result of the commotion, violence, and excitement, should be taken somewhere where she could have 'physic and attendance as were requisite for her preservation and recovery'. The council, convinced by Lady Hatton's urgent pleas, agreed that it seemed the humane thing to do under the circumstances. They drafted a letter to Coke, ordering him to bring Frances to Sir Thomas Edmondes, the Clerk of the Council, for safe-keeping at a neutral place while they deliberated further.[28]

Coke received the message that very same day, but arguing that it was late, said he would deliver Frances the following morning instead. In order to make sure that Coke would keep his word, the council issued a warrant to Lady Hatton, giving her the right to bring Frances to Clerk Edmondes should Coke not comply with the order. Mirroring Coke's earlier actions, she gathered 'three score men with pistols', who set out towards Kingston. The Privy Council also sent Edmondes to fetch Frances, but once he arrived at Kingston, she was no longer there. Coke had obeyed the council's order, put his daughter and Lady Compton in a coach, while he, Clement, and their men rode next to them, providing armed protection. Rather than going straight to Edmondes's abode in the city, Coke decided to take a detour to visit one of his other sons in Brentwood, so they met neither Edmondes nor Lady Hatton's men. Again, a potential disaster was averted, as Coke and Clem had sworn that 'they would die in the Place', rather than part with Frances. The embattled girl arrived at Edmondes's house in London later the same day. There, she was to be 'protected' by both her uncle's wife, Lady Burghley, and Lady Compton, the two matrons each representing the interests of Lady Hatton and Coke respectively. The whole affair, said one letter-writer, was like a 'Comedie'.[29] While others found the tale amusing, Frances and her parents most definitely did not.

The next day, Coke tried to explain his actions to the council. He argued that his wife had challenged his legal rights as a father by removing his child, so it was his right to retrieve her. He insisted that the warrant he obtained had given him the right to search the Withipole house, so he had broken no laws. Some of Coke's enemies within the council, like Sir Francis Bacon, viewed the events as a perfect opportunity to get the lawyer in greater trouble with the king. They argued that Coke should be arrested for overstepping the bounds of the warrant, since it only gave him the right to search the house, but not to break down doors or offer violence. Furthermore, Coke had disobeyed the council's order when he waited one night before bringing forth Frances. Some even wanted him brought to the criminal court of Star Chamber to answer for his actions there.

What Coke's enemies at court did not realize was just how much Buckingham and King James favoured the marriage between John Villiers and Frances by this point. Secretary Winwood, who had given the warrant to Coke in the first place, quickly silenced his critics within the council by showing them a letter the king had written, commending Winwood's actions in the case. Bacon would also soon realize that he had bet on the wrong horse by siding with Lady Hatton against the marriage. In order to support Lady Hatton, make trouble for Coke, and make sure that Buckingham did not get allied with his enemy through marriage, Bacon had written a letter to Buckingham outlining the reasons why the Coke–Villiers marriage was not a good match. According to Bacon, Buckingham should not pursue the marriage because neither the mother nor the bride-to-be consented, endangering the financial benefit of the match altogether, since a large portion of Frances's wealth would consist of an inheritance from her mother. In addition, the marriage would be problematic because it would tie the Villiers to a family in royal disgrace, as well as a disorderly family, where husband and wife were constantly fighting. Buckingham might also 'lose all such your friends as are adverse to Sir Edward Coke' if he persisted, although Bacon graciously inserted 'myself only except, who out of a pure love and thankfulness shall ever be firm to you'. Bacon's timing was disastrous. At the time he wrote the letter, he was unaware that Buckingham was already fully committed to the marriage. As a result, instead of dissuading Buckingham, Bacon's letter became one long series of insults towards Buckingham's future in-laws and of the favourite's judgement. Buckingham, needless to say, was not amused.[30]

Realizing his mistake, Bacon tried to correct it, but with little initial success. He soon found it necessary to explain himself further not only to Buckingham, but to the king himself, who had written to Bacon, remonstrating with him for getting involved in the business. Grudgingly, Bacon changed his course. He 'resolved to further the match', let Lady Hatton know that he would now 'in anything declare for the match' rather than support her, and promised Buckingham and Lady Compton that he would 'tender [his] performance of any good office towards the match or the advancement from the mother [Lady Hatton]'. He also asked Buckingham to stop Lady Compton and his brother John from speaking badly about him, because it was hurting his reputation. While he understood that he must excuse their passions since one was 'a Lady' and the other 'a lover' (and thus, he implied, not quite capable of controlling their emotions), he hoped that Buckingham would explain to them that he was on their side now.[31] Court politics was a tricky business indeed.

King James certainly firmly believed that Coke was in the right when he violently fetched his daughter from Oatlands. He thoroughly disliked the implication that Coke had overstepped the bounds of the warrant, since he believed in the absolute right of a father to his child. He blamed Lady Hatton for the whole trouble, because 'every wrong must be judged by the first violent and wrongous ground whereupon it proceeds, and was not the theftous stealing away of the daughter from her own father the first ground whereupon all this noise hath since proceeded?' Coke had done nothing wrong, because 'except the father of a child might be proved to be either a lunatic or idiot, we never read in any law that either it could be lawful for any creature to steal his child from him or that it was a matter of noise and streperous carriage for him to hunt for the recovery of his child again'.[32] In other words, James only recognized the rights of the father and rejected the idea that the mother might have legal claims on her children. He was fully within the bounds of the law when he made those claims: mothers had very few legal rights to their own children in early modern England.

Not surprisingly, Lady Hatton did not agree with James and fearlessly voiced her contrary opinion. With the assistance of Holles, she penned a petition to the king, in which she conceded that while the law gave the father the 'predominant power in bestowing his child', yet it was 'consonant with' both the law of England as well as the law of God that 'the mothers voice be both demanded, and obtained'. Lady Hatton also argued that it was especially important in this case, considering that Frances was heir to her estates, based on agreements she had made with Coke, the most recent of which during their Privy Council mediation earlier that summer.[33] She was unable to change the king's mind.

Young Frances, the main object of all of this commotion, continued to be tossed about from place to place, without having a say in the fight over her present and future. The council persuaded Lady Hatton and Coke to agree on a temporary abode for Frances and they settled on Thomas, Lord Knyvet's house-hold. Knyvet was a member of the Privy Council and a neutral party in the dispute. In order to give the absent Knyvet a chance to agree to that solution, Frances was first moved from Edmondes's house to the Attorney General Sir Henry Yelverton's, and then on to Knyvet. Frances had barely arrived at Knyvet's home before she was brought back to her parents at Hatton House. The council members, who at this time had not yet heard from the king about a final decision in the matter, believed that both Coke and Lady Hatton should have access to Frances, as well as jointly make decisions about their daughter. Lady Hatton, at the time temporarily mollified, agreed that Lady Compton and John Villiers could visit Frances at Hatton House, as long as she was there too. In order to both care for, and have greater influence over her daughter, Lady Hatton had to accept living in the same house as her husband, for now.

Frances was not allowed to stay at home very long: soon, the king's order arrived from Scotland: Coke, as the father, had the sole decision-making rights in all things concerning his daughter, and Lady Hatton should obey her husband. Having thus received royal support, Coke decided to remove Frances from his wife's influence altogether. He brought her back to his son, Sir Robert Coke, in Kingston. According to one account, Coke allowed Lady Hatton, as well as Frances's sister Elizabeth, to travel with them. The party stopped at the Temple Inn for dinner. The two daughters ate the meal with their father, but Lady Hatton refused to join them at the table, instead sitting at the window with some sewing. Once at Kingston, Lady Hatton was not allowed to stay with Frances any longer. It is not clear if Elizabeth was allowed to remain with her sister. Soon, Frances found herself altogether cut off from her mother, and her mother's family and friends. Trying to remain close to her daughter, Lady Hatton had rented lodgings in the town of Kingston and spent as much time with Frances as possible when Coke would allow it. She was trying to keep Villiers and Lady Compton away from her. Coke soon prevented Lady Hatton's access and arranged matters so that only the Villiers could visit Frances freely. Lady Hatton complained to the Privy Council that her daughter was held as a prisoner at Kingston and that she worried about her health and safety. She especially asked that Frances's chamber be outfitted with a proper lock that could be closed from the inside and that she be provided with a 'bed fellow' other than just a maid, since Frances was afraid of 'night disorders'. Lady Hatton and Frances worried that Villiers might spend the night in her room, thus compromising her honour, or even worse, raping her. He could then claim that marriage was the only way to restore the girl's sullied honour. A woman who had sex before marriage, even if it was not consensual, was considered dishonoured. On the other hand, if the woman married the man, her honour did not suffer in the same way, as premarital sex between betrothed or those who intended to marry was more acceptable. Considering that Buckingham secured his marriage to Katherine Manners by a similar trick three years later, it was perhaps not an entirely baseless fear.[34] Lord Holles believed that the near imprisonment of Frances at Kingston was a 'strange preamble to marriage, whose trew parts are freedom, and love with consent of the parents for the chylds benefit, not for either of their turns'.[35] While Coke did not concern himself with Frances's desires, many early modern people believed as Holles did, that the ideal marriage was one where the bride and groom freely consented, and where both sets of parents agreed to the match.

Since the attempted flight and the appeal to the Privy Council had failed to bring results, Lady Hatton turned to another strategy: she claimed that Frances was already betrothed to someone else. While they had been in hiding in Oatlands, Lady Hatton told Frances that Henry de Vere, the Earl of Oxford, had proposed to her. She then had Frances pen a response, in which she accepted Oxford's proposal and promised in very strong terms not to marry anyone else. Frances wrote:

> I vow before God and take the Almyghtie to witnesse That I Frances Coke Yonger daughter to Sir Edward Coke late lord chiefe Justice of England doe gyve myself absolutely to Wyffe to Henry Vere Viscount Balboke Earl of Oxenford to whom I plyghte my trothe and inviolate vows to keepe myself till Death do us part: and if even I brake the leaste of these I pray God Damne mee Bodye and Soule in Hell fire in the world to come: and in theis world I humbly beseech God the Erth maye open

and swallow mee up quicke to the Terror of all faythe brakers that remayne Alive. In witnesse whereof I have written alle theis with my owne hande and scald it with my owne seale (a hart crowned) which I will weare till your retourne to mayke theis goode that I have sent You. And for further witnesse I here underneath set to my Name.

FRANCES COKE

In the presence of my deare Mother.

July 10th, 1617,   *ELIZA HATTON*[36]

According to English marriage law, a betrothal established a pre-contract and people thus promised were not free to marry others. If Lady Hatton could convince others that the betrothal was real, Frances could not legally marry John Villiers. Oxford was conveniently out of the country at the time—he was travelling in Italy—and therefore could not produce any rapid responses either way. In the end, Lady Hatton's machinations came to naught: neither Coke nor the Villiers had any desire to give credence to her tactics and simply waved this obstacle aside. Oxford himself was certainly intrigued about the suggestion when he first learned about it, but quickly changed his mind when word also reached him that the king approved of the Coke–Villiers match. Friends counselled him not to get involved in the matter and he heeded their advice, delaying his response. Later, Sir John Chamberlain dryly remarked that there need not have been such a hurry about the wedding: they could have waited for Oxford's formal reply and made absolutely sure that there were no prior agreements. Other commentators believed that the pre-contract was real, so while Lady Hatton had not been able to convince the few people that mattered with her fraud, she was at least sowing some public doubt.[37]

Lady Hatton was finding it increasingly difficult to fight against the joint forces of her husband, Buckingham, the rest of the Villiers, and the king, especially since her most useful friends were also starting to desert her. When James's desires became more generally known, fewer of Lady Hatton's friends and relatives were willing to act openly in her behalf, worried that they might displease the king. After receiving a conciliatory letter from Buckingham, and after finding out how much James wanted the marriage, Lady Hatton herself finally decided to change tactics. She realized that it might be wiser to try to get some of the hoped-for benefits of the match by becoming an active party in the negotiations, rather than continue to work against it in the face of mounting opposition. She even promised to add to the settlement her husband had outlined. Chamberlain was convinced that her about-face meant that she 'would have all the honours and thanckes, and so defeat her husbands purposes, towards whom of late she has carried herself very straungely, and indeed neither like a wife nor a wise woman'. By the end of August, Chamberlain reported that husband

and wife had even been seen riding in a coach together, but could hardly believe that it meant that they had reconciled. He was correct.[38]

Once in her father's control, Frances also had to accept the marriage. While the girl was tossed to and fro between her parents, other relatives, and various officials, rarely did anyone comment on what Frances herself thought of the idea of marrying John Villiers. When she was with her mother, she wrote the letter swearing she would only marry Oxford. When she was in her father's keeping in her half-brother's house, she wrote a letter to her mother saying she accepted the marriage with John Villiers, and also wished for her mother's blessing. Considering both the content and the wording of the letter, it is highly likely that Coke dictated what Frances should write. She told her mother that

> Without your liking all the world shall never make me entangle or tie myself; but now, by my father's special commandment I presented my humble duty to you in a tedious letter, which is to know your Ladyship's pleasure, not as a thing I desire, but I resolve to be wholly ruled by my father and you, knowing your judgments to be such that I may well rely upon, hoping your conscience and the natural affection will let you do nothing but for my good, I being a mere child, not understanding the world nor what is good for myself; but resolve to be disposed by you both and my uncle and aunt Burley, who as a second father I have ever been bound to for their love and care of me.[39]

The letter points to Frances's precarious situation. She is 'a mere child' and has to rely on the directions and goodwill of her parents and relatives: she did not have the power to determine her own future. The mention of Lord and Lady Burghley, Lady Hatton's brother and sister-in-law, was in all likelihood an inclusion meant to mollify Lady Hatton. By calling Frances's maternal uncle 'a second father', the letter suggests that Lady Hatton and her family had an influence in the matter of Frances's marriage that was not consistent with reality. The next section of the letter argues that the marriage would be a boon because it could bring Coke and Lady Hatton's scandalous fighting to an end and get Coke back in the king's favour:

> That which makes me a little give way to it is that I hope it will be a means to reconcile my father and you, which I would rather prejudice myself than not accomplish it; for what a discomfort it is to you both, what a dishonour nay what an ill example to your children, what occasion of talk to the world; as I think it will be a means of the King's favour to my father, and with all them that have been opposite against it, which as they make me believe he is much offended with them, which we have no more reason the more to dislike.

The tone in this section is not that of a 'mere child' to her mother, but rather reads like Coke admonishing his wife for the scandals caused by their fighting. Coke suggests that if Lady Hatton just accepts the marriage, he will be willing to reconcile with her. This in turn would be good for both of them, since the marriage might restore the king's favour towards Coke, and, he suggests, towards Lady Hatton as well.

Regarding her intended groom, Frances writes that he is acceptable after all, since he was of a good family and likely to rise in the world through the influence of his powerful brother:

> For himself [John Villiers], your Ladyship is not to be misliked, his fortune very good, a gentleman well born; for honour it is not likely (being it is in his brother's power, and he doing it for others), but he will do something for his brother, whom they say he loves so well.

Perhaps Coke managed to convince Frances that John was in fact a good man for her, but in this letter, we mostly get the sense that she agrees that he is not too bad. Coke told Buckingham and King James that Frances in fact was 'very much in love with Sir John Villiers', but that seems to have been an exaggeration.[40] Coke said the same to Lady Hatton, who would not believe it unless she could see and hear Frances say it in person, a request which Coke refused.[41]

Lady Hatton may have feared that Coke had procured Frances's consent through violence: according to later accounts, Coke, exasperated with Frances's stubborn refusal to marry John Villiers and her insistence that she was oath-bound to marry the Earl of Oxford, had summarily tied his youngest daughter to a bed-post and whipped her until she submitted. Rumours of violence must have reached Lady Hatton, as in the closing of the letter to her mother, Frances insisted that those reports were unfounded:

> Dear mother, believe there has no violent means been used to me by words or deeds.

Other than Frances's—or perhaps more correctly Coke's—denial that violence had played any part in Frances's acceptance of the marriage, no other sources produced at the time mention the whipping episode. Frances's contemporaries certainly accepted corporeal punishment of younger children as necessary, although it was supposed to be done with measure and with the intent of instilling proper behaviour and the fear of God in misbehaving children, and not cause any long-term or permanent injury. Nonetheless, the idea of whipping a teenage girl in order to force her to marry would have been shocking to many. She may have been a 'mere child' in her father's eyes, but she was old enough to marry and of an age of reason and should not be coerced in such a manner. While it was not reported at the time, the story of the whipping later became part of the family lore of the descendants of Frances's only child and was retold in the latter part of the 1600s.[42] Sometimes, the retelling changed the parent, and said it was Lady Hatton who whipped Frances, which seems unlikely, considering how hard Lady Hatton worked against the marriage. While the story of the whipping may or may not be true, we can say with certainty that in the matter of her marriage, Frances was the pawn in the political play of her parents, the king, and the Villiers, and that she had little power to influence them. She did not herself actively choose to marry John Villiers: she was made to do so, and made to do so in quite a spectacular and forceful manner.

By 14 August, Coke had secured a marriage licence for the two. Clearly wise after the troubles created when he had married Lady Hatton with neither licence nor calling of banns, he wanted to ensure that this marriage could not be contested on those grounds. The brief licence simply states the names, ages, and home parishes of the bride and groom, and also emphasizes the fact that Frances's father consented to the match. The parish clerk did not record the consent of mothers. The marriage now seemingly assured, the king promptly rewarded Coke by restoring him to his previous position as a member of the Privy Council.[43]

Even though Lady Hatton had finally given in and at least pretended to accept the marriage, she had nonetheless tried to free Frances from her near imprisonment in her half-brother's house in Kingston, hiring some men to do the job. This last desperate plot was foiled. Lady Hatton now had to face the Privy Council again, but this time it was not of her own choosing. When she entered the chamber, Coke quickly excused himself and went to a nearby room, probably both because he could not be impartial in questioning her, and because he did not want to be in the same room with his wife. Lady Hatton's renewed attempt to gain control of Frances, as well as her continued insistence that the fraudulent betrothal to Oxford was valid, troubled the king and council enough to decide to imprison her. James sent Lady Hatton to be held in custody by the London alderman, Sir Thomas Bennett. She was later moved to the residence of another alderman, Sir William Craven. The homes of the aldermen sometimes served as alternative places of imprisonment for persons of the social elite: it was considered more appropriate—and less severe—than regular prison.[44]

Lady Hatton thus secured and out of the way, the wedding plans swiftly moved forward. In mid-September, Frances, accompanied by her father and John Villiers's mother, went to see King James at Windsor Castle. The king was hunting in the park when they arrived, so they met him there first. Frances was formally presented to the king, who graciously gave the young girl his royal hand to kiss. The king, pleased with her person and pleased that she had finally consented to the marriage and thus given his beloved George what he wanted, in turn kissed Frances and showed her 'a great deale of affection'. The party then went inside to sit down to a banquet that was prepared nearby, and during this celebration, Frances and John Villiers, who had joined them by this time, were formally betrothed in the presence of the king.[45]

On 29 September 1617, Frances and John Villiers were married in a sumptuous ceremony at the royal palace of Hampton Court, with King James, Queen Anna, and Prince Charles among the guests. Having the wedding at court was of course considered a sign of great royal favour. James had hosted the weddings of his favourites and their family members and clients before. When Philip Herbert, Earl of Montgomery, married Susan de Vere in 1604, for example, he did so in the royal presence at Whitehall Palace. Frances Howard, the daughter of the Earl of Suffolk, married twice at court, first to the third Earl of Essex, and then the Earl of Somerset. Queen Anna also hosted the weddings of favoured ladies at court, although those tended to be smaller affairs. In addition to the royal guests and the bride and groom, the entire Villiers family was there, as well as Coke's sons and their families. However, the mother of the bride was conspicuously absent from the wedding, as indeed were any members of her Cecil family. King James had sent for Lady Hatton out of her imprisonment so that she could attend the festivities, but she excused herself, saying that she was sick and thus could not come. Undoubtedly, she did not feel like participating in her husband's triumph and she was not in a position to show her disapproval in any other way. The fact that none of Lady Hatton's Cecil relations attended either certainly sent a message that the marriage was not of their choosing.[46]

And what was Frances's state of mind on this grand occasion? According to one report, Frances cried during the wedding ceremony. However, that letter-writer was not himself present at the wedding, and he also suggested that Frances's tears may have been due to the worry about her mother and her mother's family, who at the time 'remained foreclosed from the Kings grace and favor'. Perhaps some, by now familiar with the drama of the summer, were predisposed to believe that Frances would have wept as she said her reluctant vows. Those who were present at the wedding did not mention any tears: according to the courtier Thomas Paulyn, the bride was 'a fine ladie' and 'did behave her self as well that day'.[47] Considering the events that had led her to the altar, Frances was probably apprehensive about her future, although the magnificence of a court wedding might have brought some delight to the embattled girl.

After her arrival in the chapel, Coke did not take his daughter all the way to the altar and the waiting groom. Instead, he passed Frances's hand to King James, 'with some words of complement at the giving'. The king then in turn bestowed her on John Villiers.[48] The gesture was telling: Coke's agreeing to marry Frances to Villiers was clearly the result of royal pressure, but by giving Frances to the king first, Coke was essentially showing his submission to royal power and emphasizing the king's 'fatherly' authority over all his subjects. The ceremony, held in the morning as per the rules of the Anglican Church, was followed by plentiful feasting and celebrations throughout the day and evening. The wedding party was served both dinner—the midday meal—and supper in the evening as well. For special occasions like these, the guests were served a vast multitude of courses, usually centred on fancy meat dishes, like beef, deer, peacock, and swan, seasoned with exotic spices, such as clove, cinnamon, nutmeg, ginger, and pepper, either served in pies or boiled or roasted. Globe artichokes and cool salads dressed with imported salad oils were fashionable vegetables in the early seventeenth century. The meals were concluded with 'banquets', which were a sort of buffet of sweet dishes, puddings, sweet pies, comfits, and candied fruits and flowers. Traditionally, wafers and a spiced filtered wine known as hippocras or ypocras, finished off the wedding feast.[49] The seventeen-year-old heir to the throne, Prince Charles, honoured Frances by sitting with her during the meals, as did the Archbishop of Canterbury, the Lord Treasurer (the Earl of Suffolk), the Lord Chamberlain (the Earl of Pembroke), and many others. John stood behind Frances and waited upon his bride during the meals, as a sign of respect and husbandly care. King James toasted the bride both during dinner and supper, and chatted with Coke for almost half an hour. The two men spoke pleasantly about Coke's first wife and Coke's early career advances. They also talked about the absent Lady Hatton, but then the tone changed from admiration to bitterness: while they lauded the memory of Bridget Paston, neither king nor husband was quite ready to forgive Lady Hatton's stubborn resistance. Strengthened by this royal affirmation, Coke 'looked with a merrie Countenance' on the—for him—happy result of the last year's troubles.[50]

A typical marriage celebration often culminated in a formal bedding ritual. At the close of the evening's festivities, the bride and groom were prepared for bed by their guests, usually with many jokes and puns about the sexual activity that was to take place during the night. Once the couple was put to bed, and the bed blessed by a priest, the guests retreated out of the room and left the couple alone. The newlyweds were then expected to consummate the marriage, which further confirmed and solidified the matrimonial bond. King James also had a habit of checking in on wedded couples the morning after while they were still in bed, to ensure that the marriage had indeed been consummated. He had done so when his own daughter, Princess Elizabeth, married Frederick of the Palatinate in 1613. According to reports, he asked Frederick if he was now 'his true sone in lawe' and was pleased when that was confirmed.[51] Frances and John had to stay in bed until past noon the following morning, because the king had said he would visit their marriage bed, but was late in doing so. They did not want to offend the king by getting up, so they simply remained in bed until he finally arrived.[52]

Now clearly so favoured by the king, the couple received rich wedding presents from the court elite. Common wedding presents among the upper echelons of early modern English society included so called 'plate', which was a general term that could refer to any household object, but usually meant plates and dishes made of silver and gold, or some other base material overlaid with silver or gold. No detailed list of Frances's and John's wedding presents survives, but other grand court weddings recorded gifts of gold and silver plate, gold and silver candlesticks, silver fireplace tools, gilt cups, pearls, and other expensive objects. Sir Robert Sidney, Queen Anna's Lord Chamberlain, certainly grumbled over the expense he would have to incur when buying plate as a wedding gift for Frances and John. Perhaps he may have felt a little mollified if he received the traditional counter-gift from the bride and groom: a fine pair of gloves.[53]

The Michaelmas wedding brings to an end the complicated story of how and why Frances Coke became the wife of John Villiers. When the drama surrounding the negotiations and the wedding was over, the king and Buckingham pushed for reconciliations between some of the warring parties. Lady Hatton cooperated until they asked her to reconcile with her husband: that she absolutely refused to do. Ultimately, the stubborn and resourceful lady eventually was able to turn the tables on Coke, reaping benefits from the marriage she had worked so hard against, whereas Coke was left with an expensive marriage settlement and not much to show for it. The young newlyweds themselves settled into married life, which moved along rather successfully at first.

CHAPTER 3

MARRIAGE AND MADNESS

A fter the ferocious battles over her marriage, Frances's divided family still nursed ill feelings towards each other. To restore some semblance of harmony, King James and Buckingham started to work on reconciliations. After the smoothing of most, but not all, of the ruffled feathers, the first few years of married life for Frances and John were relatively calm and free of friction. The couple's life was rather typical for persons of their social standing. John's career was progressing, which led his family to be hopeful of further advancements. The first signs of trouble appeared in the early 1620s, when John's health deteriorated. John's weakening condition, and the decisions about how to deal with it, led to an increasingly bitter and distrustful relationship between Frances and her in-laws.

For a few weeks after Frances's wedding, Lady Hatton was still under house arrest at Alderman Craven's house. Her situation looked rather bleak. James was angry with her blatant disobedience and defiance of king, favourite, and husband. Disobedient women were problematic, but Lady Hatton even more so at this point, since the Privy Council had expended so much energy on reconciling her with her husband just a few months earlier. Pretending that Frances was betrothed to the Earl of Oxford was not just an act of disobedience against a husband, but also, potentially, a serious fraud. At one point, the king ordered a commission 'to examine her, of conspiracie, disobedience and many other misdemeanors, and to proceed against her according as they shall finde cause'. However, Lady Hatton became ill—or perhaps feigned illness—during her confinement, which delayed the proceedings. Chamberlain told Carleton that 'her sicknes stands her in some stead for the time, and yf she come again to herself, yt may be in that space there will grow grace'.[1] Chamberlain would prove to be correct, because in the following month, Lady Hatton's fortunes changed.

By the end of October, Lady Hatton had recovered and decided on a new guise, playing the pliable and contrite supplicant. She made her official submission to the king, asking him to forgive her errors, because as a 'woman, and a mother' she was 'too weak to wrestle with strong apprehensions'. Comparing the king with God, she pointed out that 'God whose substitute you are, requireth but for the greatest offenses but repentance, confession, and a harte to amend, all which [she] humbly presented to his Majestie'.[2] James decided Lady Hatton had been humbled enough and the charges against her were quickly dropped. Now came the time for reconciliation. The Villiers knew that it would be beneficial to bring Lady Hatton around, as she was expected to increase Coke's already hefty marriage settlement. In early November, Buckingham orchestrated Lady Hatton's elaborate ceremonial release from imprisonment by riding to fetch her himself, along with a large retinue of splendidly clad courtiers. It was a public display of her official return to royal favour. Buckingham escorted Lady Hatton to Exeter House, her father's London residence in the Strand, as she refused to return to Coke at Hatton House in Holborn. The following day, she went to court in state and the king and queen formally received her. She had now rejoined courtly society.[3]

While Lady Hatton was at court, the king reconciled her with Lady Compton and also with Frances. Frances's relationship with her mother had been strained as a result of the marriage disagreements. At first, the daughter was reluctant and she 'could not be perswaded that she could forgeve and forget'. Now irreversibly tied to the Villiers, her mother's resistance to the marriage made Frances's life with her in-laws uncomfortable, to say the least. Even if Frances had wanted to openly favour her mother, it would have been difficult for her to do so publicly once she was in her father's control and had agreed to the marriage with John. Her initial reluctance to forgive her mother certainly might have been real—it had been a traumatic few months and Frances may have felt abandoned or disappointed by her mother's failures—but it might also have been part of courtly theatre, where Frances was trying to please the king, her husband's family, and her father by feigning resistance to her mother's apologies. However, the king's desire to create harmony among his courtiers was persuasive, and just before Lady Hatton left the court, James managed to make the new bride 'sweare that she loved her [mother] as dearly as ever she did in her life'.[4]

After Lady Hatton's formal submission, the royal favours continued to rain down on her. Coke left Hatton House and his wife quickly re-established herself in her town residence and began planning a fabulous evening's entertainment, fit for a king. A few days later, she hosted a big dinner party at Hatton House, to honour the king and to celebrate her daughter's new alliance. The king arrived with Buckingham and the rest of the Villiers family in tow. Lady Hatton presented the guests with a sumptuous feast with entertainment to match. In order to emphasize their recent reconciliation, Frances and Lady Hatton both presided over the event as joint hostesses and they were granted the favoured position of standing behind the king while he partook of the plentiful dishes on offer. The king was in a merry mood the whole evening and kissed Lady Hatton multiple times, signalling to all those important people present that she was now firmly in the good graces of her sovereign and that her previous offences were forgiven (but not forgotten). For good measure, James also knighted four of Lady Hatton's faithful men before taking his leave.[5]

If Lady Hatton had been conspicuous by her absence at her daughter's wedding, this time it was Coke's turn to be absent. He was not invited. Lady Hatton had not wanted to be present for her husband's triumph at the wedding and she did not want her husband present for her own triumph. Letter-writers wryly and pointedly informed their absent correspondents that it was curious that the man of the house was not present when the king came to dinner, suggesting that they believed Lady Hatton was too forceful a woman and not a proper subservient wife, and Coke, unable to control his strong-willed wife, not a proper man and husband. For the time being, Coke was staying at the Temple Inn (one of the Inns of Court) and rather than feasting on the delicacies Lady Hatton served the king, he sent 'for his diet to goodman Gibbes, a slovenly cook'. While James liked to think of himself as a great peacemaker, he could not broker between Lady Hatton and Coke. Lady Hatton had simply had enough. She was 'so animated against her husband, that it is verily thought she wold not care to ruine herself to overthrow him'. When the king brought up the topic of reconciliation, Lady Hatton responded that if her husband 'came in at one door she would go out another'. She even left London for the Christmas season that year, because she feared that the king would continue to pressure her to reconcile with Coke. By March 1618, she was threatening to bring criminal charges against her husband, because she argued he was acting contrary to the agreement of the previous summer. There were even rumours that 'Lady Hatton has driven her husband into a numbness of the side, the forerunner of palsy [stroke]'.[6] Frances's marriage did divide the two for good: Lady Hatton and Coke never lived together again, and Coke stubbornly refused to pay Lady Hatton's annuity from then on. She had to make do with what she had and bide her time, hoping that her future widowhood would allow her greater freedom. Unfortunately for Lady Hatton, her old husband would turn out to be frustratingly long-lived.

For his part, Coke, who had such high hopes of using the marriage to get back in James's favour, would find that keeping that favour was difficult. Ultimately, he would not be able to capitalize on the king's goodwill long-term, partly because his wife continued actively to work against him and partly because he was not a very skilful courtier. He was much too stubborn, too principled, and not subtle enough to be able to make the necessary compromises and build and reshape coalitions at court. His legal opinions continued to get him into trouble with the king, as they tended to argue for limits to royal power. The king had reappointed Coke to the Privy Council just before his daughter's marriage, but then removed him again. In 1621, Coke insisted on the rights of freedom of speech for the members of the House of Commons, and meddled in the business of the future marriage of Prince Charles, both of which King James initially found outrageous and potentially treasonous. Coke found himself imprisoned in the Tower for several months, although James eventually relented.[7] In the end, the hotly contested marriage of his daughter, which cost him so much social and political capital at court, was a failure for everyone involved.

After the flurry of reconciliations, the scuttlebutt surrounding Frances and her husband died down for a year. The court observers moved on to other topics, like the growing corruption scandal surrounding the Treasurer of State, Thomas Howard, Earl of Suffolk, and his wife Katherine. A few fleeting reports mentioned the likelihood that John would receive a peerage in 1618, but he would have to wait for that until the following year.[8] The couple probably lived in rooms at court in Whitehall Palace during these early years, as neither John nor Buckingham had any London residence at the time, but rather lived and moved with the king and prince, and their courts, between Whitehall, Greenwich, Hampton Court, and the other royal palaces. Buckingham purchased both Wallingford House and York House in London in 1622 and those would later become the main town residences for the Villiers family. At that point, Frances was increasingly living apart from both her husband and her in-laws.

Another scandal involving relatives of Frances was developing in 1618: the infamous feud between the Lake family and the Earl and Countess of Exeter. Thomas Cecil, Earl of Exeter, was Frances's maternal grandfather. After the death of Frances's grandmother, Exeter had married the significantly younger Frances Brydges Smith, who then became the new Countess of Exeter and our Frances's step-grandmother. On the other side of the feud we find the Lakes. Sir Thomas Lake was James's Secretary of State since 1616. Lake and his wife, Lady Mary Lake, married their daughter Anne to William Cecil, Lord Roos, the Earl of Exeter's grandson—and thus Frances's first cousin—in 1616. The marriage turned out to be troubled. They had financial disagreements and Roos accused Lady Lake of turning her daughter against him on purpose. His mother-in-law, clearly not enamoured with her son-in-law, threatened to spread rumours about his alleged impotence and to sue for an annulment of the marriage on those grounds. While the charges of impotence were bad enough for Roos, the fighting soon grew more serious. Mother and daughter rode the opposite tack and accused Roos of sleeping with the Countess of Exeter, his own step-grandmother. In the seventeenth century, such a relationship would have been incestuous. (The definition of incest was more expansive then, including persons related by marriage in addition to blood-relatives.) Lady Lake and Lady Roos went even further and accused the Countess of Exeter of planning to poison her lover's/step-grandson's wife in order to ensure that the illicit affair remained secret. They claimed that the countess had confessed both to the affair and to the murder plans and apologized to Lady Roos for her sins and transgressions. Furthermore, they claimed, the countess had written down her confession, which they now had in their possession.

Not surprisingly, this incredibly juicy scandal exercised the newsmongers and letter-writers for quite some time in 1618 and 1619, as more and more odd and disturbing details became available. Roos decided he had had enough of both his wife and his in-laws: he secretly left the country and travelled to the continent, leaving the whole mess, as well as his mounting debts, far behind him. The Countess and Earl of Exeter were concerned about, and frustrated with, their grandson's sudden disappearance, as his actions gave more fuel to the rumours. They were also furious and outraged at the accusations coming from the Lake camp. They took their grievances to the king. James tried to mediate and settle the dispute himself at first, but he quickly realized that the charges were so severe and complex that he had to refer the matter on to the Court of Star Chamber. The Exeters formally charged the Lakes and Lady Roos with slander. During the very lengthy court proceedings, it became clear that the countess's supposed confession was in fact a fabrication and a fraud invented by Lady Lake and her daughter. Secretary Lake had also abused the powers of his position by illegally imprisoning and threatening several servants and others to testify in the Lakes' favour. In February 1619, the Lakes and Lady Roos were found guilty, heavily fined, imprisoned, and ordered to 'make submission' to the Countess of Exeter. Lake was removed from his position as Secretary. Lady Roos was the first to crack and tender her submission in May 1619 and she was soon released from prison as a result. By that time, she was a widow: Roos had reportedly died a few months after he left England, although rumours continued to surface that the death might have been staged (if he did live, he never returned to England). Lake waited until January 1620 before showing his contrition, and Lady Lake stubbornly held out all the way until May 1621.[9]

While Frances's grandfather and step-grandmother were battling the Lakes and their daughter in Star Chamber as well as in the court of public opinion, Frances herself was getting settled in her married life. The marriage certainly did not have an auspicious beginning, of course, and it would eventually break down, but that does not mean that it never worked at all. In hindsight, it is easy to dismiss John as an unfortunate choice for Frances. Seventeenth- and eighteenth-century historians writing of the reigns of the early Stuarts described John as a fool or as 'Hominem prope stupidum', as Robert Johnston did. When Arthur Wilson described Purbeck in the 1650s, he argued that the feeble-minded brother of the favourite was not capable of handling his quick rise and rich marriage and that he thus 'got a giddiness in his head, which confined him to a dark room'.[10] Later writers also added that John was too old for a beautiful and vivacious young teenager.[11]

Whatever the objections against John Villiers as an appropriate husband for Frances, age should not have been one of them. According to the marriage licence, John was twenty-five at the time of the marriage, although he may in fact have been at least twenty-six.[12] Clearly, he was older than Frances, but only by a little over a decade. In Stuart England, husbands were often a few years older than their wives. When the age difference between young wives and old husbands was very large, people sometimes commented and felt that the match was inappropriate or that it was a set-up for failure. But in the case of Frances and John, no one participating in or commenting on the marriage 'negotiations' mentioned John's age as in any way problematic.

As far as looks go, John seems to have been perfectly adequate. While he did not have the dashing attractiveness of his famous brother—few did, after all—no one mentions his appearance as in any way objectionable. One portrait of John exists. It is a Villiers family portrait, featuring Buckingham, his wife, and their children most prominently. The central couple is flanked by Buckingham's siblings and his mother. None of the sibling's spouses or children is included in the picture. John, casually leaning on the back of Buckingham's chair, is dressed in a darkly coloured doublet and hose, a large lace ruff around his neck, with fashionably free-flowing long, wavy dark hair and a small, carefully manicured pointy beard and a matching moustache. The artist does not hint at any particularly disturbing features (see Fig. 3.1).

When Frances had finally given in and consented to the marriage with John, she had written to her mother that John was not to be 'misliked', since he had much promise, especially considering his close relationship with his powerful brother. By 1618, Buckingham had further solidified his position by winning over the rather awkward teenage heir to the throne, Prince Charles. Charles had initially felt threatened by James's affection and clear preference for Buckingham, and had acted against him, once even by soaking the favourite with water from a garden fountain. James, who almost always took Buckingham's side in these disputes, was furious with Charles, 'boxed his ears', and made the seething and humiliated young prince apologize to the favourite. While Charles's humiliation and the king's loving assurances gave Buckingham personal satisfaction, he was savvy enough to realize

Fig. 3.1. The Villiers family. Adults from left to right: Susan Villiers Fielding, Countess of Denbigh; Katherine Manners Villiers, Duchess of Buckingham; George Villiers, Duke of Buckingham; John Villiers, Viscount Purbeck; Mary Villiers, Countess of Buckingham (mother of John, Susan, George, and Christopher); Christopher Villiers, Earl of Anglesey. The children in the picture are Buckingham's eldest daughters and son: Mary, Katherine, and baby George. William Greatbach, after George Perfect Harding (mid-nineteenth century), after original seventeenth-century painting. National Portrait Gallery, London.

that it was better to have the future king as his ally rather than as his enemy. As a result, he worked hard to make up with Charles and set about winning him over with his famous charm. He succeeded: the two became fast friends, a friendship that would only grow deeper as Prince Charles matured. While Buckingham was James's beloved, he served as a substitute elder brother for the young prince, who had lost his real brother Henry in 1613. In the summer of 1618, Prince Charles, temporarily in disfavour with his father, asked Buckingham to mediate and help him make things right. Buckingham obliged and threw a grand party for James and Charles, who were reconciled. Afterwards, the party would fondly be remembered as the Friends' Feast. Buckingham's mother and sister, as well as Lady Hatton and Frances, attended the event and dined at the same table. Thus, by 1618, Buckingham now had the affections of the prince in his pocket as well as the king's, and the king declared that he desired to advance the Villiers family above all others.[13]

As Buckingham's star continued to rise, so did John's. In the years following the marriage, John disappointed neither his young bride nor her parents. In June of

1619, he joined the peerage when the king created him Baron of Stoke and Viscount Purbeck, also making Frances both a baroness and viscountess in one swoop. John's titles were in name only, however, because even though James had put considerable pressure on Lady Hatton to give up Corfe Castle and her land holdings on the Isle of Purbeck to Villiers, she refused. James tried to sweeten the deal by suggesting that Lady Hatton may receive a title of her own if she acquiesced, but to no avail. Frustrated, James even threatened to make Coke a baron just to annoy Lady Hatton. She still refused, so John became a viscount without an accompanying estate.[14]

John also had become quite an influential person at the Jacobean court by 1619 and all signs pointed to a continued rise. When he married Frances, he had already been knighted and served as Prince Charles's Master of the Wardrobe and Groom of the Bedchamber since 1616.[15] By early 1620, he rose to Charles's Master of the Horse.[16] When Queen Anna died in March of 1619, James gave her London residence, Denmark House, to Prince Charles. John was promptly appointed Keeper of the large and sprawling property, which faced the Strand on one side and the Thames on the other. As a result of John's appointment, Frances often lodged in rooms at Denmark House thereafter.[17] (Denmark House would later be renamed Somerset House. It fell into disrepair in the eighteenth century, was torn down and rebuilt, so that the current Somerset House stands roughly in the same place as the old palace.) Chamberlain reported hearing about a plan that Buckingham would resign his position as the king's Master of the Horse, so that John would be appointed to that office in his stead. That did not happen, but it clearly points to a perception that John's career had an upward trajectory.[18]

At the beginning of 1620, Chamberlain reported that Buckingham was so busy that he delegated some of his work to John. Buckingham was very fond of his brother, appreciating his simple honesty, modesty, and ability to 'speake plaine English to him' when necessary, and so trusted him.[19] In addition, John also served as a go-between for potential suitors, so that people who wanted favours from Buckingham had to go through his brother first.[20] Ambassadors, ever sensitive to court the people they perceived as the most helpful to gain inside access to the royals, began to take note of John as well. The Venetian ambassador entertained John and many of his friends and clients in January of 1620, and John promptly returned the favour. When the Venetian wanted an appointment with Buckingham, he asked John to set it up.[21] The French ambassador also entertained both Buckingham and John during the same month.[22] John was clearly becoming a person of some note and influence at the Jacobean court.

While John was moving along in his career, Frances, as the wife of an official and courtier and the daughter of influential parents, participated in the entertainments of the court. Lady Hatton regularly entertained the 'gallants and great ones about the court' and her daughter and son-in-law were usually among those invited. Throughout the winter of 1619–20, Lady Hatton decided to hold weekly entertainments every Thursday night until Lent. Frances and John were standing guests, as was Lady Hatton's step-daughter from her first marriage, Frances Hatton. Frances Hatton's husband, Robert Rich, Earl of Warwick, also attended the regular soirées.[23] Being part of the Villiers family ensured that Frances was in the inner circle at court. In December of 1621, when bad weather hindered the king from keeping a 'great store of companie' as he had planned, the people of note among those few who remained with the king were Buckingham, his wife and mother, and Frances. A month later, Frances was part of a dinner party the Bishop of London threw for Buckingham and his family. The company amused themselves by having the bishop conduct confirmation 'as children use to be in his chappell where they had choice musicke and all the ceremonies belonging to that action'. A bishop presiding over a pretend church ritual purely for entertainment seems rather irreverent, but perhaps mocking sacredness made the evening more titillating for the bored courtiers.[24]

John's health, specifically his mental health, worsened in the early 1620s. The earliest—brief—indicators of John's troubles surfaced during the marriage negotiations and immediately surrounding the wedding. While reporting the marriage, Chamberlain argued that John was 'in no such perfect health but that wedlock was rather like to hurt than heal him'.[25] He also believed that John was a weak man who was not likely to live long, so all the hullaballoo of the marriage seemed entirely unnecessary. Chamberlain was wrong: like his feisty father-in-law Coke, John proved to be a stubbornly long-lived man.

While struggling with Lady Hatton over control of Frances during the summer before the marriage, Sir Edward Coke quite forcefully tried to suppress what he considered 'slanderous speeches' about reports of John's 'soar legg'. These reports were coming from friends and allies of Lady Hatton who were against the match, so it is perhaps not surprising that Coke wanted to silence the opposition. Lord Holles, Lady Hatton's friend, was already outraged when Coke and the Archbishop of Canterbury brought him in for questioning and examined him about his potential involvement in the removal of Frances from London. He felt Coke was acting far beyond his authority and that he had been treated poorly by the questioners. Holles also complained to his friends that Coke had brought in 'a woman that sells chickens' and examined her 'for some scandalous words of Sir Jhon Villars soar leg'. Coke also brought in, examined, and imprisoned two male servants of Lady Withipole's (in whose house Frances had been in hiding from her father) for their 'slaunderous speeches of Sir Jhon Villars soar legg'.[26]

Why would Coke consider reports of a sore leg slanderous and go to such lengths to silence reports of the ailment? The implication that John's health was not optimal certainly threw a shadow over his suitability as a bridegroom. The injured leg might also have been a euphemism for sexual impotency, or at the very least temporary inability to consummate a marriage. When Frances was held in her step-brother's house in Kingston, John and his family were allowed to visit her, although Coke denied access to Lady Hatton. Holles reported that John visited Frances

> when his soar legg will give him leave, which recovereth more slowly the more the fault to thrust him into such toilsome work, unless his chapps could have chawed the beans better, this being a business for a whole man, both in boddy and mynd, least while the boddy is in paine the mynd suffer, and is less able to operate wher it would, and should, neither can a wound heal while the mind is distracted, both must draw together, both are compatible of the good, or hurt of either.[27]

Holles is here also making a connection between John's physical and mental health. The mental health was going to become more troublesome for John and his family.

Just a few short weeks after the wedding, another brief report of John's ill health appeared. This time, Frances had been sent away to stay at her husband's aunt's house 'some say upon discontent, others more likely that the humor in Villiers's leg burst forth again, so that her company might do him some harm'. The notion that Frances was sent away 'upon discontent' suggests that observers were aware that Frances had been forced into the marriage. In the future, Frances would prove to be a very stubborn and outspoken person: she may very well have voiced some discontent to her in-laws, prompting them to send her away for a few weeks. However, another letter-writer was more direct, reporting rumours that John was 'ill of his leg, that being sore before hath been made worse by the conjunction copulative'. According to these rumours, John's mother had 'lately sayd that his sonne must not be so frequent with his wife, and a lady by told hir it was *durus sermo* [hard words] for the yong tender Lady'. Here, the implication is not that John is impotent, but rather that his frequent copulation with his new bride was slowing down the healing of his leg. In addition, the lady who commented on Lady Compton's complaints about John's over-zealous sex life believed that restricting the newlywed's sexual activities would be disappointing for Frances, suggesting that she was enjoying herself. The report and the comments could of course be a joke, a common trope of poking fun at the enthusiasm of newlyweds, rather than a factual comment on John's health and Frances's reactions.[28]

John was healthy throughout 1618 and 1619, but then trouble began in the early 1620s, when he suffered from shorter spells of an unidentified illness, which in all likelihood was the same mental illness which would afflict him for the rest of his life. In August and September of 1620, John and Frances went to take the curative waters and enjoy the baths at Spa in Flanders, hoping that it would help him. It did not work, as Chamberlain reported that the 'Lord Purbecke is come home, (they say) little amended'.[29] John may also have had plans to go to Italy, specifically to Padua, known for its medical schools, to seek expertise there. He told the Venetian ambassador that he was curious to visit Italy. For whatever reason, the trip never happened. In the 1621 Parliament, John was present in the House of Lords only three days out of the total of ninety-three: once in January, once in February, and once in March, but not at all in April, May, June, November, or December, indicating that he was perhaps not in good health. In October the same year, he was too ill to take care of his position as the Master of the Wardrobe to Prince Charles. This time, it was definitely a mental illness that plagued him, as Chamberlain reported that someone else would be performing John's duties as long as his 'witts be out of the way'. Buckingham rented a manor house in Buckinghamshire called Stanton Berry, and temporarily placed John there under the treatment of Dr Richard Napier, a rector also trained in the astrological and medical arts.[30]

It is hard to determine which mental illness afflicted John, but the descriptions of his symptoms suggest that perhaps he had a bipolar disorder. When he was ill, he fluctuated between depression and some sort of manic episodes, which led him to act in outrageous ways. John's sister-in-law described observing the shift from mania, when his behaviour was uncontrollable and unpredictable, to his 'melancholy' or 'dull fits', when he became pliable and easier to handle. In 1623, when John was again 'distempered', Buckingham's wife told Secretary Conway that it was best to wait 'till the dull fit be upon' John before trying to remove him from London, because if there should be 'violent courses taken with him' while he was in his manic stages, she thought 'he would be much the worse for it' and that it would 'drive him quite besides himself'.[31]

Notwithstanding his emerging illness, John was not replaced in his official positions; he merely had substitutes fill in for him when needed. Furthermore, he enjoyed periods of better health as well, and during those periods, he participated fully in courtly life. In August of 1621, Buckingham celebrated his purchase of a country estate, Burley-on-the-Hill in Rutland, and he invited the king and court to elaborate festivities as a sort of house warming. Buckingham had married Katherine Manners, daughter of the Earl of Rutland, the year before. Unlike the splendid nuptials of John and Frances, the favourite's wedding had been a private affair without any pomp. The simplicity had to do with the contested courtship: while Katherine Manners was very keen on marrying Buckingham, her father did not approve. Buckingham would not marry if he would not profit from the bargain, so the father's approval was necessary in order to get a good dowry. Buckingham and his mother colluded to have Katherine Manners stay the night at his mother's without a chaperone, while Buckingham was also present. The Earl of Rutland felt his unattended daughter's honour was compromised and, after some more back and forth where Buckingham was holding out for a higher dowry, finally acquiesced to the match.[32] So, while there had been no wedding feast the year before, Buckingham pulled out all the stops for the celebrations at Burley. He ensured that his family, including those who were now related to him by marriage, were all present.

As part of the festivities, the famous playwright and poet Ben Johnson was hired to write *A Masque of the Metamorphosed Gipsies* to mark the occasion.[33] In the masque, a band of gypsies welcome the king to Burley, 'the house your bounty built, and still doth rear', referring to the fact that everything Buckingham had, he owed to the king's great favour. Buckingham himself played the captain of the gypsies, and John had a part as a gypsy as well.[34] Amidst the song and dance that were requisite parts of the masques, the Burley 'gypsies' then proceeded to tell the fortunes—all highly flattering—of the most prominent guests, beginning with the king, moving on to Prince Charles, and then to the members of Buckingham's family who were present: Katherine Manners Villiers, Marchioness of Buckingham (Buckingham's new wife), the Countess of Rutland (Buckingham's wife's step-mother), the Countess of Exeter (Frances's step-grandmother), the Countess of Buckingham (Buckingham's mother), Frances (Buckingham's sister-in-law, of course), and finally Lady Hatton (Buckingham's brother's mother-in-law). The verse directed to Frances was, like all the others, full of flattery and courtly fluff. The gypsy addressing her—which might have been John—extolled her great beauty, named her Queen of Love, and argued that even wise men could not help but fall for her loveliness, and that she would set all men's hearts aflame:

> Help me, wonder, here's a book.
> Where I would for ever look
> Never did Gipsy trace
> Smoother lines in hands or face:
> Venus here doth Saturn move,
> That you should be Queen of Love,
> And the other stars consent,
> Only Cupid's not content;
> For, though you the theft disguise,
> You have robb'd him of his eyes;
> And, to shew his envy further,
> He charges you with murther;
> Says, although that at your sight
> He must all his torches light,—

Though your either cheek discloses
Mingled bath of milk and roses,—
Though your lips be banks of blisses,
Where he plants, and gathers, kisses,—
And yourself the reason why
Wisest men for love may die,—
You will turn all hearts to tinder,
And shall make the world one cinder.

The gypsy's predictions that Frances would inspire a burning love was certainly true at least, and both Frances and her future lover would set aside their better judgements and pay dearly for their passion. The masque was a great success, so much so that it was performed two more times for the king and court. Only two days after the original performance at Burley, the king saw it again at Belvoir Castle (the estate of the Earl of Rutland, Buckingham's father-in-law), and then at the royal castle at Windsor the following month. Presumably, John continued to play a gypsy the two extra times, and Frances also attended.[35]

While John was thus ably assisting in his brother's triumphant celebration in the summer of 1621, a troubling episode occurred the following summer, this time publicly. At this point, John's illness also became entwined with his shifting religious convictions. By the spring of 1622, John had converted to Catholicism, apparently having been persuaded by a Jesuit priest operating secretly in England. John introduced the priest to his mother, who also considered conversion. The troubled King James sent William Laud, at the time Bishop of St David's, to the Countess of Buckingham to try to persuade her to remain in the Anglican faith. The Countess wavered for some time, but did eventually settle on Catholicism.[36] While staying at Wallingford House, Buckingham's new London home near Whitehall Palace, John had a severe manic episode, perhaps in response to attempts to get him to abandon his new-found faith. In a state of panic, John beat and broke a glass window in a room facing the open street below, cutting his hands in the process, and 'all bloodied, cried out to the people that passed by that he was a Catholique and wold spend his bloud in the cause'.[37] No doubt the people who witnessed it would note and remember the dramatic scene: the broken window, the frantic, bloody nobleman in the throes of mental anguish heightened by disease, desperate to declare his faith. Being Catholic in England was illegal at the time, but because of his illness, and more significantly because of his connection with Buckingham, John was largely protected from the negative consequences of nonconformity. In 1624, there was a drive to remove Catholics from official positions, but John was granted an exception at least twice.[38]

John's public displays of madness made the king order his removal from the public view altogether the following year. By the autumn of 1623, a flurry of letters issued from various court officials all had the same purpose: to get John out of London so that he would not be able to dishonour his brother or endanger himself or others. The two Secretaries of State took care of most of the practical issues, like the orders, warrants, and monies supplied to one of Buckingham's close friends, Sir John Hippisley, to escort John to the countryside. Hippisley seemed not too keen on his task, as he wrote from Hampton Court that he had done his duty by bringing John out of the city, but that John now refused to go any further without an express command from the king. Furthermore, Hippisley requested that he be relieved of the task of being responsible for John any further, and recommended the services of a Mr Aimes in his place, since Aimes had the 'power to persuade' John when needed.[39] Hippisley may have been uncomfortable with dealing forcefully with Buckingham's brother, or with dealing with a mentally disturbed person. King James himself wrote a letter to John in which he told him that he 'had tender respect to one so near and dear to the Duke of Buckingham' and that he therefore 'desires him for his own good' to 'abide at such a place as shall be appointed him by the Earl of Middlesex [the Lord Treasurer]'.[40] When the king summoned Parliament to meet in February of 1624, John did not attend: Buckingham was entered as his proxy.[41] By the summer of 1624, John was better and returned to court for some time, but it did not last long: he soon had an even more severe relapse.[42]

While John was ill, Frances lived mostly apart from her husband. She remained in London, either at Denmark House, or at her mother's at Hatton House. Mother and daughter also spent the summer and early autumn of 1623 abroad. They went to The Hague in the Netherlands, visiting the court of the English Princess Elizabeth, James's only surviving daughter. She had married Frederick, ruler of the German territories called the Palatinate. When her Protestant husband was also offered the throne of Bohemia in 1618 by the Protestant nobles there, Elizabeth received the title Queen of Bohemia. The royal couple is sometimes referred to as the Winter King and Queen, since they only ruled in Bohemia for a single winter. After that, the Catholic troops of the Holy Roman Emperor forced them out of both Bohemia and the Palatinate, and they took up residence at The Hague. These battles in central Europe were the beginning of the violent Thirty Years War, Europe's largest and bloodiest religious war between Catholics and Protestants, lasting from 1618 until 1648. As a result of the royal exile, many members of the English elite would make their way to the Netherlands to visit the king and queen without a country. Lady Hatton and Frances were also friends with Sir Dudley Carleton, the English ambassador to the court at The Hague (the recipient of Chamberlain's and others' regular reports about English court news), and his wife, and were looking forward to renewing that acquaintance. Mother and daughter travelled together with the Earl of Essex, and the travelling company wrote a complimentary letter to Carleton after their landing in Rotterdam, informing him and the royal couple of their imminent arrival (the spelling and punctuation of Lady Hatton's original is tricky, so what follows is a modernized version):

My Lord Ambassador,

Here are certain noble company landed at Rotterdam who have long lived under the government of the land gods, and now put themselves into the protection of Neptune, who have been so favourable to direct our course to this coast, which country we hear is so ennobled by the possessing of two excellent princes, the King and Queen of Bohemia. Hearing of their fame [we] have long desired to be an eyewitness thereof, which desire we hope to be accomplished by your interest in them, hearing of your faithful services you daily desire to deserve of them, and the care you take of all the wanderers of Great Britain, from whence we come. Though we be travellers accompanied with such misfortunes as we cannot appear but under the mournful weeds that belong to [?] noble dear deceased father, for which we hope you will crave leave of her [the Queen's] excellent eyes, nether to be offended nor to debar the same.

All the requital we poor weather-beaten travellers can make you, is to bring you word, in what good health we have left in the land from whence we came, some good friends of yours, although many hath been so prevalent, to debar us of some of our worthy company. The rest of us here all of us with one consent put ourselves under your direction and protection.

To witness the same we sign
Essex
    Hatton
        F. Purbeck
           Essex[43]

Lady Hatton's father, Frances's grandfather, had died in February 1623, which is why she was explaining that she was wearing mourning clothes. Unfortunately, Carleton's wife was out of town temporarily, and so missed the visitors, who 'much wanted her company', especially as their return journey was delayed for a full two weeks because of contrary winds. Carleton reported that Lady Hatton 'took it so unkindly at Aeolus' hand that [she] vowed she would never come more in his

Fig. 3.2. Frances Coke Villiers, Viscountess Purbeck. This portrait of Frances was painted when she and her mother visited the exiled King and Queen of Bohemia in The Hague in 1623. Michiel van Miereveldt, c.1623. Ashdown House, Lambourn, UK. National Trust.

danger, having never in her life being [sic] so absolutely overruled, as she confessed herself'.[44] After all, one could not write petitions or rely on powerful friends to change the weather in ones favour.

The only portrait that currently exists of Frances was painted during this visit to the Netherlands (see Fig. 3.2). The artist, Michiel van Miereveldt, was a famous and fashionable Dutch portrait painter, employed as court painter by the Prince of Orange-Nassau, and sought after by many. Miereveldt never travelled to England, but he painted portraits of Queen Elizabeth of Bohemia, Sir Dudley Carleton and his wife, as well as many other members of the English elite visiting in the Netherlands, including both Lady Hatton's father as well as Buckingham. Perhaps Frances and Lady Hatton left the portrait behind when they returned to England, because the painting became part of Elizabeth of Bohemia's extensive collection, which she brought with her when she returned to England in the 1660s, some fifteen years after Frances's death. The portrait of Frances is now on view at Ashdown House in

Fig. 3.3. Ashdown House, Lambourn. William Lord Craven had this house built for Elizabeth, Queen of Bohemia, after she returned to England in the 1660s. She died before she was able to occupy it. It now holds a portion of her portrait collection, which she willed to Craven. Most of the paintings in Ashdown House are portraits of Elizabeth and her large family, with one exception: at the very top of the stairs hangs the only surviving portrait of Frances Coke Villiers, Viscountess Purbeck. Photo: Stocker1970/Shutterstock.

Lambourn, Berkshire, where it sits at the very top of the winding staircase, with a pleasant view of the rolling hills outside (see Fig. 3.3).

When Frances and her mother returned from The Hague, a tragedy befell the family. Frances's elder sister Elizabeth died in November 1623, shortly after having given birth to a daughter named Frances, after her aunt, no doubt. We know frustratingly little about Elizabeth. For reasons unclear, she remained unmarried longer than any of her sisters. Perhaps her father was loath to pay yet another hefty dowry, because when she finally married Sir Maurice Berkeley in December 1622, her dowry of £4,000—not all of which was paid—was significantly smaller than the hefty settlement the Villiers enjoyed from their alliance with Frances.[45] During her short life, Elizabeth had constantly lived in the shadows of her beautiful and spirited younger sister, whose life at court seemed as charmed as her private life was troubled. Elizabeth would not be there to see her sister's downfall, or able to help or support her when she most needed friends.

Frances always maintained that the separation from her husband was not her choice, but rather enforced by Buckingham and the Villiers family. Those may have been mostly tactical statements, however, since Frances's primary concern was her increasingly troubled finances. Frances's problems were the same as those her mother had faced in her marriage to Coke: she had no real control over the substantial wealth she had brought to the marriage. With John so often in the care of physicians and hidden away in the country, Buckingham took control of his brother's finances. He may have been involved in John's affairs even earlier. In an account of payments listed by Buckingham's man Endymion Porter, probably around 1620, £200 was to be paid out to 'Lady Purbeck'.[46] However, Buckingham did not provide any regular payments to Frances from the Purbeck estate, causing Frances to continue to complain of her lack of funds, squarely blaming her brother-in-law and his mother for the situation. At one point, she said that Buckingham's mother and 'her Agents' literally threw her out, or, in the words of Frances, 'most barbarously carried [her] into the open street by force' when she came to them to seek financial relief.[47]

Frances found her situation increasingly difficult to bear, and eventually she had enough. In an undated letter to Buckingham, probably written in 1622, Frances angrily complained about her forced separation from her husband, her poor financial situation, and the mistreatment she received from the Villiers family. It is a forceful appeal, especially considering that it is addressed to one of the most powerful men in England at the time. This letter is the first time we hear Frances's voice directly, without the heavy influence or dictation of her mother or father, as in the letters before her marriage. Frances began by proclaiming herself to be an affectionate and exceptionally dutiful wife, who truly wished to comfort her husband no matter how unpleasant his illness made him:

> My Lord,
>
> Though you may judge what pleasure there is in the conversation of a man in the distemper you see your Brother in; yet the dutie I owe to a husband, and the affection I bear him, (which sicknesse shall not diminish,) makes me much desire to be with him, to adde what comfort I can to his afflicted mind, since his onely desire is my Companie. Which if it please you to satisfie him in, I shall with a very good will suffer with him, and think all but my dutie, though I think every wife would not do so.

But Buckingham was not willing to let Frances be with her husband, and he made her already trying situation even more difficult by not providing her with financial means to live comfortably while separated from him. The letter continued:

But if you can so far dispense with the laws of God, as to keep me from my Husband, yet aggravate it not by restraining from me his means, and all other contentments, but which I think is rather the part of a Christian, you especially ought much rather to studie comforts for me, then to adde ills to ills, since it is the marriage of your Brother makes me thus miserable. For if you please but to consider not only the lamentable state I am in, deprived of all comforts of a husband, and having no means to live of : besides falling from the hopes my fortune then did promise me, for you know very well I came no beggar to you, though I am like so to be turned off.

Frances was reminding Buckingham that the wealth of his brother was in fact the wealth that she brought to the marriage, and it was therefore patently unfair for Buckingham to deprive her of those means, especially considering the hardships John's illness has caused her. She also threatened to expose Buckingham publicly as a man who did not take care of his own. Seething with anger and desiring revenge, she continued:

For your own honor, and conscience sake, take some course to give me satisfaction, to tye my tongue from crying to God, and the world for vengeance for the unworthy dealing I have received. And think not to send me again to my Mothers, where I have stayed this quarter of a year, hoping (for that my Mother said you promised) order should be taken for me, but I never received pennie from you. Her confidence of your Nobleness made me so long silent, but now believe me, I will sooner beg my bread in the streets to all your dishonours, then any more trouble my friends, especially my Mother, who was not only content for afford us part of the little means she hath left her, but while I was with her, was continually distempered with devised Tales, which came from your Familie, and withal lost your good opinion, which before she either had, or you made shew of it; but had it been real, I cannot think her words would have been so translated, nor in the power of discontented servants Tales to have ended it.

Frances here also refers to the falling out between herself and the Villiers and that her mother had been forced to listen to false rumours spread by them, although she does not specify of what those rumours might have consisted. In addition, Buckingham clearly was no longer friendly with Lady Hatton either, although Frances thought that if the friendship had been real to begin with, it would not have been adversely affected by the slanderous words of what she termed unhappy former servants. At the end of the letter, Frances appeals to Buckingham's honour and nobility, implying that if he were truly an honourable man, he would treat her better:

My Lord, if the great honour you are in, can suffer you to have such a mean a thought as of so miserable a creature as I am, so made by too much Credulitie of your fair promises, which I have waited for performance of almost these five years: And now it were time to despair, but that I hope you will one day be your self, and be governed by your own noble thoughts, and then I am assured to obtain what I desire, since my desires are so reasonable, and but for mine own. Which wether you grant or no, the affliction my poor husband is in (if it continue) will keep my mind in a continual purgatorie for him and will suffer me to sign my self no other, but

Your unfortunate Sister,

F. Purbeck[48]

When Frances wrote this letter, she was around twenty-one years of age. She was no longer an insecure teenager, but a tenacious and resilient young woman. After several years of navigating both her increasingly troubled married life—including a sick husband and unfriendly in-laws—and life at courts both foreign and domestic, Frances clearly had found a new confidence, manifested in her appeal to Buckingham. We begin to see the development of the incredible stubbornness and fighting spirit which became an integral part of Frances's personality in the years to come.

Buckingham was still slow in responding, and Frances decided to make good on her threat and make her brother-in-law's neglect of her public. In June of 1622, she petitioned the king for a financial agreement of a set amount for maintenance or alimony, like her mother had previously received from Coke. Chamberlain, who reported the event, suggested that Frances's petition reflected poorly on the Villiers family, as it seemed rather callous to leave Frances without support. The petition prompted Buckingham, who was present, to promise that he would 'take such order hereafter that she shold be furnish to the full and [have] no more cause to complaine'.[49] Frances eventually succeeded in convincing Buckingham to provide her with some financial relief: in a petition to the House of Lords almost two decades later, Frances mentioned that Buckingham agreed to give her 1000 marks per year, in addition to her 'Jewels, Apparel, and Housholdstuff', as long as she did not cohabit with her husband.[50] The payment would be the rough equivalent of £160,000 in today's value and would have afforded Frances a comfortable living, although not quite as luxurious as that of her mother. Having thus secured some semblance of financial stability, Frances would soon face other troubles. Those 'troubles' were the consequences of her growing attachment to Sir Robert Howard.

CHAPTER 4

THE LOVER

As her husband suffered through his increasingly frequent and severe episodes of mental illness Frances continued to struggle with her in-laws. Diversions such as her trip to The Hague with her mother no doubt presented welcome respite, but the death of her elder sister Elizabeth in 1623 added sorrow and grief to her difficulties. Increasingly, Frances sought solace in the growing and deepening relationship with the man who would come to play a central role in her life: Sir Robert Howard. By 1623, the two were lovers and the clandestine liaison triggered a whole host of new challenges for Frances.

Sir Robert Howard came from the influential and rich Howard family, but he made no mark on society. Individuals from the various branches of the large Howard family served at the Tudor as well as the early Stuart courts, with earldoms and baronetcies as their rewards. Robert was the son of Thomas Howard, Earl of Suffolk, and his countess Katherine, born Knyvet. Thomas Howard began his court career under Queen Elizabeth: she gave him a title, Baron de Walden, and he became her Lord Chamberlain towards the very end of her reign. When James came to the English throne in 1603, Thomas Howard managed to secure his position at the new court: James made him Earl of Suffolk, and he served as Lord Chamberlain from 1603 to 1613 and as Lord Treasurer from 1614 to 1618. Similarly, the Countess of Suffolk became an important and influential figure at court, serving as Queen Anna's Lady of the Privy Chamber and Keeper of the Queen's Jewels, receiving the very positions that Lady Hatton had so coveted. As it turned out, the rapacious greed and ambition of the Earl and Countess of Suffolk eventually led to their temporary downfall.[1]

The Suffolk union was a fruitful one: Robert Howard was one of fourteen children, ten of whom survived into adulthood. (I will call Sir Robert Howard 'Howard' from now on, in order to distinguish him from his and Frances's son, also named Robert.) Howard was the fifth of eight sons. He was born in 1598, which made him four years older than Frances.[2] Since he was a younger son, he was not in the immediate line to inherit Suffolk's titles; those went to his eldest brother Theophilus. Howard's many siblings married into other prominent families like the Humes, Knollys, Devereauxes, and Cecils among others, extending the already expansive Howard connections like so many tentacles through the English elite. The English nobility was rather small, leading to intertwined family trees. Frances and her lover were related by marriage twice over: two of Frances's first cousins, William Cecil, Earl of Salisbury, and Elizabeth Cecil, married Howard's sister Katherine and his brother Thomas, later Earl of Berkshire, in 1608 and 1614 respectively (see Appendix). Moreover, Howard was also related to Frances's brother-in-law through marriage: Buckingham's wife Katherine Manners was Howard's first cousin on his mother's side, and in 1623, Howard's brother Edward married one of Buckingham's nieces.[3]

While the Suffolks and some of their offspring were able to rise to great heights at the court of King James, other family members fell into disgrace. Most spectacular were the double scandals involving Howard's elder sister, also named Frances. In 1606, when Frances Howard was just thirteen years old, she had been married to the fourteen-year-old Earl of Essex, as part of King James's attempt at reconciling rival noble families. The marriage was not successful and in early 1613 Frances Howard decided that she no longer wished to remain married, as she had fallen in love and begun an illicit relationship with Robert Carr. Carr, later created Earl of Somerset, was a handsome young Scot who had managed to capture the king's affection and by 1612 was a powerful royal favorite. Initially, Frances Howard and Carr's love seemed doomed to a lifetime of illegitimacy, as the modern version of divorce did not exist. Spouses could go through a legal separation, called a 'separation from bed and board', but could not remarry. The only option for a person to end a marriage and enter a new one—while both parties still lived—was an annulment, which declared that some impediment made the marriage null and void. The Howard family realized that a marriage with the political comet Somerset could be much more beneficial than the Essex alliance in the long run and therefore decided to support Frances in her quest for an annulment. The Suffolks argued that their daughter's marriage to Essex had never been consummated, that it stood no chance to be consummated in the future, and that it therefore was no true marriage and the Church should release her from her dysfunctional bond so she could fulfil her desire to become a mother elsewhere.

The court case quickly became a *cause célèbre*. Some of the commentators were troubled by the potential precedent of the case: what would happen to social order if marriages could be annulled simply because of a wife's whims and desires? Others were titillated, amused, and outraged because the judges and witnesses had to discuss intimate details of the failed sex lives of these members of the court elite. When reporting on the case, Chamberlain asked Carleton with feigned outrage and thinly covered delight: 'what wold you say yf you shold heare a churchman in open audience demaund of him [Essex] and desire to be resolved: whether he had affection, erection, application, penetration, ejaculation with a great deal of ampli-fication upon every one of these points'.[4] For Essex, admitting that he was impotent would not only be embarrassing and question his manhood (male impotency was often treated with derision in the early modern period), but it would also potentially damage his ability to marry again, since consummation and procreation were considered crucial and central parts of marriage. The solution to the embarrassing situation was to claim that he was impotent only with his wife, probably as a result of black magic, but that he had no difficulty sustaining a robust erection with other women. Since James knew that his favourite Somerset had a special interest in the outcome of the annulment trial, he ensured that the trial ended up freeing Somerset's lover from the unwanted marriage. When the judges initially proved split down the middle, James stacked the commission with extra judges who all voted for the annulment. By September 1613, Frances Howard was no longer Essex's wife. Three months later, she openly shared Somerset's bed as his loving new bride.[5]

The annulment was only one of the hurdles Frances Howard had to face before she could marry Somerset. One of Somerset's clients and friends, Sir Thomas Overbury, found Somerset's relationship with Frances distasteful and detrimental to his political career and he was not shy to share his opinion with his patron. Overbury and Somerset consequently had a falling out. In order to silence his friend and smooth the way for the annulment and his marriage with Frances, Somerset orchestrated a situation that led to Overbury being jailed in the Tower for refusing to follow the king's order. While at the Tower, Overbury died of an apparent acute stomach ailment. No one paid much attention to the death of a disgraced and imprisoned man at the time, but two years later, evidence surfaced suggesting that Overbury had been poisoned. As the story unravelled further, it became clear that Frances Howard had been deeply involved in the murder. Pretending to be a caring and concerned friend, Frances had sent Overbury tasty treats several times to alleviate his suffering in the dank prison. Cruelly, the tarts, pies, and jellies that the grateful Overbury devoured were laced with poison, slowly sickening, and finally killing him over a period of several weeks. Frances's husband, the favourite Somerset, was also implicated. In the spring of 1616, the couple went on trial for accessory to murder. Frances Coke's father, Sir Edward Coke, then still Lord Chief Justice of the King's Bench, was the main prosecutor of the case, zealously pursuing the noble defendants. The countess pleaded guilty, but Somerset insisted he was innocent. Nevertheless, the judges quickly found both guilty and sentenced them to death, but the king commuted the death sentences to imprisonment. Although their lives were spared, the Earl and Countess of Somerset never returned to court or to any position of power. They spent a few years in the Tower, but were then pardoned and lived a retired life in the country, their reputations in tatters. Their accomplices, the servants who had procured the poison, prepared the food, and delivered it to Overbury, were shielded by neither noble status nor royal favour. They were promptly convicted and hanged, the victims of their master and mistress's desires.[6]

Surprisingly, the careers of Frances Howard's parents and siblings seemed not to have suffered greatly as a result of her downfall. While they had fully supported their daughter during the annulment proceedings in 1613, the Suffolks quickly distanced themselves from her during the murder trial in 1616 and their positions at court remained intact for the time being. In fact, in a show of royal favour, three of the younger Suffolk sons, including Robert as well as his brothers William and Edward, were created Knights of the Bath in November 1616, only about half a year after their sister's conviction and imprisonment. The three-day ceremony, which actually did include ritual bathing as the title suggests, was part of the larger and elaborate celebrations of Prince Charles's installation as Prince of Wales (and thus as official heir to the throne). Twenty-three other sons of the nobility and gentry also shared the honour of becoming Knights of the Bath alongside the Howard brothers.[7]

The Suffolks' penchant for scandals continued. By the late autumn of 1618, the Earl and Countess of Suffolk themselves became the focus of royal and public outrage and this time it would temporarily affect their children. While serving as James's Lord Treasurer Suffolk succumbed to the temptation to line his own pockets. Modest graft was almost institutionalized at the early modern courts. Many officials made extra money from their offices in various ways: that was not unusual or even really frowned upon. Suffolk's downfall was his outsized greed and the fact that his wife was so closely involved in the corruption. The countess had accepted an annual payment from the Spanish ambassador in order to further Spanish interests at the English court. She also profited handsomely from taking bribes in return for her husband's political favours and influence. Female greed was usually interpreted as worse than male greed, and a wife who—Eve-like—influenced her husband to bite the wrong apples was seen as even more problematic, since the husband was supposed to be the ruler of the family and in full control of his wife. Suffolk was tried and convicted in the Court of Star Chamber, and both he and his countess found themselves imprisoned in the Tower and liable for a huge fine of £30,000 (roughly £7.2 million in current money). Coke, at this point restored to the Privy Council after his daughter's marriage, had called for an even larger fine of £100,000, but his fellow counsellors and judges believed it was excessive and reduced it.[8]

Despite public outcry and heavy penalties, the couple only remained in prison for a few weeks. Their fine was substantially reduced, largely because they agreed that their sons should give up their profitable offices and places at court. The eldest son, Theophilus, was Captain of the Pensioners and Thomas Howard served as a gentleman-in-waiting to Prince Charles. Now adults with their own ambitions, Theophilus and Thomas were not willing to give up their positions because of their parents' misdeeds, which spoiled Suffolk's plans: the king was not so interested in a fine reduction anymore. The couple then tried to hide some assets in order to claim poverty and reduce their liability that way, which further damaged their relationship with the king when the truth surfaced. In a show of goodwill to the Suffolk children and to demonstrate that he did not fault them for their parents' sins, the king promised to be godfather to Theophilus's newborn baby son in January 1620. By summer and autumn of the same year, the Suffolks slowly were able to extricate themselves from the worst of their troubles, eventually reconciling with the king and paying a much reduced fine of only £7,000.[9]

Although he came from this prominent, if problematic, family, Sir Robert Howard himself does not seem to have been a very ambitious man. He never reached the same levels of political or financial prominence his father, mother, and siblings achieved. In fact, Howard never rose above the status of a knight, although two of his brothers managed to receive noble titles (three if you count Theophilus, although he simply inherited their father's title) and three of his sisters became countesses through marriage.[10] Howard did not have any property of his own until his brother Charles died in 1622 and left him the lordship of Clun in Shropshire. He did not have full access to his inheritance until 21 June 1626, but he served as an MP for Bishops Castle (the borough was part of the Clun estate) for the Parliaments of 1624, 1625, and 1626, and then again in 1628. He spent most of his Parliamentary career in silence, observing the wits and oratory of those more skilled than himself.[11]

Young Howard was thus a man at the periphery of power. While he did not have the benefit of significant personal wealth and influence, he did enjoy a great deal of freedom, unburdened as he was by heavy responsibilities. His birth rights allowed him many privileges. He could live comfortably at the various Suffolk properties, the most magnificent of which was Audley End just outside Saffron Walden in Essex (see Fig. 7.2). When in London, he usually stayed at Suffolk House in Charing Cross, which first belonged to his father, and then to his elder brother Theophilus (see Fig. 6.1). Through the connections of his parents and siblings, he had access to the splendid entertainments and festivities both at court and at the homes of the rich and famous.[12]

No known portraits of Sir Robert Howard exist. His mother and sister Frances were both celebrated court beauties and Queen Anna deemed his mother and his three of his sisters worthy of participating in her extravagant courtly masque performances.[13] We can assume Howard enjoyed similar good looks. Portraits of family members, including the Earl and Countess of Suffolk, Howard's older brother Theophilus, as well as his sisters Elizabeth and Frances show a few common family traits, such as slim and slender bodies, voluminous wavy or curled hair of various shades of brown, dark brown eyes, rather narrow rosebud mouths, and pleasingly symmetrical, oval-shaped faces.

Frances and Howard moved in the same social circles, so it is likely that they knew each other long before they became lovers. In 1617, during the dramatic quarrels about Frances's marriage to John, a brief rumour surfaced that Lady Hatton intended to marry Frances to 'a younger sonne of the Lord treasurers [Suffolk, Howard's father]'.[14] Undoubtedly, Frances's life would have been very different, and much happier, had Howard become her 'yoke-fellow', instead of the sickly John Villiers. A couple of years after Frances's marriage to John, Lady Hatton actively favoured the Suffolks and tried to get them restored to the king's good graces after their corruption debacle. She had help from Buckingham, who also interceded with the king on Suffolk's behalf. Lady Hatton hosted elaborate entertainments and invited 'all the gallants and great ones about the court, but especially the Howards', which also could have brought Robert Howard further into Frances's sphere. At that time, Lady Hatton was also trying to tie Buckingham closer by working towards a match between the favourite and her niece, Diana Cecil. That particular scheme did not work, as Buckingham chose Katherine Manners for his bride instead. Diana Cecil later ended up marrying the Earl of Oxford, the unwitting subject of Frances's fraudulent betrothal in the summer of 1617. Buckingham also cultivated even closer ties with the Howards. In November 1623, the duke hosted a wedding at York House (Fig. 4.1): the bride was Buckingham's niece, a daughter of his elder half-sister, and the groom was Sir Edward Howard, Robert Howard's brother. In all likelihood, Frances and Howard both would have attended the wedding.[15]

Frances and Howard's relationship evolved from casual contacts to a romantic and sexual liaison around 1623. According to the witness depositions in Buckingham's later investigation in the spring of 1625, Robert had 'for the space of neer two yeers past' had 'verye often & familiar access to the Lady [Frances]'.[16] At this point, Frances lived separately from John, which gave her more freedom of movement. Frances spent most of her time in Denmark House, Prince Charles's London palace (see Fig. 6.1). His illness notwithstanding, John was still the Prince's Keeper of Denmark House and as a result his wife had rooms available to her there. John, depending on the swings of his fragile nerves, split his time between treatment and isolation in the countryside and one of Buckingham's London residences, Wallingford House.

Fig. 4.1. York Watergate, Victoria Embankment Garden, London. This gate is all that remains of Buckingham's elaborate London residence, York House. Visitors arriving by water from the Thames would have crossed under this gate in order to get to the main house. Photo: Chris Dorney/Shutterstock.

While Frances and Howard certainly were meeting each other openly at various functions and entertainments, it was the revelations of their secretive and private meetings which later presented the damning evidence of their illicit affair. In the intense stages of an early relationship, the two lovers took great risks to be together. Howard's frequent visits to Denmark House sometimes lasted until the early morning hours. To avoid curious eyes, Howard sneaked into Frances's room by going through a neighbour's house, climbing over the roof, and slipping in through Frances's window, like an acrobatic Romeo. The couple also met secretly at the same accommodating neighbour's house, a man named Mr Peel. It is not entirely clear why Mr Peel would allow the couple's transgressions to take place in his house. Perhaps he was compensated, or perhaps he was a friend of Frances and Howard. The lovers had intimate suppers in their coach in Knightsbridge and at Ilford several times. Sometimes, they left the city altogether; they went to the wells in Essex, no doubt drinking what was believed to be the holy waters. They spent nights at inns in Lambeth, Maidenhead, and Ware, where they rented rooms located right next to each other, which later interrogators interpreted as suspiciously close, although Frances and Howard claimed it was innocent. Perhaps the couple stayed at the White Heart Inn in Ware, which featured the famous Great Bed of Ware, a giant bed more than three metres wide, built as a special attraction to lure more visitors and customers to the establishment. Over the course of many centuries, overnight guests have left their marks on the bed by carving in their initials or leaving wax seals on the wooden posts. If they slept in the bed and left their marks, centuries of later couples have rendered Frances and Howard's initials unreadable. Considering that the bed was associated with bawdy puns and stories and that it was so famous that both Shakespeare and Ben Johnson mentioned it in plays and poetry, it would have been wiser for the couple to stay somewhere more discreet and not leave any tell-tale signs behind.[17]

In addition to their secret meetings, Frances and Howard also sought the services of John Lambe, a medical practitioner, astrologer, fortune-teller, convicted witch, and rapist. Before he ran into legal troubles, Lambe had managed to build up a large and varied clientele, including members of the artisan classes in London as well as women from the gentry and nobility. It was not at all unusual for both men and women of all classes to consult astrologers and it was not unusual for astrologers to combine their astrological knowledge with medical and magical arts. Perhaps the most famous practitioner of such a combination was Dr Simon Forman, who had featured heavily in the trial of Howard's sister Frances for the murder of Overbury in 1616.[18] Desperate to get out of her marriage to the Earl of Essex, Frances Howard had paid Forman to ensure, through magical means, that the Earl of Essex remained impotent and incapable of consummating the marriage. She had also asked that he magically 'bind' Somerset to her, so that she could be assured of his love throughout her difficult annulment proceedings. As the word spread of Frances Howard's desire to use magic to rid herself of an unwanted husband and supply her with a new one, London society and beyond were horrified. The countess's contemporaries condemned her occult schemes as particularly sinister, presaging her further downward spiral into evil, eventually culminating in the cold-blooded poisoning of Overbury.[19]

Performing such services could be dangerous business. The line between accept-able and benevolent semi-magical, semi-medical practices and black magic was very fine. In 1623, Lambe discovered where the line lay. He found himself in the King's Bench Prison on witchcraft charges, accused of having bewitched Lord Windsor's 'ymplement': in other words, having rendered him impotent. In 1624, Lambe was further accused and convicted of having raped an eleven-year-old girl who came to his prison cell to bring him some herbs. Although convicted of both the witchcraft accusations and the rape, Lambe somehow managed to obtain a reprieve from the usual death sentences and eventually even a royal pardon. When in prison in 1623–4, he was not kept 'close prisoner', which meant that people could still visit him, he had access to pen and paper, and he could move about freely within the confines of the prison walls. He thus was able to stay in business even from prison, as Frances and many other clients, burdened by problems in need of magical solutions, went to consult with him there.[20] Twice Frances went to see Lambe wearing a disguise, having borrowed her chambermaid's clothes for the occasion. But she visited Lambe as herself as well, and Howard accompanied her at least six or seven times, according to witnesses. While the witness depositions do not say specifically why Frances went to see Lambe, some implied that she went there to have him practise some sort of 'sorcerye or charmes, wth pictures of waxe, &ct'.[21] Frances may have wished to bind Howard's love to her, or have her future told, or perhaps even see if there was a way to get rid of her burdensome husband and bring trouble to her in-laws. Buckingham later worried that Frances and Lambe may have hurt John and perhaps even caused his mental illness with magic or poisons. Frances certainly rewarded Lambe well for whatever services he provided: she gave him money, a gown, and her own garters, both of which he wore frequently. She also paid money towards securing his pardon.[22] Lambe may have escaped the gallows, but ultimately he could not escape the judgement and punishment of the London crowds. In June 1628, Lambe was attacked and brutally beaten to death by an angry mob.[23]

Later, Frances and Howard's association with this ambivalent character certainly gave Buckingham more fuel for his fire, once he discovered their relationship and began preparing the case against them. But for the time being, the pair were safe. Throughout 1623 and 1624, Frances juggled her relationship with Howard and battled with Buckingham over money at the same time. The meetings with her lover provided pleasant breaks from her fractious relationship with her in-laws, but those pleasures proved expensive. In the spring of 1624, Frances discovered she was pregnant. Suddenly, the stakes became much, much higher and Frances's difficulties rapidly multiplied.

Frances's pregnancy threatened to expose the lovers' illicit affair, which could have dire consequences. According to both secular and ecclesiastical law in England, any sex outside of the bonds of marriage was illegal, but the laws were directed by a clear double standard. It was considered much more serious if a woman, especially a married woman, engaged in illicit sex than if a man did the same. The law defined adultery largely as a female crime: a married woman having sex with anyone other than her husband was committing adultery, whereas a married man could only be found guilty of adultery if he was having sex with another man's wife. A married man having sex with an unmarried woman committed the less serious crime of fornication. A woman could only be guilty of fornication if she herself was unmarried.[24] In the case of Frances and Howard, they were both guilty of adultery: although Howard was unmarried, he was having sex with a married woman. The punishment for adultery varied, but included fines, whipping, stocking, and other public shaming, like being forced to stand dressed in a white sheet in a churchyard or marketplace, publicly confessing one's sins and asking for forgiveness, in a ceremony called penance.

For Frances and other women during the early seventeenth century, the options for preventing unwanted pregnancies were relatively few and the moral condemnation for using any form of birth control heavy.[25] This made illicit sex very risky, especially for women. Like most medical knowledge, the understanding of the human reproductive process was incomplete in the early seventeenth century. It was based on ancient theories of the operations, balances, or imbalances of the four basic bodily substances, or humors (blood, phlegm, and black and yellow bile). Some medical doctors believed that conception simply required the depositing of the male semen in the uterus in proper conditions (not too hot, not too cold, and with a good humoral balance), whereas others argued that both male and female ejaculate was necessary for conception, placing greater importance on female sexual pleasure. It was not until the first half of the seventeenth century that William Harvey and Hieronymus Fabricius developed their theories of the existence of a human egg or ovum. Anthony van Leuwenheok first observed live sperm through a microscope in the 1670s. Those discoveries led to much argument before it was recognized in the nineteenth century that both egg and sperm were necessary for conception. Not until the beginning of the twentieth century did doctors properly understand the timing of ovulation in the menstrual cycle.[26]

The lack of knowledge about the process made the prevention of pregnancy especially tricky, but many birth control methods were not necessarily based on the science of the medical doctors, but rather the trial and error practices of regular women and men who wanted to avoid pregnancy. Some rudimentary barrier methods existed, like condoms made of linen and silk, and pessaries of various kinds, but those probably were not very common. The condoms were meant to limit exposure to venereal diseases rather than prevent pregnancy, and considering the porosity of the material used, they could hardly have been very effective at either. In all likelihood, the most common form of contraception during the early modern period was coitus interruptus, or withdrawal before ejaculation. That required a great deal of cooperation and control by both parties, but especially the man, and was not a very reliable method. Different forms of non-penetrative or non-vaginal sex could also ensure that no pregnancy would ensue, but according to the teachings of the Church, sexual acts which could not at least in theory end in conception were sinful and should be avoided.

According to early seventeenth-century medical consensus, a pregnancy was not fully confirmed until the moment of 'quickening', which was the first time a woman could feel the foetus move in her uterus. According to religious and medical teachings, that was the moment when the foetus became a separate entity from the mother. Abortion was illegal and considered a serious crime and sin but only action taken to abort a foetus *after* quickening was considered to be a true abortion. Medical treatises and advice books discussed at length various methods to 'bring on the flowers', or restore menstruation that had ceased, such as herbal concoctions of parsley, pennyroyal, savin, mint, and others. Of course, these treatments could be both for amenorrhea (cessation of menstruation) as a way to improve fertility, as well as for ending early pregnancies, as a pre-quickening abortion restored the menses too.[27] Lambe, in addition to being an astrologer and practitioner of magic, also provided medical services, so it is perhaps possible that Frances asked him for some sort of treatment to restore menstruation. Options, possibilities, and efforts aside, one thing was certain: a new life was attached to Frances's uterine wall, a product of passion and a producer of endless new problems.

Since the stigma of having illegitimate children was heavy, desperate women who carried unwanted babies to term on rare occasions killed or abandoned the child after birth. A new statute in 1624 equated infanticide with murder and the punishment was death. The statue was especially severe in the case of unmarried women: whereas married women were presumed innocent until proven guilty, the opposite was true for unmarried women. It assumed that if an unmarried woman gave birth secretly, she would be more likely to submit to the temptation to kill the baby and thus 'get away' without anyone finding out about her sexual sin. So, even if a baby was stillborn, if the unmarried mother had no witnesses that could swear that the child was dead at birth, the law assumed that it was a case of infanticide. It made the consequences of secret births for unmarried women especially dire. The idea behind the law was to encourage unmarried women to confess their illicit pregnancies, to discourage them from giving birth secretly, and to protect the lives of illegitimate children. Once the illegitimate children were born and out in the world, however, there was not much legal protection for them.[28]

If Frances had not been separated from her husband at the time when she became pregnant she might have been able to get away with claiming that the child was legitimate. English ecclesiastical law generally assumed that the child of a wife was the husband's as long as he was 'alive and in England', unless the circumstances clearly made it impossible for the husband to be the father. Furthermore, if the husband accepted paternity, the courts most likely would not challenge it.[29] However, because of the long separation between the spouses, and because John was under the influence of her hostile in-laws, Frances found a pregnancy very difficult to explain. She knew that her only chance was to conceal everything: the pregnancy, the birth, as well as the child.

As other desperate and 'unfortunate' women of the era, Frances did succeed in concealing her pregnancy. The most common way of hiding an illicit pregnancy was to escape prying eyes altogether by going to some obscure place in the countryside or perhaps even abroad and only re-emerge after the child had been born, pretending that nothing had happened. Other prominent women had been able to pull it off at least temporarily, like Elizabeth Throckmorton, Queen Elizabeth's maid-of-honour in the 1590s. In order to hide her pregnancy and secret marriage to Sir Walter Raleigh, Throckmorton excused herself from her service, claimed illness, went to the country, gave birth, and then returned to court, her health magically restored. Later on, the rumour mill exposed her childbirth and secret marriage. As a result of the deception, the queen imprisoned her for several months. Nonetheless, people at court did not know about her pregnancy until months after she gave birth. Anne Vavasour, another Elizabethan court woman, managed to *stay* at court and yet conceal her entire illicit pregnancy until the birth itself, which also took place at court, gave her away.[30]

The fashion that had developed by the 1620s was especially helpful for a person trying to hide a swelling belly. The previous late Elizabethan and early Jacobean style had been very unforgiving: it featured exaggerated long and narrow waists, accomplished with the help of tightly laced bone- or wood strip-enforced stays (corset) and a long, pointy stomacher. A stomacher was a stiff, triangular-shaped piece, usually heavily decorated, that was attached to the front of the stays and went over the top of the skirt, pointy end down. It made the torso appear longer and the stomach flatter. By the 1620s, that older, stiffer style had been replaced by dresses with significantly higher waistlines and more voluminous and loosely flowing skirts.[31]

In the one existing portrait of Frances painted in 1623, she is wearing such a dress (see Fig. 3.2). A pregnant belly could conceivably be hidden in the large folds of the dress, especially with some assistance of a corset and a servant or two with particular skills in draping and arranging clothing just so.

Frances did not go to the country: she stayed in London, at Denmark House, throughout her pregnancy. A few people, on whose assistance Frances had to rely, were surely aware of her condition. Her closest female servants, who knew about her relationship with Howard and who would be the ones regularly to come into close physical contact with Frances while dressing her and taking care of other bodily needs, must have known. Three of Frances's gentlewomen servants accompanied her to the secret location where she gave birth and helped with the complex arrangements.

Buckingham and the Villiers family did not know about Frances's pregnancy, although they might have suspected it at some point. In a petition written seventeen years after the event, Frances claimed that Buckingham's mother, as well as his half-brother Sir Edward Villiers, a midwife, and others besides had burst into her room at night and forcibly attempted to search her body for signs of pregnancy. Frances did not say whether they succeeded in discovering anything, although in her version, she was 'with Child near her time' when the night visitors came. At the time when Frances gave that account, she was actively trying to seek financial payments from the Villiers, and establish her son as her husband's lawful heir. As a result, she was attempting to explain away the secrecy of the birth: she argued that the child was her husband's and that after this rough treatment from her in-laws she felt forced to hide the birth in order to save both the child and herself from further harm. She does not explain why her in-laws would have been so upset at the idea of Frances being pregnant with her own husband's child.[32] Perhaps Frances had a close call, with her in-laws either suspecting her but not able to conclude their physical inspection for whatever reason, or perhaps her pregnancy was not quite as advanced as she said later and she was still able to hide it. In any case, whether or not the story of the bodily inspection was true, the Villiers did nothing and said nothing about Frances's condition until January of 1625, several months after the birth of the baby. In the autumn of 1624, the rumour mongers and the news writers, who constantly kept abreast of all the goings on at court, did not know about this pregnancy either.

Normally, the birth of a child of a wealthy noble or gentry family would be associated with a series of elaborate rituals. First, the pregnant woman chose the most appropriate place for her 'lying-in', as the period surrounding the birth was known. If the woman had access to multiple homes, as many elite women did, she chose the one that best suited her particular needs and situation. Then came the preparation of the lying-in chamber: stocking it with clean linens, covering the windows as fresh air and daylight were considered to be harmful to mother and child, bringing in a birthing-chair, and so forth. The pregnant woman also had to make decisions about which women would assist and attend her at the birth. Usually, the chosen women were female family members, friends, servants, and a hired-in midwife. The lying-in chamber generally was an all-female space with no men allowed. After a successful birth, the mother would rest in her lying-in chamber for four weeks, while others cared for the infant. After the period of rest followed the religious ceremony of churching, which officially ended the new mother's lying-in period and cleansed her of the impurity of birth, thus receiving her back into the Christian community.[33]

A few weeks after the birth, or sooner if the child seemed weak, parents would have their children baptized. As in the case of Frances's elder sister Elizabeth, christening ceremonies and celebrations could be quite elaborate parties and the guests were expected to provide the infant with rich gifts. The selection of godparents, or 'gossips' for the christening was also an important process, as this was a way to establish or confirm friendships, alliances, and honours. Because of the special importance of blood lines and inheritance for social, political, and economic power and prestige in early modern England, the births and baptisms of children, especially the children of the elite, elicited much commentary in letters. Writers who were reporting to absent friends or patrons about what was happening at court or among the powerful often included information about the lying-in of notable women, the christenings of their babies, the selection of godparents, and of the generosity—or stinginess—of the gifts.

Naturally, Frances was not interested in making arrangements for a lying-in or baptism. Wanting to ensure that the news writers would have nothing to report about the birth of her child, she made an intricate and cunning plan. In early October of 1624, Frances left her lodgings at Denmark House in her coach. Once she arrived in Watling Street, just to the east of St Paul's Cathedral, she changed from her own coach to a hired coach. She told her coachman and footman to wait at a nearby inn until she sent for them again, ensuring that they would not know where she was going. She did not trust them enough to take them into her confidence, which turned out to be a correct decision. Accompanied by her three trusted gentlewomen, Elizabeth Ashley, Dorothy Wingfield, and Anne Elwick, she directed her hired coach to take her to a Mr Manning's house in White Cross Street, outside of the city walls (see Fig. 6.1). There, she stayed in Manning's 'Garden-House' under the assumed name of 'Mrs Wright', wife of John Wright of Bishopthorpe, Yorkshire. Shortly thereafter she gave birth to a baby boy, assisted by a hastily hired midwife.

The next day, the child was privately and hurriedly baptized and given the name Robert Wright. One of Frances's accompanying gentlewomen, along with two of the midwife's sons, served as impromptu godparents. The baby was quickly sent away to be cared for by a wet-nurse. That evening, Frances returned to Denmark House sans baby, again under the cover of secrecy. She hired another coach to travel part of the way, then sent to the inn for her waiting footman and coachman, and thus travelled back to Denmark House in her own coach.[34] Concealing the birth demonstrated Frances's impressive planning skills, and uncanny ability to get other people to assist her in difficult situations. It also shows the strong loyalty she inspired in some of her servants.

It is hard not to notice the choice of name for the baby: Robert, like his father. Although the last name 'Wright' was part of the boy's 'disguise', the choice of his first name signals the baby's true paternity. Robert was a very common name, of course, and early modern parents generally did not favour unusual or unique names for their children. A quick look through any number of seventeenth-century genealogies will find a rather narrow use of names: William, James, John, Robert, Thomas, Edward, Charles, George, Richard, Henry, Francis for males, and Elizabeth, Katherine, Mary, Anne, Susan, Frances, Margaret, and one or two Dorothys and Lucys for females. It was common to name sons, especially firstborns, after the father or after other close male relatives from the father's family. Notably, while there were several Roberts on Frances's side of the family, both among the Cecils and among the Cokes, there were no Roberts at all in the immediate Villiers family. Frances's choice of the name for the newborn thus distanced him not just from her husband, but also from her husband's family.

Frances could not rest as other women recuperating from childbirth were able to do. She had to try to go about her business as usual, so that no one would suspect that she was a new mother. While struggling to keep up appearances, she received another blow: only two months after the birth, she contracted smallpox. Smallpox is a dangerous viral disease, which during this period was sometimes fatal. Victims suffer from high fever, severe head- and backaches, nausea and vomiting, and a skin rash which develops into liquid-filled pustules covering large parts of the body. The pustules often burst in later stages of the disease, and sometimes smallpox survivors can be horribly disfigured by the scarring from the healing pustules. Howard's mother, the Countess of Suffolk, lost some of her celebrated looks after a bout of smallpox in 1619.[35] If the pustules appeared in the eyes, the scarring could cause blindness and other complications. No later sources mention anything about lasting disfigurements or effects from the disease, so it seems Frances managed to escape both with her life and with her good looks.

The curious part about Frances's illness was the fact that her husband John was 'so kind that he stirres not from her beds feet' the whole time while she was ill.[36] The couple had been separated for most of the last two years, but here they were spending time under the same roof again, albeit under difficult circumstances. John, who was clearly attached to his wife, was tending to her less than two months after she had given birth to another man's child. He did not know about the child at the time. Buckingham would have to work hard to convince his brother of Frances's guilt in the months to come. His mental state was not very stable during 1624: he had been better during the summer, but he soon suffered another episode, apparently more severe than previous ones. It is not clear what his health condition was like during his vigil by Frances's sickbed, but it is notable that his family did not prevent him, or at least did not successfully prevent him, from tending to her. The episode certainly points to John's great affection and concern for his wayward wife.

The difficulties of pregnancy and childbirth, the stress and strain of keeping both secret, and the suffering associated with the smallpox ensured that 1624 was a very difficult year for Frances. The lull of the early years of marriage was definitely a thing of the past and Frances's troubles would only get worse. By January 1625, Frances's secret relationship, pregnancy, and baby were secrets no more and her renewed battles with Buckingham and the Villiers would become very public indeed, as she fought against them in the Court of High Commission, in front of the Privy Council, and through Parliamentary petitions, investigations, and decisions. As had been the case during her marriage negotiations, her personal life now would become intensely political.

CHAPTER 5

THE LEGAL TROUBLES

B y February of 1625, Frances and Robert's affair, and especially the birth of their love-child, had become the new public scandal which 'exercised this whole towne'. For the next few years, Frances struggled against the powerful forces hell-bent on making her pay the price for her illicit actions. Frances fought back with all the vigour she could muster, proving herself to be a formidable force, and, as Chamberlain remarked, perhaps with some reluctant admiration, 'Her mothers owne daughter'.[1]

Considering that Frances was complaining about dissatisfied servants spreading rumours about her in her earlier letter to Buckingham, and that both former and current servants would play crucial roles as witnesses against her during the investigation and adultery trial, some of these same servants were the likely conduits of information about the illegitimate newborn to Buckingham. By late January 1625, the news about the birth of Frances's son began to spread more widely. Bishop William Laud noted in his diary on 21 January that this was the day when the 'business of my Lord of Purbeck' was 'made known unto me by my Lord Duke [Buckingham]'.[2] Buckingham had become Laud's patron at this point, and Laud would soon rise from his position as Bishop of St David's to Bishop of Bath and Wells in 1626, Bishop of London in 1628, and finally to Archbishop of Canterbury, the highest church office in England, in 1633. He would become deeply involved in the prosecution of Frances.

As soon as he found out about the birth of baby Robert, Buckingham moved quickly and restrained both Frances and Howard. Howard was put into the custody of London Alderman Ralph Freeman of Bishopsgate and Frances was held in her lodgings at Denmark House, 'kept somewhat straightly so that none of her frends or acquaintances come neere her'.[3] Buckingham was furious: how dared his sister-in-law shame his newly exalted family in such a manner? Initially, he wanted to throw both of the offenders in prison, lose the key, and be done with it, but he could not persuade King James to agree to such a course of action. James wanted the matter to be dealt with according to 'justice and no favour'.[4] In other words, he did not want others to think that he was imprisoning Frances and Howard simply because his beloved Buckingham had asked him to do it. Throughout his reign, James had carefully cultivated the image of a just, lawgiving king, a Solomon for the English people, and he did not want that image tarnished.[5] Buckingham found that he had to temper his anger and proceed more cautiously.

The crimes of adultery and having a child out of wedlock could be punished in ecclesiastical and secular courts alike. In the 1620s, Frances and Howard potentially faced fines, whipping, stocking, and imprisonment from secular courts, and fines and public penance from church courts. Some lawmakers had tried to make the punishment for adultery more severe in the latter part of the sixteenth century and early seventeenth century. Parliamentary committees discussed the bills and brought them to the floor, but they never made it through both houses in Parliament until 1650. One major dispute for the lawmakers concerned what constituted appropriate punishments and who should have the power to enforce them. Some worried that punishing offenders by making them forfeit dowries or jointures or inheritance, as some MPs suggested, potentially gave church courts too much power over what many considered to be secular financial affairs. In the 1620s, enough MPs either believed that the punishments were harsh enough already, or did not consider adultery a serious enough crime to warrant a change in the law. Some were no doubt also concerned that the topic might hit too close to home.[6]

Having children outside of marriage was also illegal, usually referred to as 'bastardy'. While church courts tended to focus on punishing the religious sin that illicit sex constituted, the main concern for secular courts when dealing with bastardy was to ensure that the parents of the illegitimate child were able to support their offspring financially. The whole idea was to prevent the sinful and irresponsible behaviour of two people from negatively affecting the whole community, as each parish was required to provide for its poor. An illegitimate child unclaimed or ignored by its father would be much more likely to fall into poverty, thus adding to the parish poor rolls. According to the Poor Laws, relief should be reserved for the 'deserving poor': in other words, to those who were unable to work because of physical disabilities or old age, rather than those who became poor or socially stigmatized as a result of sexual sin. Keeping their eyes on the economics, secular courts usually focused on fining fathers of illegitimate children, or ordering that they pay for the upkeep of the child. Mothers, on the other hand, carried more of the social stigma. They were usually physically punished, either whipped or put in the stocks, or, after a new law in 1609, incarcerated, hoping to thereby prevent them from committing a similar crime again and also to deter other women from jeopardizing their sexual virtue.[7]

As was the case with many laws, those against sexual offences did not impact the nobility the same way as they did commoners. The nobility and the elite enjoyed many legal privileges, in addition to the economic, social, and political ones. During the Elizabethan and early Stuart reigns, it was highly unusual for noblemen and noblewomen to answer charges of illicit sexual offences in legal courts. Early modern ideas of nobility argued that those with titles and high positions were better fitted to rule and more honourable than commoners. In order to promote the stability of the social order, it was important that commoners and nobility both understood the differences between them, which mostly meant upholding various kinds of noble privileges. As a result, any sort of punishments designed to publicly shame the convicted person, like penance, whipping, or stocking, would usually not be applied to a noble person. The elite worried that commoners may lose respect for their 'betters' if they saw them humiliated in that fashion, which might lead them to question society's very foundation: the nobility's right to rule. This principle becomes very clear in one of the suggestions to change the punishment for adultery in 1628: commoners would receive corporal punishment, but upper classes would be fined instead.[8]

The fact that the nobility were not brought to court did not necessarily mean that they could escape punishment for their sexual offences. Quite often, the monarch punished the nobility directly, especially if they were courtiers, family members of courtiers, or from a high noble family. The unmarried 'Virgin Queen', Elizabeth I, punished sexual offenders quite harshly. She regularly sent philandering and fornicating courtiers to the Tower or other prisons. She tended to punish women more severely than men: while some male courtiers managed to get back into Elizabeth's good graces after a sexual misstep, female courtiers rarely received such forgiveness. Elizabeth reacted strongly to her courtiers' sexual offences because she viewed them as slights of her authority. She was everyone's 'mother' and 'mistress' at court, and when her courtiers misbehaved, it reflected badly on her. Elizabeth had to be especially vigilant, because as a woman—and especially as an unmarried one—many people questioned her ability to wield power effectively. Queenly rule rested on shaky foundations. John Knox's 1558 treatise *The First Blast of the Trumpet Against the Monstrous Regiment of Women*, in which he argues that female rule was contrary to both natural and divine order, gives the gist of the opposition. If her court had a reputation for being a place of immorality, Elizabeth's critics would get more fuel for their fires. For King James, keeping his courtiers on the straight and narrow was not quite as important: he was a married man with children, so his role as a 'father' and ruler of the people was not questioned. At the Jacobean court, it became a little less dangerous for courtiers to have sex outside of marriage: generally speaking, James did not punish sexual offences in and of themselves; he only punished sexual offences if they were part of some other, more serious crime. That was the case for

Frances Howard and the Earl of Somerset. The couple were punished for their involvement in the murder of Overbury, but not for their adulterous affair, although the illicit sex became an integral part of the public scandal. People who carried on affairs discreetly, and who did not get involved in other scandals, could be relatively safe from any royal furore. For example, the widowed Lady Mary Wroth had a long-standing affair with her first cousin, William Herbert, Earl of Pembroke and Lord Chamberlain to King James. Wroth even had two children with Pembroke, but the lovers did not suffer any punishment from the king.[9]

So, when Buckingham insisted that his wayward sister-in-law should not just be closely examined, but tried at law as well, his was an uncommon approach. As a result, the people around Buckingham were at first hesitant to act against both Frances and Howard, due to their high social positions. When Buckingham demanded that the offending pair be thrown into prison, the Attorney General, Thomas, Baron Coventry, and the Solicitor General, Sir Robert Heath, argued that prison was 'unadvisable' as it was 'unusual for persons of their rank'.[10] Coventry and Heath did not mean that it was unusual to send noblewomen and noblemen to prison. King James had certainly jailed other members of the nobility and court plenty of times, such as the Somersets for accessory to murder, the Suffolks for corruption, and Sir Edward Coke for challenging the king's prerogative and arguing for the right to free speech in Parliament. Rather, the two lawyers argued that it was unusual to imprison nobility for mere sexual offences. King James himself was 'tender (at the first mention of this business) of the hande of a Lady of her quallity', but Buckingham felt that if the king fully knew 'how dishonorably she hath carried herself he would have no more support showen to her than to an ordinary Lady'. By her 'ill carriage', Buckingham argued, Frances had 'forfyted that hand', throwing out the usual protection her noble status afforded her.[11]

Why was Buckingham so intent on making an official case of Frances's adultery? He could have tried to handle the business privately, within the family, instead of involving the machineries of state and Church. First, the matter became a question of honour. Buckingham was working hard to raise his family into prominence and a scandal was harmful not just to himself but to that project as a whole. By using the legal courts, he could publicly distance the Villiers family from Frances, in order to minimize the damage. Buckingham also deeply loved his brother and felt protective of him, especially considering his fragile mental state, and did not want to see him openly cuckolded and ridiculed. More importantly, John was Buckingham's legal heir. While Buckingham had married in 1620, by early 1625, he had only a daughter, and no sons. As a result, John, and any male children of John's, would inherit Buckingham's titles and estates should the duke die.[12] By making Frances answer for her offences in a court of law, Buckingham could ensure that the illicit affair became official and public knowledge, so that no bastard child of Frances and Robert Howard would ever get the titles and wealth he had worked so hard to acquire.

At Buckingham's insistence, King James signed a warrant for Sir Ranulphe Crewe, Lord Chief Justice, to begin the investigation in January and the hearing of witnesses commenced right away.[13] Crewe questioned a total of nineteen witnesses, including Howard. Many of the witnesses were either servants or clients of Frances and the Villiers, although not all of them can be fully identified. Dorothy Wingfield, Elizabeth Ashley, and Anne Elwick were Frances's gentlewoman servants, who had accompanied her from Denmark House when she went to give birth secretly. All three of them gave detailed testimony about the arrangements surrounding the pregnancy and birth. The same three women, along with Isabell Peel, Isabell Hobell, Richard Gralye, James Blint, Richard Grimes, and Daniel Dickinson testified about the progression of the relationship, how Howard 'for the space of neer two yeers past' had 'verye often & very familiar access to the Lady'. The servants also shared with the interrogators the many ways and places the two lovers had met, such as Howard's visits to Frances in Denmark House at unseemly hours, and the trips they took out of town to Ware, Maidenhead, Knightsbridge, Essex, and Ilford. Isabell Peele was probably a female family member of the neighbour named Peele, in whose house the couple had sometimes met, and from where Howard climbed into Frances's rooms in Denmark House. Daniel Dickinson was one of Frances's former footmen who had moved on first to her husband's service, and then to yet another master. He would feature again in a related investigation. The identities and roles of Hobell, Grimes, Blint, and Gralye remain vaguer. Other witnesses included Rebecca Babington and Frances or Francis Fuller. In all likelihood, one of these women was the midwife who had attended to Frances when she gave birth. John Shawe, Christopher Phillipson, Robert Yeoman, and John Squire were also brought in for questioning. Robert and John were in all likelihood servants, but it is not clear who employed them. According to the Lord Chief Justice, almost all of these witnesses concurred that Frances and Howard had visited the problematic John Lambe, the astrologer and medical practitioner, in the King's Bench Prison many times.[14]

Howard and Frances were also both brought in for questioning. While Frances's servants were in all likelihood very frightened by the seriousness of the situation and worried about getting into trouble with authorities, Frances and her lover, both members of the upper classes and thus used to conversing with powerful people as equals, were not as easily intimidated by the investigators. When questioned, Howard was very tight-lipped and refused to admit to anything that could incriminate either Frances or himself. While he freely confessed 'his often address and familiarity with the ladye', in all other matters, such as the paternity of Frances's baby, he was 'very restrained'.[15] On 19 February, when the Lord Chief Justice and his assistants examined Frances at the Sergeants Inn, she was very defiant. When she first arrived, she said she 'marvayled what those old cuckolds had to say to her'.[16] The 'old cuckolds', as she called the officers of state, had clearly expected to be challenged by her, because they had spent the morning further examining other witnesses in order to make sure they were fully informed of all the facts before facing the determined Lady Purbeck herself.[17] The records of Frances's examination have not survived, but she likely denied the adultery, as she would continue to do later.

Frances's connection with Lambe acquired sinister overtones during the examinations. Buckingham became convinced that Lambe had been using black magic in order to harm both his brother John as well as himself, both at Frances's behest. Some of the witnesses said that Lambe had used 'sorcery and charmes, with pictures of waxe' during Frances's visits, all evidence of magic.[18] At one point, Buckingham wondered if Frances and Lambe were behind his brother's mental illness and had 'with powders and potions intoxicate[d] her husbands braines'.[19] Buckingham's fears were not unusual or exaggerated. Belief in the reality and imminent danger of witchcraft and black magic was widespread and common in the early seventeenth century: this is the period when witchcraft accusations, trials, and executions were at their very peak in early modern Europe. Victims of witches often suffered 'fits', where their bodies contorted in unnatural ways, and they sometimes also seemed to become crazed, raving nonsensically, or conversely, fall into a comatose state. Many of these symptoms could of course fit a variety of mental illnesses as well, and judging which was which was tricky. John experienced fits of irrational, frenzied behaviour, mixed with periods of deep melancholy. Buckingham, who desperately sought to help his ailing brother, was also clearly worried about the fine line between medical treatments and magic. Two years earlier, he had consulted with Bishop Laud, by then his personal chaplain, about the claims of a healer who said he could cure John by simply touching his forehead. Buckingham wanted to help his brother if possible, but he was sceptical that a simple laying of hands could be anything but magic. When the healer tried to demonstrate his technique on Buckingham, the duke shrank back from his touch and could not be easy again until he had consulted Laud about the matter. After the break of Frances's scandal, Buckingham again spoke with Laud about witchcraft.[20] Thus Buckingham, like so many others, was prone to fear magic. The fact that Lambe already had an established record, having been convicted of witchcraft but escaped the death penalty, only made Frances's visits to see the man more suspicious.

Frances's contemporaries also believed that witchcraft and sinful sexual desires were closely connected. Thus, it was natural for them to believe that a woman like Frances, who had succumbed to unlawful sexual desires, had also created a connection with evil. In order to get new recruits to his army of darkness, the Devil exploited people's greatest weaknesses. During the early modern period, the religious, social, and cultural convention taught that women's greatest weakness was their flesh and its insatiable, unruly desires. Thus, the Devil, or his demon minions, literally seduced women, and then forced them to renounce their Christian baptism and instead give their souls to Satan. It was after this initial seduction that women, and a few men, began their careers as witches, causing death, destruction, and discord in their communities. This connection between illicit sex and black magic formed a large part of the narrative of Howard's sister's scandal after her involvement in the murder of her husband's former friend Overbury.[21]

Buckingham's suspicions notwithstanding, Lambe vehemently denied all charges that he had used witchcraft to harm either John or Buckingham. Humphrey Frodsham, another suspected wizard, was also brought in and accused of the same crime. Frodsham was in the same business as Lambe, and had been striving to build up a similar practice, since he saw how well it could pay. However, once Frodsham got into trouble, he worried more about this own health than that of others, and he quickly insisted he had no magical skills. He was only 'juggling', meaning defrauding his trusting customers. Although Buckingham put significant pressure on Lambe and Frodsham to 'speak more directly and truly to the point' so that he could discover 'the knot of this villainy', the two men would not say anything further, only continued to insist that they were impostors, in the business for the money only, and that they had not actually performed any magic.[22] Once the case came to trial, 'all matters of sorcerie, witchcraft, and the like' were omitted.[23]

When Buckingham heard the more substantial evidence of Frances's affair with Howard from the witness depositions, he insisted on her removal from Denmark House, as he argued that Prince Charles 'often speaks in distast of her continuance' in his royal palace.[24] Instead, she was put into the custody of Alderman Edward Barkham in mid-February where she was to be 'close kept'. While Buckingham had worried that the custody of the London aldermen was really more of a 'honour than disparagement' and that it was rather a 'place of entertainment' than a true prison, Heath and Coventry comforted him by saying that both Frances and Howard probably would 'be more closely restrained [at the aldermen's houses] than in prison'. Perhaps it soothed Buckingham a little to learn that Frances had been 'dismayed' when she received word that she would be moved to Barkham's house. When Barkham received his charge, however, the Privy Council informed him that his custody of Frances should be 'with that latitude of libertie that becomes a ladie of her birth and quallitie'.[25] Frances's imprisonment also meant a brief separation from her little son, contributing further to her grief. Since the discovery of her affair, Frances had brought her son back to Denmark House, where she could tend to him with the help of the hired wet-nurse. When Barkham took custody of Frances, Buckingham initially insisted she had to leave baby Robert behind. After a while, the duke relented and allowed both the baby and the nurse to join Frances in her captivity.[26]

In addition to appeasing Prince Charles's 'distaste' for housing an adulteress, Buckingham had another reason for wanting Frances in custody or prison. He was worried that he would not be able to keep John away from his wife, and that she would be able to influence him in her favour. Buckingham and John were with the king at Newmarket Palace in Suffolk while the examinations of the first batch of witnesses were taking place. Buckingham was concerned that Frances should be put into prison before the court returned to London. If she was still in Denmark House at the time, Buckingham argued: 'My brother who hopes to be going hence, will not be kept from her and she will (if he should come to her) so worke on him by her subtilty as that she will draw from him something to the advantage of her dishonourable ends and to his prejudice.'[27] John's affection for Frances, so tenderly displayed just a few months earlier when he refused to leave her side while she lay sick of the smallpox, had clearly not entirely diminished, and Buckingham knew it. John had to be protected from his own emotions, or Frances might succeed in convincing her pliable husband that she was innocent.

By late February, after consulting with various legal experts, Buckingham had determined his course of action. He would bring Frances and Howard in front of the ecclesiastical Court of High Commission, which the king could call to 'sit without delay', even though it was not the regular law term. He would get Frances convicted for adultery, and then use that conviction as a foundation for filing for a divorce from bed and board, a legal separation, between Frances and John, thus ensuring that no spurious issue of Frances's would inherit the Villiers name, titles, or fortunes. The High Commission ended up taking a full two years to come to a conclusion, but no record exists of a separation ever being filed or seriously bruited at any time after the spring of 1625, so Buckingham's initial plan did not come to fruition. John probably did not agree to a separation, and since he was a Catholic, he would in all likelihood not have accepted an Anglican divorce from bed and board anyway. Furthermore, after the spring of 1625, Buckingham's desire to formally separate Frances and John may have flagged. In May of that year, Buckingham received good news from his wife: she was pregnant again.[28] Buckingham's hopes for a male heir were realized in November, when the duchess finally gave birth to the couple's first son, promptly named Charles after the new king.[29] The birth of a son meant that John was no longer Buckingham's immediate heir, which in turn meant that the need for a divorce was less pressing.

The Court of High Commission, the court set to try both Frances and Howard, was created during the Reformation period in the sixteenth century. The crown had put together this special church court with the initial purpose of ensuring that people adhered to the proper form of the new Protestantism. As a result, the court tended to direct its attention to nonconformists on both ends of the spectrum, both Catholics and Puritans, who disagreed with the settled Anglican doctrine. It could also deal with other matters over which the church courts had jurisdiction, such as disputed marriages, divorces from bed and board, annulments, and sexual crimes, although that was less common. The court tried both office and instance causes. In instance causes, plaintiffs brought cases against defendants to the court for adjudication. In the office causes, the court itself was the instigator of the trial against a person, in order to correct problematic behaviour, whether religious misconceptions or sinful actions, that had become scandalous, or part of the 'common fame', and therefore needed correction for the good of the community. Legally, Frances's case classifies as an instance cause, where first Buckingham, and then his brother Kit Villiers, Earl of Anglesey, acted as plaintiffs on their brother's behalf. The court did not have juries, but rather a commission of around one hundred members forming a pool for a smaller group who heard cases and voted on their decision. Twelve members heard the case in 1625, and at the conclusion two years later, the number had swelled to nineteen judges deciding Frances's case. The court commissioners consisted of church officials, such as archbishops, bishops, deans, lawyers specialized in canon (religious) law, and representatives of the crown, usually men in high state positions and members of the royal Privy Council. In Frances's and Howard's 1625 proceedings, the Archbishop of Canterbury, as well as the Bishops of Lincoln and London, King James's Lord High Treasurer and President of the Privy Council (Edward Montagu, Viscount Mandeville), and Oliver St John, Viscount Grandison, were part of the commission, as were Sir Henry Marten, Sir John Suckling, and five other persons.[30] Unfortunately, the High Commission court records only survive for the period 1633–41, with a few exceptions, so Frances's court case has to be reconstructed using both letters of state, Laud's diary notations and autobiography, as well as comments on the trials in private letters.[31]

The charge against Frances was adultery, but not bastardy, although she had given birth to an illegitimate child. While no one made any specific comment about the limited charges at the time, the secret birth was of course an integral part of the case, so it is possible that it was not deemed necessary to pile on extra charges. In addition, as bastardy cases were usually brought forward to ensure that fathers would provide for the child, the commissioners probably had no major concerns that Robert, the child of a noblewoman and the son of an earl, would fall into severe poverty and require public support.

In early March, Frances's and Howard's High Commission trials began at Lambeth Palace (Fig. 5.1), the centre of operations for the Bishop of London, on the southern banks of the River Thames (see Fig. 6.1).[32] At the start of the trial, Howard had already been freed from Alderman Freeman's custody. Howard's brother, Sir William Howard, who served as one of Prince Charles's Gentlemen of the Privy Chamber, had successfully managed to lobby for his release. King James now claimed that he had not given the Lord Chief Justice permission to imprison Howard and especially not to keep him 'close prisoner'.[33] This development presaged a trend that would continue for years: Frances would always find herself the main target of prosecution,

Fig. 5.1. Lambeth Palace, London. Lambeth was, and is still, the London seat of the Archbishops of Canterbury. It was also where the Court of High Commission sat, and thus where Frances and Howard were brought to trial. Photo: Pete Spiro/Shutterstock.

and the consequences of their love affair would never be as dire for Howard as they were for her. Both King James and King Charles remained reluctant to approve of harsh treatment of a male member of the powerful Howard family, for what they considered a sexual misdemeanour.

By the time of his release, Howard had developed an effective two-fold defence strategy. First, he simply refused to swear the *ex officio* oath the court required. The accused had to swear to give truthful answers to all charges brought by the court before the actual charges were read. Howard, who clearly did not want to risk having to lie under oath, had refused to swear before. When the Lord Chief Justice had examined him in February, the justice's notes showed that Howard was examined without oath, whereas all the other witnesses, except Lambe, had given their testimonies under oath. When he refused to swear the oath in front of the High Commission, he also made it impossible for the court to proceed properly, as it required that all those charged were sworn in first. Second, Howard argued that as a Member of Parliament (he had been elected to represent Bishop's Castle for the upcoming 1625 session), the High Commission did not have the right to try him, as MPs had that privilege while Parliament was in session.[34] Howard appeared before the court several times, and each time, he stubbornly refused to take the oath. At one point, he also tried to stall the proceedings, arguing that he did not have appropriate legal counsel and that he needed to wait for his lawyers to come to town. The commissioners, finding themselves unable to convince Howard to swear, initially sent him to Fleet Prison for his refusal. Howard petitioned the Lord Keeper for *habeas corpus*, which was allowed, so he was discharged after only a few days in jail. When he was brought in front of the High Commission again, he brought evidence of his election to Parliament, again insisted on his MP privilege, and refused to swear. The commissioners waved aside the evidence of his election as not valid, arguing that Parliament had not officially begun yet, and decided to try to put an end to the business. When investigating what legal weapons were at their disposal to put pressure on Howard, they were discouraged to find that the only action allowed them was 'the rustie sword of the church excommunication'. Ironically, it was Sir Edward Coke and William Cecil, Earl of Salisbury (Howard's brother-in-law and Lady Hatton's first cousin), who, years earlier, had worked to remove the commission's ability to fine people for refusing the oath.[35]

On 20 March, church officials declared Howard's excommunication from the pulpit of St Paul's Cathedral.[36] Being excommunicated meant being cut off from the Christian community, not being able to attend church services, receive communion, or in any way participate in religious life. Furthermore, the Church expected the community to shun the excommunicate entirely: if they did not, they could themselves be subject to excommunication. The excommunicated person was not allowed to buy or sell anything, receive employment, sue in a law court, make wills, serve as an administrator or guardian, or even receive a legacy from another person. However, it is unlikely that Howard suffered such dire consequences, as not everyone followed the letter of this church law so closely. Historian R. B. Outhwaite has suggested that some excommunicates 'may have even gone about their everyday lives little disturbed by their technical state', depending on where they lived, and how serious people in their community perceived the crimes for which they had been excommunicated. Financial resources also played an important part: the economic restrictions placed on excommunicates barely affected the elites.[37] The commissioners had been disappointed that all they had to wield was 'the rustie sword of excommunication', showing that they saw the limits of their power. The events that followed would also indicate that Howard's excommunication was not a very serious imposition. While the High Commission had questioned his initial election to the 1625 Parliament in March, he was actually re-elected to the Parliament a month later, even though he was at that point under excommunication.[38]

Mimicking her lover, Frances also tried to refuse to swear the oath when she was brought in front of the High Commission. She told the commissioners that the burden of proof of her supposed crimes 'lay upon her accusers' and that until they had presented their evidence against her, she would not swear, since she should have the right not to incriminate herself. The commissioners answered that 'the Oath imposed by the Laws and Customs of the Realm was not to be refused; nor could there be any immorality for an innocent Person to take it'. Frances responded by suggesting that the judges should make their own wives swear that they were 'free from all faults' first and thus provide her with a good example. If, as the judges claimed, innocent people had nothing to fear, then all their wives should be happy to swear the oath in front of the court. Although the bystanders were amused by Frances's pointed wittiness, the judges were not. Eventually, they wore her down and she reluctantly swore the oath. Thus, the proceedings began.[39]

Following the events closely, Lady Hatton was so worried about her daughter that she swallowed her pride and went to seek help from a person she knew had excellent knowledge of the law, and who might be able to help Frances in her predicament: her estranged and hated husband. She left London and set out to visit Coke at Stoke, hoping that the experienced lawyer would care enough for his daughter to help her. However, her trip to Stoke would prove to be in vain. Coke was not interested in assisting his daughter or his wife. Lady Hatton barely had time to state her business before Coke brusquely told her to leave. As the Lord Keeper Williams gleefully reported to Buckingham, Coke had simply 'dismist her

Ladiship, when she had stayed with him very lovingly half a quarter of an hour'.[40] Coke did not approve of Frances's adultery and thus did not lift a finger in her defence. It would take a full seven years before father and daughter reconciled. Lady Hatton travelled back to Hatton House in London, seething at the humiliation and determined not to have anything to do with her hateful husband again, if she could help it.

Like Lady Hatton, Howard's mother, the Countess of Suffolk, also tried to 'help' her son, although Howard probably did not welcome that help greatly. Lady Suffolk argued that Howard was in fact 'insufficient', or impotent, and therefore it was simply not possible that he could be the father of Frances's baby.[41] As we have seen in the case of Howard's brother-in-law, the Earl of Essex, male impotence was usually a matter of ridicule and dishonour in the seventeenth century. Clearly, Lady Suffolk was wrong; Howard was not impotent. If the birth of Robert was not enough proof, the birth of his three children when he actually did marry over two decades later, certainly was. John, on the other hand, married twice and never had any children at all, so perhaps the accusation of impotence would have been more correctly levied at him.

Although she received no assistance from her lawyer father, Frances defended herself 'reasonalie well' in court, considering the seriousness of the accusations and the power and influence of the accusers. She began by complaining that she in fact was the victim in the situation and that she had been treated very cruelly, 'deprived of her Husband's Company, loaded with the Imputation of Adultery, her subsistence taken from her, & tho' endowed with a very great Fortune, was reduced to such necessity as hardly to have wherewith to buy herself Cloaths'. She readily admitted that there were rumours of an adulterous relationship with Howard, but she argued that those had been purposely and falsely spread by the Villiers. Her main defence consisted of denial: she admitted to a close friendship with Howard, but she denied that they were lovers and that the baby was his. Instead, she argued that the child was her husband's. When her accusers pointed out that she had been separated from her husband for close to two years and that the two had been living far apart from each other, Frances responded that they had happily been able to sneak away from the prying eyes of the rest of the Villiers family and had private meetings, which then had resulted in the pregnancy.[42] John had been willing to go along with the version that he was the father, at least initially, which was the reason why Buckingham was so keen on keeping him away from Frances, especially while the examinations of witnesses were conducted. Buckingham wanted to ensure he had a preponderance of evidence so he could convince both King James and his brother of Frances's guilt. He needed to overcome both the king's initial instinct to treat her leniently, and John's wish to be convinced and manipulated by the wife he adored. Had John not been mentally unstable, and had Buckingham not been so powerful, John's initial insistence that the baby was his would have made it legally very difficult for an ecclesiastical court to try Frances.

The court case attracted much attention, turning into entertainment for the leisured class. While Buckingham had the weight of the political and legal powers behind him, Frances and Robert clearly had at least some people rooting for them, either out of empathy or bemusement. Commentators on the case were often impressed by Frances's wit. Chamberlain was certainly amused by Frances calling the justices 'poore old cuckolds' when they were getting ready to examine her. He also reported Frances's response when the High Commission asked her to pay bail or go to prison, because the alderman no longer wanted to be responsible for the charges of keeping her in his custody. Frances replied that if Alderman Barkham was 'wearie of her she was not wearie of him wher she found such good usage'.[43]

Humour was indeed a rather common response to sexual scandals. It offered a way to talk about illicit sex without appearing to approve of the sins of others. Lord Holles, when reporting the news of Frances's scandal to his brother, quipped: 'You have long since heard of my Lady Purbeck (and her servant Sir Robert Howard) who is becum a mother, without the helpe of her husband.' When the Puritan MP Ignatius Jourdain wished to discuss a new bill with stricter punishments for adultery in the Parliament of 1628, a jester in the House responded to Jourdain's motion for 'the bill for adultery' with a loud cry: 'Committ it, Mr. Jourdain, commit it!' The chamber exploded with laughter. Jourdain did not appreciate the joke at his expense, and was assisted by dour Sir Edward Coke, who felt the need to kill the joke by unnecessarily explaining that 'it was the bill, and not the sin, we would have committed'. The bill made its way to committee, only to die a quiet death there.[44]

Frances also seems to have inspired pity. Some felt sorry for her since she had been forced to marry to a man who was mentally ill. As Robert Johnston remarked when discussing the trial, 'The Standers by were so much the more moved at her Distress, in that she had been married quite against her Consent, to a man disordered in his Senses, & the crimes of adultery urged against her.'[45] This idea was nothing new, of course: Frances's forced marriage had been a topic of discussion during the fraught marriage negotiations in 1617. John's mental illness was not as much part of the gossip then, since it had not yet fully manifested itself at that time. As soon as the birth of her child became common knowledge, Frances also would always defend herself in the same vein, emphasizing her unfortunate marriage and the enmity of the Villiers, and downplaying her relationship with Howard. However, expressing support for Frances was not entirely safe. A servant of the Archbishop of

Canterbury, named Bembridge, found himself imprisoned after commenting on how 'hardly [roughly]' Frances 'was used' by the commissioners. He clearly uttered his opinion to the wrong person, because one of Frances's adversaries brought it up with Buckingham, who in turn promptly had Bembridge arrested and thrown in prison. Frances took to calling Bembridge 'one of her martirs'.[46]

People who valued loyalty and romance also believed that Howard was behaving commendably, both for refusing the oath (and thus challenging the authority of the High Commission) and for refusing to admit to adultery with Frances. Although the Lord Keeper John Williams dismissed Howard's supporters as the 'Hee and Shee good fellowes of the town', these people clearly believed Howard was very chivalric for 'his closeness and secrecie', since his refusal also ensured that he did not further incriminate his beloved Frances. 'Although he refuseth to be a Confessor, yet [he] is sure to die a Martyr, and most of the Ladies in town will offer at his shrine', Williams surmised.[47]

After Frances's initial court appearances, and Howard's excommunication, much official business was interrupted by the death of the king. James, aged fifty-nine in 1625, had been increasingly sick over the last year. He suffered from gout, severe arthritis, and kidney stones. The Christmas season was rather quiet at court, since the king did not participate in the grand entertainments usually marking the holidays. During the spring of 1625, his health deteriorated further. By March, he fell into bouts of increasingly severe 'tertian agues', or intermittent fevers, causing fits of chills and shaking. Initially, the doctors did not think he was in any immediate danger, but as the fits continued and grew worse, they started to fear that he might not recover. Buckingham and his mother, both present during the king's illness, hoped that some plasters, which had previously helped the duke when he was sick, might also relieve the king. They applied the treatments without the approval of the official royal doctors, and when James grew worse rather than better, the two came under a cloud of suspicion of having poisoned the king and thus hastened his demise. It became part of the growing list of complaints against Buckingham, although there is little evidence of actual poisoning. On 25 March, James also suffered a stroke, which partly paralyzed his face. In addition, a severe case of dysentery caused dangerous dehydration. Realizing that the end was near, the Archbishop of Canterbury prayed with the king and administered the Communion. As the king slowly lost the ability to speak, the room filled with servants, lords, bishops, and chaplains, kneeling and praying by the bedside. Just before noon on Sunday, 27 March, the much weakened king drew his last breath.[48]

After James's death, Frances's High Commission case entered a lull, with just one more brief appearance in early June. More than two years would pass before

Frances's court case actually came to a conclusion. It was not unusual for court cases to last several years, as court sessions tended to be relatively short and as delays often occurred when the necessary people and documents could not always be present at short notice. Many cases appeared multiple times at different stages, before the court made a final decision.[49] However, Buckingham had desired a speedy trial: he wanted Frances found guilty as soon as possible, so that he could proceed with the divorce. The case was surely delayed because of the changes occurring in England as a result of the new reign.

CHAPTER 6

COUNTERS AND CONVICTION

King James died at a very hectic and fraught time. Charles's negotiated marriage had to be concluded, dangerous and complex foreign affairs loomed, the new king's first Parliament was about to open, and a deadly plague epidemic hit London. In the crosswinds of bigger issues, the scandal surrounding Frances faded from the public spotlight. Even Buckingham and the Villiers family began focusing their attentions elsewhere. In the shadow of the new developments, Frances continued to assert and defend herself, trying her best to make the High Commission case go away. But while they were temporarily preoccupied, the Villiers certainly did not forget about John's troublesome wife. They were only biding their time.

The king's death necessitated the planning of a grand funeral, fitting for England's Solomon. James died at the end of March, but the funeral was not held until 7 May. After his death and autopsy at Theobalds, James's body was embalmed and encased in a lead coffin. The king's corpse remained almost as active as it was when the king was alive. On its way to London, the coffin rested for a few nights in each of the royal palaces in and around the city. Everywhere the body was moved, a large number of people dressed in black mourning clothes attended to it with great reverence. The need for cloth caused a mad scramble among London merchants. One of the major expenses for the king's funeral was the purchase and distribution of black cloth of various quality, both to the official mourners as well as to their servants. A contemporary observer estimated that more than nine thousand people received 'blacks' from the crown. In addition to the clothes, reams of black velvet, taffeta, and other varieties of fine black cloth draped the rooms and furniture in the palaces wherever the body rested, the hearse which carried the body, the horses that drew the hearse, and everything else that came in contact with the royal corpse. In the funeral procession to the king's final resting place in Westminster Abbey, the entire royal household took part, from the lowest positions such as page-boys, grooms of the poultry and pastry, spaniel keepers and actors, to the great officers of state, such as the Treasurer, the Lord Chamberlain, the Lord Keeper, and everyone in between. The members of the procession marched in groups, and at the head of each group, a groom led a magnificent black velvet-attired horse without a rider, symbolizing the dead master. James's son Charles, now the new king of England at the age of twenty-five, served as chief mourner in the procession and followed his father's body on foot. Buckingham also marched. John's participation is not certain, but if present, he would have marched with the groups of noblemen, carefully arranged according to precedence. Only men participated in the procession, so even if Frances had been in good standing with king and favourite, she would not have had a role in the mournful parade.[1]

As soon as James was buried, the English court turned its attention to the next big event: Charles's marriage and the arrival of the new queen. Deciding on a bride for Charles had been part of England's foreign policy throughout the early 1620s. Initially, James had intended that Charles marry Maria Ana, sister of the Spanish king Philip IV. When the negotiations stalled by 1623, Buckingham and Charles decided to make a dramatic and romantic gesture by travelling incognito—although their identities were discovered rather rapidly—through France to Spain, so that the prince could woo the Spanish Infanta in person. Having had no previous romantic experiences, Charles now fell head over heels in love with the princess, who frustratingly did not return his ardour. More importantly, neither did the Spanish king nor state officials, who were not pleased with this surprise royal visit. After having stayed in Spain for half a year, it became painfully clear to both Buckingham and Charles that the Spanish were stalling and not really serious in their negotiations. Charles was especially interested in getting the Spanish king to support the return of lost territories to his sister and brother-in-law, the exiled King and Queen of Bohemia in The Hague, but the Spanish clearly had no intentions of doing so. Disillusioned and humiliated, Charles and Buckingham returned home, where they were nonetheless warmly welcomed by both King James and the population at large. The king had written passionate letters expressing his longing for the absent Steenie, and now he was bursting with joy, having his beloved back home again. The English population were rejoicing that the only heir to the throne was safely back in his own kingdom, rather than gallivanting through Europe. Once back, Charles and Buckingham both firmly followed an anti-Spanish agenda, the memory of the Spanish slight still smarting.[2]

Next, James and Charles turned towards France, where King Louis XIII's youngest sister, Princess Henriette Marie, or Henrietta Maria, as the English called her, presented another possible choice for Charles. The marriage negotiations began in 1624. One main sticking point was the issue of religion: Henrietta Maria was Catholic, and the French wanted to ensure that she would be able to practise her religion freely in Protestant England. Furthermore, they pushed for a more liberal treatment of Catholics in England overall as a condition of the alliance. The foreign affairs of the 1620s were increasingly tricky. England had to balance Catholic France and Spain against English Protestant interests in the growing conflict on the continent, later known as the Thirty Years War (1618–48). This war was the last, and largest, of the religious wars that had wracked Europe since the start of the Reformation in the sixteenth century. A complex mix of secular and religious issues ensured that Catholic France eventually ended up fighting with the northern Protestant countries against the Catholic Holy Roman Emperor and Spanish king, both from the same powerful Habsburg family. To the chagrin of other Protestant countries and territories, England stayed out of the major continental fighting of the Thirty Years War. However, at the time of Charles's marriage, England's role in the war was not at all settled. Even though they would not engage in the larger conflict with the Holy Roman Empire in central Europe, England would still end up fighting a quasi-war with both Spain and France in the second half of the 1620s, Charles's developing new ties with France notwithstanding.

After much wrangling, James and Louis concluded the marriage treaty in the autumn of 1624. The wedding itself had to be postponed until Henrietta Maria could receive a papal dispensation to allow her to marry a Protestant, and then James's illness, death, and funeral preparations created further delays. Charles and Henrietta Maria were finally married by proxy in France on 1 May 1625, six days before James's funeral. Initially, Buckingham had been selected to act as the stand-in for Charles, but since he had to stay in England for the imminent funeral of James, the kings settled on the French Duke of Chevreuse as a stand-in for the stand-in. Even though the groom was not personally present, the French court put on a rich display for the ceremony and the subsequent feasting. The English lords who were present were impressed by the splendid grandeur and reported it all in great detail.[3]

Two weeks after the proxy wedding, Buckingham arrived in Paris to escort the new queen back to England. He had outfitted himself handsomely for the occasion. Sporting one elaborately rich suit after another during a full week of entertainments in his honour, he was making quite an impact on the court ladies, according to observers. One of his outfits was decorated with hundreds of pearls, purposely sewn on very loosely. As Buckingham moved through the crowded court, some of the pearls came off, scattering rich little souvenirs for the impressed bystanders. Also of particular note was his 'white satin uncut velvet suit, set all over, both suit and cloak, with diamonds, the value whereof is thought to be fourscore thousand pounds, besides a feather made with great diamonds; with sword, girdle, hatband and spurs with diamonds'. One person who especially noticed the quite literally sparkling duke was none other than Queen Anne, the neglected wife of Louis XIII. Buckingham, rather recklessly, pursued an arduous flirtation with the queen, who, while flattered and impressed with him, was clearheaded enough to realize the dangers and ensured that the affair remained strictly platonic. One evening, when Buckingham was walking with Anne in a garden, the couple turned a corner and temporarily disappeared from the view of their companions and attendants. Suddenly, a cry pierced the quiet night, and when the others reached the queen, she looked flushed and flustered, whereas Buckingham was some distance away, seemingly troubled. It seems likely that the lovelorn Buckingham tried to embrace or kiss or otherwise touch the queen, and that she, unable to get him to stop, cried out.[4]

Buckingham had a chance for one more indiscretion while in France. When Henrietta Maria began her travels towards the coast and her new life, she was at first accompanied by her family: the French king, queen, and queen mother, along with Buckingham and the English party, escorted her. The party travelled slowly, as there were elaborate celebrations and displays in the towns along the way. King Louis came down with a bad cold, and had to stop. Soon after, the queen mother also fell ill. Henrietta Maria initially halted her travel, but because Charles was impatient and insisted she come as soon as possible, she eventually continued on without her family, as Queen Anne also decided to remain with her sick mother-in-law. At one point on their journey, Buckingham left Henrietta Maria, doubled back on some excuse, only to kneel at the bedside of Queen Anne, speaking softly to her and touching her bed sheets. The queen's female attendants in the room were uncomfortable with his overly informal address, but he ignored them. The affair went no further, and Buckingham and Anne never saw each other again after this incident. King Louis was informed of Buckingham's behaviour and was not pleased. Although Louis did not pursue any formal censures as evidence of a sexual relationship did not exist, Buckingham thus managed to make himself *persona non grata* at the French court.[5]

It is rather astonishing that Buckingham allowed himself such a politically dangerous flirtation at a time of so much uncertainty in the new reign. It points to a streak of recklessness and thoughtlessness. It also offers another example of the early modern sexual double standard: at the same time as Buckingham was persecuting Frances for her adultery, he, a married man, was openly pursuing a dangerous flirtation with a foreign queen. While the dalliance with Queen Anne was platonic, Buckingham's relationships with other women were not. Buckingham's patient wife, who loved her handsome and charming husband beyond measure, bemoaned his 'one sin [of] loving women so well', but was unable to make her lustful spouse reform. When rumours of Buckingham's behaviour in France reached England, it was not only his wife who reacted to the troubling news, but also his long-time mistress, Lucy Hay, Countess of Carlisle. Since men had so much more sexual freedom, the patent unfairness of Buckingham's expectations that Frances should live chastely whereas he did not, probably did not even cross his mind.[6]

After some additional delays, the new queen finally set sail and arrived at Dover on 12 June, where an impatient Charles hurried to meet her. While the first meeting appeared successful, the first three years of the new marriage would become increasingly stormy and troubled. Like Frances, Henrietta Maria was a young bride, only fifteen years old when she married King Charles. She was inexperienced in both politics and marriage, and she was in a foreign land, whose language she did not speak and with whose customs she was unfamiliar. In England, she was surrounded by the Catholic servants she had brought with her from France, and she resisted the king and Buckingham's attempts to remove her own servants and replace them with English ones, among others Buckingham's female relatives as well as his mistress. The queen came to despise Buckingham, who now found himself at odds with another headstrong young woman, this one trickier to bully and control than Frances, considering Henrietta Maria's exalted position. At times, Buckingham tried to reconcile the fighting spouses, but for the most part, he created larger rifts between them instead by telling Charles that he should expect more submission from his recalcitrant wife. Charles, convinced that his wife's French servants were the ones creating strife and feeding discord, eventually outright dismissed most of them, notwithstanding his wife's desperate pleas to keep them. He relented a little and allowed a small number to remain, but most of them were summarily sent packing. It certainly did not seem like a good beginning for the royal union, but in time it would significantly improve and turn into a remarkable love story once the real main obstacle—Buckingham—was out of the picture.[7]

While the rest of high society were busy either participating in, or talking and speculating about, the events set into motion by the death of King James and the accession and marriage of Charles, Frances had other matters on her mind. After her initial appearances in the High Commission court in March, she had been released from the alderman's house by April and was living with her little son and servants in a house owned by Sir Giles Brydges in Stepney, west of the City of London. Brydges was a relation, the brother of Frances's step-grandmother, Frances Brydges Cecil, Countess of Exeter (whom the Lakes had falsely accused of incest and attempted murder in 1618, see Chapter 3).[8] From her position of greater safety with relatives in Stepney, Frances now turned the tables and became the accuser rather than the accused: she asked the Privy Council to investigate a death threat against herself, her son, and her servants and attendants.

According to Frances, Thomas Worley and Daniel Dickinson, two of her former footmen, had acted in a suspicious and threatening manner, making her fear for her very life. Worley had gone to the family of baby Robert's wet-nurse and asked them how he could 'come to speake wth the Ladie Purbeck wth manie other unnecessary questions', such as 'the way upp unto her [Frances's] owne chamber'. Worley's visit raised the suspicions of the family, especially since he had not 'carried himself well towarde the Ladie Purbecke' since he had quit her service and entered the service of her husband instead. Worley had then made his way to Frances's house in Stepney, where he had entered the hall, his odd behaviour raising concerns. With a sword by his side, he had walked up and down the hall in a 'melancholie and discontented manner', but never talked to anyone in the house, although several servants had been moving through the room. When Frances's solicitor Richard Elwick (husband to Ann Elwick, Frances's gentlewoman servant) saw Worley in the hall, he asked him what his business was there. Worley, 'shakinge his head and gryndinge his teeth' replied that his business was none of Elwick's business and then he attempted to push past the solicitor further up into the house, into the rooms of Frances and her son. Elwick stopped Worley, told him that neither Lady Purbeck nor anyone in the house wanted to have anything to do with him, and briskly 'bid him begone'. Worley, furious, stormed out of the house, swearing that he would have his revenge on Elwick.

In the presence of Daniel Dickinson, Worley later discussed his encounter with Elwick with a woman he was courting. Other people at the inn and alehouse where Worley's sweetheart was staying heard the story. During that conversation, both Worley and Dickinson swore revenge on Elwick and his wife by either stabbing or poisoning them, and the two also wished an evil destiny to befall the whole house of Lady Purbeck. When others in the inn asked Worley and Dickinson why they were intent on so dark a crime as murder, Worley replied that it was because Elwick had 'hindered him from coming to his purpose wth the Ladie Purbeck'. By happenstance, Elwick had come by the inn while Worley and Dickinson were still there, fuming in an upper room, and had other guests not warned him to leave, he surely would have been murdered by the two vengeful footmen.

Even more suspicious and troubling, Frances continued, was the fact that Worley had said that once he 'had done his intended purpose', he would have eight or ten pounds in his purse, or perhaps even as much as thirty or forty pounds. Thus enriched, he would go to France and then all 'suche deede and matters wilbe pardoned'. Supposedly, he was banking on getting a coronation pardon for his murders when Charles was officially crowned king. Frances was implying that Worley was taking both orders and payments from people who wished her gone, suggesting—without actually mentioning any names—that her in-laws were behind the plot. Worley and yet a third man, a servant of either Buckingham's wife or Buckingham's mother, had also armed themselves with cudgels and rapiers and walked up and down the street in front of a house where they believed that Elwick would appear, waiting to pounce.[9]

Frances's version of events implies that Worley's 'intended purpose' was to kill Frances and potentially her son as well. The violent threats against Elwick came about as a result of his hindering Worley's murderous plan. The Lord Chief Justice, the Attorney General, and the Solicitor General—Crewe, Coventry, and Heath, the very same men who had examined Frances, Howard, and others about the adultery—now examined Thomas Worley to try to get to the bottom of Frances's accusations. According to Worley, his only 'intent' was to try to contact Frances to see if his service with her could be renewed, or if he should consider himself fully discharged. When he arrived at the house in Stepney, one of Frances's gentlewomen had noted his presence but said she was busy and left without speaking further to him. Worley then entered the kitchen, where he met Elwick, who promptly called him a rogue, asked him how he dared to show his face in the house, and bade him 'get out of doors'. Worley had then written a letter to Frances and enquired about how to get it delivered to her without letting her servants know who it came from, since at least some of Frances's attendants did not like him and might not give the letter to the viscountess. Worley admitted to having spoken some words in anger regarding Elwick when he was in his cups with Dickinson at the alehouse. He contritely expressed his remorse to the Chief Justice and Solicitor General, assuring them that he had not really meant anything by his drunken rant. He had indeed started to go downstairs in the alehouse to the room where Elwick had arrived, but it was not to do Elwick any harm: he had simply already paid his bill and was ready to leave the establishment. He denied that he had ever said that he was about to come into money and go to France. He thought that someone might have just overheard fragments and misunderstood when he had discussed possible finances with the woman he was wooing. By the way, Worley added, in all the time that he had served Lady Purbeck, he 'could never get eather the good will or good word of Mr Elwick', implying that Elwick had never liked him and was not going to be an objective witness of his actions.[10]

The evidence for a murder plot against Frances and her son was rather weak, and the Privy Councillors did not take any actions beyond the initial investigation. The threats against Elwick seem to be more credible, especially considering the number of witnesses who heard Worley and Dickinson talk about killing Elwick in the alehouse, as well as his confession of having said some regrettable drunken words against Elwick. Clearly, there had been bad blood between Worley and Elwick for some time. Perhaps Frances really did feel seriously threatened by her former servants, or perhaps she was exaggerating her accusations in order to discredit witnesses who were giving evidence against her in her High Commission case. In these accusations, Frances argues that Worley was a former servant who clearly did not leave her service on the best of terms and therefore would be more likely to be recruited to work against her. Worley had connections with Buckingham's family, her main persecutors in the adultery case. Furthermore, Dickinson was also a former servant, who now was employed by a person who 'followes the Cause against the Ladie Purbeck'. Unfortunately, the name of that employer is unreadable in the document. Dickinson himself had testified in the adultery case against Frances.[11]

The case offers an interesting window into the complicated and often precarious upstairs–downstairs relationships in larger households. Nobility and gentry relied on their servants for their every need, including comfort and companionship. As a consequence, servants were witnesses to numerous private and potentially compromising conversations and deeds. As long as the relationship between mistress/master and servants was cordial, intimacy was not problematic. However, if the relationship broke down, and the service terminated, former servants' intimate knowledge of their former employers' lives could serve as a powerful weapon. Naturally, in a hierarchical society like early modern England, the masters and mistresses usually had the upper hand vis-à-vis their servants. While the sources do not mention the precise chronology of Worley and Dickinson's employment, given the context, it seems highly likely that they had been in Frances's household while she was having her affair with Howard. This would be especially true of Dickinson, since the Chief Justice had formally questioned him as a witness.

Buckingham's name does not appear anywhere in the documents dealing with potentially murderous former servants. In order to have more time for other, at this point more pressing, business, Buckingham had enlisted the assistance of his younger brother, Christopher 'Kit' Villiers, to take over the prosecution of Frances. Kit was not a very clever person, but Buckingham must have trusted him enough to ensure that the dishonourable Frances would get her punishment. All the royal bounty Kit had received was linked to his brother's political ascent. To please Buckingham, James had appointed Kit Gentleman of the King's Bed Chamber and Master of the Robes in 1617. As had been the case with John, Buckingham and his mother were looking for a rich marriage for Kit, but initially finding only unwilling candidates. Two prospective brides, the daughter of the wealthy Lord Mayor of London, and the daughter of the Earl of Berkshire, were uncooperative, and their families showed no great enthusiasm for the unions either. While the Villiers were well-connected, it is no wonder that the drama surrounding Frances's marriage might have triggered trepidation among other elite families. By 1622, Kit finally secured a marriage with Elizabeth Sheldon of Howley. A year later, James gave him a peerage and he became the Earl of Anglesey. At that point, the king had delayed Kit's earldom for over a year, hoping to 'take him off his wench' first. In other words, James tried to entice Kit to give up his mistress and be more loyal to his new wife. In addition to his womanizing, Kit also gained himself an apparently quite well-deserved reputation as a drunkard. James, himself known to indulge in alcohol, did not mind, but Charles was not fond of heavy drinkers. While as a prince Charles had to endure Kit Villiers in his father's entourage, he 'would have no drunkards of his chamber' as a king. He refused to reappoint Kit to the Bed Chamber position.[12] Kit's release from royal household service in late March ensured he had time to devote to the prosecution of his sister-in-law.

The incompetent Kit did not have much to do in Frances's case after the initial March appearances. Frances briefly reappeared in front of the High Commission again in early June, when the commission was having regular court days. In these early summer proceedings, Frances had temporarily run out of witticisms and effective strategies of resistance. The Lord Keeper Williams informed the out-of-town Buckingham that Frances's defence 'proves to be modest and without aspersion of other parties', but divulged no other details.[13]

The meetings of the High Commission were possibly suspended or delayed by the virulent plague epidemic that broke out in London during the summer of 1625. Ever since the devastation of the Black Death in the mid-1300s, the horrific disease regularly returned to various parts of Europe throughout the early modern period. The symptoms of the bubonic plague, a bacterial disease, included pounding headaches, high fevers, large swellings of the lymph nodes, boils, blisters, and reddish and black splotches developing under the skin's surface. In its advanced stages, plague caused coma, and for 60–80 per cent of those who fell ill, death followed shortly. This version of the disease was usually spread through rodents and fleas: when a flea bit an infected rodent and then bit a human, it would spread the infection. The pneumonic version of the plague infected the lungs, and could spread very rapidly through contact with infected phlegm or blood. The disease was swift: many people died within a few days of first noticing symptoms.[14]

While early modern outbreaks were not as devastating as the fourteenth-century version, the plague was still a major killer. Seventeenth-century doctors did not know anything about bacteria and their spread, so they did not fully understand the cause of the disease. Nor did they have any effective medical cures, although they tried desperately to find something that would work. The most effective way to prevent the spread of the disease was isolating infected people and areas. By 1625, England had an official plague protocol in place, which ordered that dead bodies be inspected, and if found to be dead of plague, the whole household would be quarantined for up to six weeks, a mark placed on the door to alert others of the dangers within. The quarantine was a brutal necessity. While it protected the neighbours, the household members shut in with the sick were not likely to escape with their lives. As a result, people sometimes lied to inspectors about the causes of death of their loved ones, hoping to avoid the lockdown with death. The clothes and bedding that had been in contact with the ill and dying were also supposed to be burned, but textiles were expensive and precious, and people sometimes could not bring themselves to destroy them. Due to widespread poverty, the rules and regulation worked imperfectly.[15]

The spread of the 1625 plague started slowly, but by the peak of the summer it had grown to a terrifying menace. During the height of the epidemic, several thousands were buried each week in London. Frances probably fled the infested city for the relative safety of the more sparsely populated countryside, as people who could afford it generally did. She may have joined her mother at Corfe Castle, hoping that the old Norman stronghold could protect them. The royal court also left the city, although it commonly spent the warmer summer months away from the city anyway. More unusually, Parliament, which opened in June and met until August, was moved to the city of Oxford in July, mid-session. Frances's husband John had fled London too: he was present during three of the eleven days that the House of Lords met in Oxford. Her lover Howard, an MP, probably went to the Oxford Parliament as well, although there is no definite record of his presence. If not in Oxford, he likely rode out the epidemic at Audley End, his brother's country estate in Essex. Buckingham, attending the king, had already followed the court out of town.[16]

The plague eased by the autumn of 1625, and life for the survivors slowly returned to normal. The disease had hit hard: it killed about 35,000–40,000 people, which amounted to a loss of almost 13 per cent of the population of London and its suburbs.[17] The fortunate who had fled started to file back to the capital, reopening their abandoned town dwellings amidst the large number of freshly dug graves. Buckingham was again concerned about his brother John returning to London and to the proximity of Frances. With the High Commission case still pending, Buckingham continued to worry that Frances might influence John in some way if given the chance. The duke found it necessary to ensure that she would not get anywhere near him. In the autumn, Buckingham had to go abroad on a diplomatic mission to The Hague in Holland. Rather than leave his vulnerable brother behind, he decided to include him in his entourage. It was a potentially risky move, considering John's fragile mental state. Perhaps as a way to keep his brother busy and out of trouble, Buckingham also brought along his young nephew, son of their sister Susan, Countess of Denbigh. While in The Hague, Buckingham posed for a portrait with Michiel van Mieereveldt, the same artist who had painted Frances's portrait two years earlier. In the portrait, he is wearing the fancy pearl-studded suit that had made a sensation in Paris earlier that year.[18]

Having returned to Stepney, Frances found that she had to fight a different kind of foe: creditors. Charles's second Parliament opened early in 1626, and on 25 February, the Lord Keeper 'signified unto the House that he had received a petition from the Viscountess of Purbeck complaining that she was arrested this parliament time and her coach horses attached at the suit'.[19] Simply put, Frances had many unpaid debts and some of her creditors had tired of waiting, had her arrested, and held her coach horses as collateral. The problem for the creditors, however, was that getting members of the nobility to pay what they owed was not always easy. One of the many privileges of the nobility included their immunity from arrest for debts, specifically during the time when Parliament sat. This privilege had been debated earlier, most notably in a Star Chamber case in 1605, when the Countess of Rutland had been arrested for unpaid debts, but it had remained in effect.[20] Unsurprisingly, the nobles were not very keen on getting rid of such a convenient privilege and they would quickly move to ensure that those who had dared to act against Lady Purbeck would have to answer for it.

The Lords promptly brought in the creditors (one of whom was a baker in Stepney) and the sergeants and bailiffs who had carried out the arrest for questioning. The creditors tried to defend themselves by first insisting they had intended to arrest Dorothy Wingfield, Frances's gentlewoman, rather than Frances herself. However, the testimony of Wingfield, Elizabeth Ashley (Frances's other gentlewoman servant), as well as of Frances's coachman, convinced the Lords that the creditors were lying. The Lords also sent a person outside the chamber to ask for Frances's version again and she reiterated that she had been the one arrested. Frances was not allowed to come inside, as 'it is not fit that she come to the bar', meaning that the Lords considered it inappropriate for the wife of a peer to be present in the chamber. All those involved in the arrest of Frances and the taking of the coach horses received their prompt punishments: they were sent to the Fleet Prison for a time, although the imprisonment seems to have been relatively brief, a few weeks at the longest. The 'offenders' sent humble petitions to the Lords for their release, arguing that they had been ignorant of the rule of noble privilege and promised not to do anything like it in the future. The Lords ordered them released as long as they paid their fines. The two sergeants who had taken Frances's coach horses had even petitioned Frances herself and told the Lords that she had forgiven them their trespasses and was 'willing that they should be discharged if your honors so think fit'. The Lords' willingness to let the creditors and bailiffs go so soon reflect that fact that they did not consider the incident very serious—they called it a 'misdemeanor'—but that they nonetheless wanted to protect noble privilege. However, squabbles about the right to arrest some of Frances's servants, and re-arrests of other persons, as the Lords received piecemeal information about who served who when, and who arrested who when, continued to pop up in the records of the 1626 Parliament until mid-June. John was not present while the Lords discussed his wife's case: he had entered the Earl of Cleveland as his proxy on the first day of Parliament, and did not attend at all throughout the five months Parliament met that year. Presumably, he was away from the capital, perhaps again under the care of doctors in the countryside.[21]

Howard, despite his excommunication the year before, returned to the Commons once more as the representative for Bishop's Castle in 1626. Like Frances, he would find this Parliament particularly helpful. Charles had called Parliament because he badly needed money for his worsening conflict with France: the situation demanded careful balancing, as only Parliament could levy taxes. To the king and Buckingham's displeasure, MPs were set on using the Parliament to express their growing grievances, including their dislike of Buckingham. Many had hoped that the death of James would end Buckingham's monopoly on the king's affections and favour, only to be disappointed when it became clear that Charles remained frustratingly loyal to his friend. Some MPs viewed Buckingham's insistence on the trial and imprisonment of Howard, a fellow MP, as yet another example of his repeated abuses of power. Even the High Commission, and especially the court's use of the ex officio oath, came in for the MPs' ire, as they viewed it as a form of arbitrary power. More reform-minded MPs introduced a bill to abolish the use of the oath altogether, but it did not pass. The problem with Howard's excommunication also came up: technically, the other MPs would themselves risk a lesser form of excommunication if they associated with him, but yet he had been re-elected and had a right to sit. The Commons formed a committee to further investigate the fact that the High Commission had ignored Howard's MP privileges the previous year, which had allowed them to excommunicate him in the first place. After hearing and investigating MPs who had sat on the High Commission at the time of Howard's appearance, the committee decided that the Commission had been in the wrong, that Howard's privileges should have been granted him, and that the court should not just lift the excommunication, but erase Howard's case from their records, which they did. Howard was now in the clear, but not Frances.[22]

The rest of the year passed without any notable incidents and without any further actions in the High Commission. Frances remained in Stepney with her son, and Howard's movements cannot be discerned. In March the following year, Buckingham was struck with a tragedy: his only son Charles died, just over a year old, leaving his parents distraught and Buckingham without a male heir. By summer, his wife was pregnant again, giving the couple some new hope. However, Buckingham could not be assured of a boy, or that the pregnancy would be successful, or, if born, that the child would live. Should Buckingham die without a son, John would inherit. The High Commission case against Frances had still not concluded: what if she still might be able to convince her husband that little Robert was in fact his child, especially if Buckingham was no longer there to protect him? Buckingham again had to worry that his estate might fall into the hands of Frances's bastard. The international situation heightened his fears. Buckingham was set to lead a military expedition against France in the autumn: war certainly increased the risk of a premature death, forcing him to think about how to arrange his affairs for posterity. King Charles wanted to ease his best friend's troubled mind: in August of 1627 the king decreed that Buckingham's young daughter Mary would inherit all his titles and dignities, should the duke and duchess fail to have a son.[23] Even though the worry that Robert might inherit now had somewhat dissipated, Buckingham was still pushing to bring the High Commission case against Frances to its conclusion. Perhaps he simply wanted to finish what he started: more likely, he wanted to ensure that Frances would never be part of his family again, and that her schemes would not hurt or trick his brother any further.

More than two years after it had begun, the High Commission made its final decision in the case of Frances's adultery on Thursday, 19 November 1627. The proceedings took over six hours that day, beginning at two in the afternoon and not ending until after eight o'clock in the evening, highly unusual at a time when most court cases reached a conclusion in a few minutes. Nineteen members of the commission sat on their benches to give final judgement. As the court could sit and operate officially with only three judges, nineteen was a high number, suggesting the case's great importance. Five of them were extraordinary commissioners, high officials at the royal court: Sir Thomas Coventry, by now Lord Keeper of the Great Seal; Henry Montagu, Earl of Manchester and the Lord President of the Privy Council; William Herbert, Earl of Pembroke and Lord Steward; Phillip Herbert, Earl of Montgomery and Lord Chamberlain; and Sir John Coke, Secretary of State (no relation to Frances). Two additional noblemen were present: Edward Sackville, Earl of Dorset, and Oliver St John, Viscount Grandison, both also members of the Privy Council. Since this was the highest ecclesiastical court in

England, the court commissioners also included five bishops, representing London, Durham, Norwich, Rochester, and Bath and Wells; the Deans of St Paul's and Rochester; and Thomas Worrall, doctor of divinity. In addition, three Doctors of Law sat on the commission: Edmund Pope, Hugh Barker, and Sir Charles Caesar. Sir Henry Marten, who was Dean of Arches, the judge in the ecclesiastical court of the Archbishop of Canterbury, was also present. He had been one of the MPs who sat on the commission in the spring of 1625, and who had been censored by Parliament for dismissing Howard's demand for parliamentary privilege, as well as imprisoning and excommunicating him. The Earl of Manchester, Viscount Grandison, and George Montaigne, the Bishop of London, had also been part of the earlier proceedings.

The prosecutors' case was largely the same as during the 1625 hearings, with a few added details: Frances, in maidservant disguise and with a basket of food, had met Howard in Dr Lambe's chamber and witnesses had seen them both together on the bed. Lambe had drawn the bed curtains around them and locked them into the room to ensure that no one disturbed them. The outing to the inn at Ware received another recounting, as did the fact that Howard had visited Frances in her lodgings at Denmark House at unseemly hours and that he had entered her lodgings through a secret passageway. Frances's defence remained unchanged and unwavering: those who accused her were her 'sworn enemies' and people who had 'threatened her mischief'. She also argued that the former Lord Keeper had threatened the witnesses to speak 'against their consciences to accuse her', and if they did not, they would 'be in chains all their days'. By the end of the day, Frances's defence did not move the judges: eighteen of the nineteen voted to find her guilty. The nineteenth member, Sir Charles Caesar, one of the Doctors of Law, 'desired to be spared, and so gave no Sentence'.[24] Unfortunately, Caesar did not leave any clues as to why he chose to abstain from voting.

The court also decided on Frances's punishment: she was to be imprisoned 'at the pleasure of the court', fined 500 marks (a mark was not a coin, but an accounting unit, roughly the equivalence of two-thirds of a pound in seventeenth-century England), and—most notably—she was to do public penance in the Savoy church.[25] The penance hit a proud woman hard. The convicted sinner stood in front of the congregation, or in a public place such as a church or at a market, barefoot, bareheaded, and clad in the penitent's simple white robes. The penitent then humbly confessed her sins and asked for forgiveness, both from God, the community, and the people injured by her misdeeds. This ceremony both publicly humiliated and made an open example of sinners, as well as enabled their readmittance to the Christian community afterwards. A person could not be forgiven until she had admitted her sin. The news of the High Commission decision spread rapidly, and many Londoners were no doubt relishing and looking forward to the spectacle of a humiliated viscountess without all her finery, stepping with her bare feet in the mud and filth.[26]

Not surprisingly, Frances did not want to do the penance. Noblewomen's convictions for adultery were rare in the first place, and it was even more unusual for noblewomen to be placed in such humiliating positions. Frances herself had been careful to protect her noble privilege when she had been arrested for debts the year before and she would use and emphasize her status in the future as well: she was a noblewoman and resented being treated like a commoner. She would *not* be publicly humiliated and jeered by the crowds, she would *not* give Buckingham and the rest of the Villiers the satisfaction of the spectacle, she would *not* adhere to the ruling of the High Commission: she would simply *not* do the penance.

Frances at first refused to appear on the appointed day for the penance. When it became clear that she would not comply of her own accord, the Privy Council issued a warrant for her arrest and sent two officers to apprehend her. As Lord Holles described it in a letter to his son, Frances, 'smelling the storm, tooke a tree, and can not be found'.[27] Frances's well-instructed, brave, and loyal servants told the arresting officers that Lady Purbeck was not there and then simply refused to let them in, indeed even threatening that if the officers 'came in there, they should never go out againe'.[28] Enraged at Frances's overt flaunting of the High Commission's authority, the Privy Council issued a new warrant for her arrest on 19 December. The council empowered John Bennet, one the King's Sergeants at Arms, to carry out the arrest. They told him immediately to go to 'Lady Purbeck in the Strand, or to any other house or place as well privileged as otherwise' where he might find her (Fig. 6.1). Clearly, Frances was no longer in Stepney, and not with her mother at Hatton House in Holborn either. She may have been staying with her grandfather, the Earl of Exeter, in Exeter House, situated along the Strand. As the warrant made clear, however, Frances would not be able to hide anywhere, not even in the houses of the powerful. The council also told Bennet that he had the right to request the help of 'all mayors, sheriffs, justices of the peace, constables, head boroughs and all others His Majestie's officers, whome it may concern', in the event that he should meet with any resistance. Bennet was warned that he 'may not fayle' in his task, as he would then have to answer to the council at his own 'uttermost perills'.[29]

Finally, Buckingham received word from his spies that Frances was hiding out in a house adjacent to Cesare Allessandro Scaglia, the ambassador of the Duke of Savoy. In order to assist Sergeant Bennet in his tricky task, one of Buckingham's mother's gentlemen went to Scaglia and asked for his assistance in the matter. The Countess

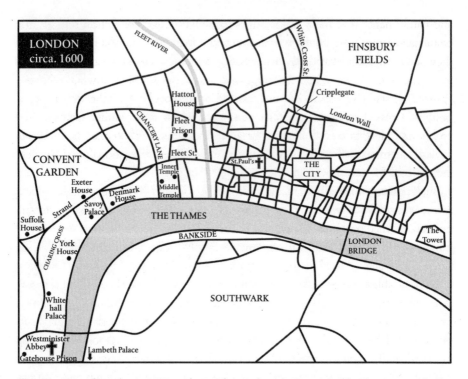

Fig. 6.1. Map of London, *c*.1600, with significant places in Frances's life. The map marks the approximate locations of various places in London mentioned in the text.

of Buckingham wanted sergeants and other officers to be able to pass through the ambassador's house and gardens in their process of catching the recalcitrant Frances in the neighbouring house. Scaglia was not pleased about this request, as he found the whole business distasteful. He thought it was unseemly to ask him to open up his house to 'such persons' (meaning the sergeants) and to make him party to 'the surprise and arrest of a fair Lady his neighbor'. After considering the situation's political complexities, he reluctantly let the authorities in.[30]

The sergeants were lying in wait at Scaglia's, trying to determine the best time to strike. Suddenly, they were forced into action. On the street side of the house, a young woman rushed out, darted into the ambassador's coach, and drove off at high speed. The sergeants and the officers scrambled to catch up, leading to a mad chase down the Strand: galloping horses pulled Scaglia's coach at the front and the sergeants, both by foot and by horse, dashed behind. Curious onlookers lined the streets and windows, and fleet-footed youngsters ran along, so not to miss the conclusion of the spectacle. When the sergeants finally caught up with the coach and triumphantly got their hands on its passenger, their satisfaction turned into embarrassed rage. The young woman they had been chasing was not Frances, as they had thought, but rather the ambassador's page, 'a handsome Fair Boy' dressed in women's clothing. While the sergeants were busy chasing down the coach, Frances herself had quietly slipped away under the cover of the diversionary hubbub. Dressed as a man, with her young son in tow, she climbed into another coach and disappeared.[31] To his great dismay, Sergeant Bennet had indeed 'fayled', outsmarted by a fugitive lady. As a consequence he soon found himself behind bars for several weeks.[32]

Buckingham's rage was palpable when he found out that Frances had slipped away. Most of his fury was directed towards Scaglia, as he felt the ambassador had publicly scorned him by helping Frances, 'she being Wife to his Brother, & bringing him Children of anothers begetting', he seethed. Scaglia was placed in a difficult situation: he needed to be in good standing with Buckingham and King Charles in order to be able to serve the interests of his master, the Duke of Savoy. The Savoyard thus sought to rectify matters with Buckingham right away, only to find his entrance into Whitehall Palace denied. When he tried to get the Lord Chamberlain to intervene on his behalf, he received a curt message from Buckingham, 'who took his proceeding so unkindly as he was resolved not to speak with him'. Scaglia was disappointed, but hoped that time would heal the wounds. After further mediation by the Earls of Carlisle and Holland, Buckingham finally agreed to see Scaglia a week later, and after an hour's discussion, they were able to reconcile.[33]

It was not just the ambassador of Savoy who was favouring Frances's cause. Friends of Frances and Lady Hatton found both the conviction questionable and the punishment outrageous. John Holles, now the Earl of Clare, argued that the evidence presented in court against Frances was not very convincing. With a great deal of sarcasm, Holles told his son that because Howard had 'lodged the next chamber' to Frances at a few inns, and 'was found sitting by her bed side at another place, with his hand over her pillow, and such hayneous misdemeanors, and adulteries', the High Commission had found Frances guilty. He made no mention of the birth of Robert, the most difficult evidence to explain away. Holles also said that he was not alone in his judgement, as 'all the town is friendly to her in opinion'.[34] When London resident Joseph Mead reported on Frances's escape to Sir Martin Stuteville, the words he chose suggest that he too thought Frances was treated harshly. He said that Frances, who was 'hotly pursued' to do the penance, was 'rescued' by the ambassador of Savoy and thus had 'escaped their clutches'.[35] Robert Johnston, a Scotsman working in London as Clerk of the Deliveries of Ordnance, witnessed the chase and reported that Frances's flight 'afforded Matter of Mirth to People at that time', suggesting that the hullabaloo surrounding Frances's absconding might have been a good and entertaining replacement for people who missed out on seeing the scheduled penance.[36]

After her brazen escape, Frances went even deeper into hiding. The Privy Council was still actively trying to find and arrest Frances in the early months of 1628. Her flight and disappearance also caused difficulties for her loyal servants. A few weeks after the dramatic coach-chase, the Privy Council brought in Dorothy Wingfield, Elizabeth Ashley, Anne Elwick, and Sir Giles Brydges (in whose house in Stepney she had been staying), for examination. The council, trying to scare Brydges and the servants with its power, questioned them about their particular roles in resisting the apprehension and arrest of Frances. Implying serious consequences, the Privy Council was openly pondering if they had grounds to draw up criminal charges against them in the Court of Star Chamber. The tactic failed. Frances's gentlewomen were clearly made of similar stock to their mistress, because when asked where Frances was at present, one of them cheekily replied that 'she knew not, except her ladyship was gone to the Isle of Rhé, now called the Isle of Rue'. She was not actually implying that Frances had fled to the French west-coast island: instead, she was making a pun at the expense of Buckingham. The previous autumn, Buckingham had led an expedition to the Isle of Ré in order to assist the beleaguered Protestants in conflict with the French Catholic king in the region around the city of La Rochelle. The expedition turned out to be a humiliating failure and Buckingham had to retreat after a three-month-long siege attempt, having lost more than half of his troops and accomplished nothing but a much worsened relationship between England and France. In fact, he had just returned to England before the conclusion of Frances's High Commission case. The councillors were not pleased with the gentlewoman's 'untoward' sarcastic comment about the 'Isle of Rue'. According to one report, she was 'laid by the heels', meaning imprisoned.[37]

While the Privy Council was trying to ascertain the whereabouts of Frances, her sister-in-law, the Duchess of Buckingham, had other pressing matters occupying her time. Having prepared her lying-in, she gave birth to a much-welcomed baby boy on 30 January at Wallingford House. Two weeks after the birth, William Laud, at the time Bishop of Bath and Wells as well as Buckingham's chaplain and political protégé, arrived to christen the little boy. The parents named him George after his father. Baby George had illustrious gossips, or godparents, as King Charles and Queen Henrietta Maria had agreed to serve in that capacity. While the king actually attended the christening, Henrietta Maria sent the Duchess of Richmond to stand in for her, as the Catholic queen could not participate in the Anglican ceremony. In addition to the royal couple, Buckingham also selected Theophilus Howard,

Howard's elder brother and now Earl of Suffolk since the death of their father, as a third attending godparent. Clearly, Buckingham attempted to clarify that his enmity against Frances and her lover did not extend to the rest of the powerful Howard family.[38]

Notably, no record of the Privy Council questioning or apprehending Howard in connection with Frances's flight and disappearance exists. Perhaps he had nothing to do with it, or perhaps they were chastened by the 1626 Parliament's dismissal of Howard's excommunication and insistence on Parliamentary privileges and did not want to bring more fuel to the fire for the upcoming Parliament. Charles, still desperate for money for his battles with the French, officially opened yet another Parliament on 17 March, demanding that they vote for new taxes. Howard had yet again been returned for Bishop's Castle, and was thus enveloped in the protective cloak of Parliamentary privileges.

Frances was still hiding and could not be found to perform the penance despite repeated attempts, but the High Commission did not want to leave her entirely unpunished. Since she refused to either admit to, or repent, her crime and thus be spiritually redeemed, they decided to excommunicate her instead. In her now characteristically stubborn fashion, Frances fought back. In late March, she petitioned the House of Lords and insisted that her noble privileges be properly protected from the wrongful and illegal actions of the High Commission. She claimed that as the wife of a member of the House of Lords, the High Commission did not have the right to excommunicate her during a Parliamentary session. She also asked that the Lords consider the fact that she had been denied the Parliamentary privilege when she was brought in front of the High Commission initially.[39] In essence, she was taking a page out of Howard's playbook, arguing that the High Commission had never had the right to try her and was thus hoping to overturn not just the excommunication, but ultimately the adultery conviction as well.

The House of Lords took her petition seriously, as they usually did in cases of noble privileges. Frances had asked for legal counsel and they provided her with two lawyers, both members of the House of Commons. The Lords then sent her petition to the Parliamentary Committee of Privileges for further study. Presumably, Frances was able to operate more in the open while the case progressed. The latest turns did not please Buckingham. As the weeks went by without any resolution, he became impatient with the sluggish wheels of justice. He told the Lords they needed to speed up the proceedings, as his brother John 'has stayed long in town about it, which is contrary to his health'. However, even powerful Buckingham could not get his way in this case. The Lords essentially told him that the matter was proceeding in committee and that it would be done when it was done. John was not present for most of these proceedings: he had not entered a proxy for the 1628 Parliament, but he was in the House only one day, on 7 April, out of the total of 81 days. While the deliberations of the committee took place during the month of April, no discussion or decision was made in Frances's case on the one day that John attended.[40]

The debate in Frances's case centred on whether she could enjoy privileges as a Lord's wife when she lived separately from her husband and had been found guilty of adultery. To Frances's great disappointment, the Lords were not interested in questioning the adultery conviction at all, but focused solely on the issue of the excommunication. If she had a right to the privileges, the High Commission would have been wrong to excommunicate her. The main question was a complex one. Did the privileges always follow her person inherently and regardless of her relationship with her husband, or were the privileges of a peer's wife only in effect if the marriage was intact and the spouses living together? In addition, John had written a letter to the committee in which he 'absolutely disavow[s] all privileges which she claims as his wife'. So, could a Lord's privileges be extended to his wife *against* his express wishes? Those friendly to Frances's case argued that since she still was the legal wife of a peer, the 'privilege of honor cannot be separated from her'. While John and Frances certainly were estranged and did not live together, they had not gone through the legal process of separation, with required a church court decision for a divorce '*a mensa et thoro*', or a 'separation from bed and board'. However, argued the other side, Frances had been found guilty of adultery in the highest church court in England. The Parliamentary privilege was her husband's and she could 'derive no privilege but from the bed whence she is departed'. If she committed adultery and thus betrayed the marriage bed, her husband had the right to rescind her privileges.

After a spirited debate, the Committee of Privileges came to the conclusion that Frances had forfeited her privileges when she committed adultery. She could not claim them against the express wishes of her cuckolded husband, even though, as Frances pointed out, the charges against her in the High Commission had been brought by her brother-in-law Kit Villiers, Earl of Anglesey, rather than by her own husband. When the committee presented their decision to the full House of Lords, several Lords protested so vehemently against the decision that it was resolved that the whole House should vote on whether to accept the committee's verdict. Some members were reluctant to participate in the proceedings, claiming either that they were too closely related to Frances to be impartial, or that they had not heard the entire debate and therefore were not sufficiently informed to vote. Their qualms were waved aside and those who had already excused themselves and left the chamber were promptly told to return and cast their vote. In the end, a majority voted in line with the committee. However, the Lords were also careful to point out that their decision only applied to this particular case and was not to be treated as setting any sort of precedent. They were concerned about inadvertently curtailing Parliamentary and noble privileges in the future. Unfortunately, the records do not tell us who of the 139 Lords and bishops present cast the yay or nay votes, but we can safely assume that Buckingham, his brother the Earl of Anglesey, and brother-in-law the Earl of Denbigh, who were all present, voted against Frances. Lady Hatton's friend the Earl of Clare in all likelihood voted for Frances, as he had been one of the Lords who had argued for allowing her privileges during the debates. Perhaps Howard's brother Theophilus, also present, voted in favour of Frances as well. Thus, while Frances had friends in the House of Lords, it was not enough. As the Lords denied her privileges, they did decide to show Frances some mercy: because of Frances's status as 'a lady', they argued, they granted her a temporary grace period of privileges for twenty days, during which she could not be arrested or detained.[41] Now, no hiding place in London would suffice: this was Frances's signal to escape the capital.

CHAPTER 7

TOWN AND COUNTRY

The House of Lords denied Frances's privileges on 29 April 1628. The twenty-day grace period gave Frances a respite from the fear of arrest and some freedom of movement until 19 May. Not able to accomplish much in London, and only protected from arrest for a precious few weeks, Frances needed to leave London and stay away for some time. She was as determined as ever not to perform the penance, but how could she be safe from Buckingham and his men, the lords of the Privy Council, the High Commission, and the king? At this juncture, her lover offered her a refuge at his recently acquired estate in Clun, Shropshire. Seeking security in the remote countryside, Frances rather naively hoped that if she stayed out of sight long enough, the world would forget about her transgressions. Had she chosen to break with Howard, instead of moving in with him, perhaps it would have worked.[1]

Clun, then as now, is in a sparsely populated area along the Welsh border in Shropshire (see Figs. 7.1 and 7.2). The loveliness of its vast vistas and thick forests surely would have provided at least some initial solace for a woman who had been under pressure for several years, with continuous strife, fear, and uncertainty. The medieval Clun Castle was long the original home of the Lords of Clun, but the castle was in ruins already in the seventeenth century, no longer fit for habitation. Instead, Howard and Frances may have been living in nearby Hopesay, or in The Hall in the Forest outside Clun. The Hall in the Forest was aptly named: built in the late sixteenth century, it was a large house, secluded in the midst of the large, sprawling Clun woods. It was a perfect spot to stay out of sight, but also a very lonely and boring place for someone used to the faster pace of the city, including life at court with its constant stream of entertainments and socializing. Her lover provided solace, but Howard's Parliamentary duties also forced his return to London for both the remainder of the 1628 session and the session early the following year, leaving Frances alone with her thoughts.[2]

Only a few short months after arriving in Shropshire, Frances received the startling news that set the whole of England abuzz: the mighty Buckingham had finally fallen. He was dead, murdered by a disgruntled army officer. Buckingham's monopoly on the new king's affection had made him increasingly unpopular, and

Fig. 7.1. Rural landscape in Clun, Shropshire, where Frances spent several years hiding after her adultery conviction. The top of the church of St George is visible in the lower left corner, which is where Sir Robert Howard was buried. The church still has a plaque commemorating Howard. Photo: Andrew Roland/Shutterstock.

the failure of his French expeditions had only added to the grievances against him. The House of Commons of both 1626 and 1628 presented remonstrances to the king, outlining what they considered Buckingham's many misdeeds, trying to chip away at least some of his influence. While he was able to defend himself against Parliamentary displeasure with the king's solid and loyal support, the tide of public opinion was turning against him. During the summer of 1628, a bloody event offered an ominous warning. The people of London had come to associate John Lambe, that problematic medical healer Frances had consulted, with Buckingham. Presumably, Lambe had been providing services to the duke after the debacle with Buckingham's adulterous sister-in-law. In June, an angry and murderous mob in London killed Lambe. A lover of theatre, Lambe had attended a play. As he left the playhouse and entered the street, a crowd of people identified him as 'The Duke's Wizard'. Fuelled by outrage against Buckingham, fear and hatred of witchcraft, and desire for revenge for Lambe's rape-victim, several groups of young men began the merciless attack. Lambe's 'skull was broken, one of his eyes hung out of his head, all partes of his body bruised and wounded so much, that no part was left to receive a

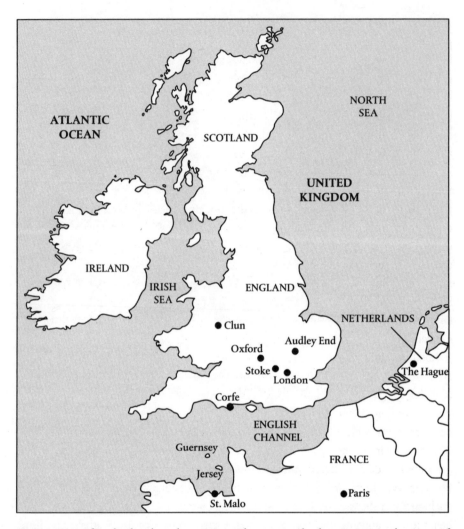

Fig. 7.2. Map of England and northern France. The map marks the approximate locations of the main residences and places where Frances and Howard stayed at various points in their life.

wound'. Unable to find people willing to help him against his attackers, the old man died of his injuries the following day. Despite several inquests, ultimately no one was held accountable. The mob's verdict and execution stood as the last word on his life.[3]

In the months following Lambe's murder, threatening verses predicted that Buckingham would meet a similar fate. One of many foreboding messages emphasized that royal protection would not help against the people's anger: 'let Charles & George [Buckingham] do what they can, Yet George shall dye like Doctor Lambe'.

A newsletter relating the killing of Lambe also argued that had Buckingham been present at the time of the attack, the young men threatened that they would have killed him as well, 'minced his flesh, & have had every one a bitt of him'.[4] Others also predicted the duke's demise, albeit less violently. Lady Eleanor Davis, who claimed to be able to foretell the future, stated on multiple occasions that August 1628 would be the month of Buckingham's death. Aware of the threat, Buckingham still hesitated to display public concern. He did not want people to see him afraid, although his friends, including the king, certainly wished he would take precautions. In August, Buckingham travelled to Portsmouth to oversee the supplying of naval ships. His wife and sister-in-law (Kit's wife) accompanied the expedition and the party lodged at the Greyhound Inn. On the morning of 22 August, Buckingham was downstairs in the inn, discussing business with the local representatives. The place teemed with all the duke's men, other officials, and townspeople. Amidst the throngs moved Lieutenant John Felton, an ambitious young officer burning with rage over failing to acquire a promotion. His anger was both personal and political; he also shared the general opinion that Buckingham was a bad influence on the king. He decided that it was he who should solve the problem. Felton manoeuvred himself close to Buckingham, and without warning, stepped forward and swiftly stabbed the duke in the left side of the chest. Stunned and shocked, Buckingham cried 'villain!', removed the knife from his own body, and just had time to half-way draw his sword before he fell. The confused and horrified people around him caught the duke before he hit the floor. They laid the dying man on a table, blood pouring both from his mouth and from the wound in his chest. Buckingham's wife had stayed in their rooms upstairs while her husband went down to begin the day's business. The duchess heard the commotion and stepped out to the top of the stairs. Looking over the railing, she saw her dying husband on the table below, blood gushing from the now still body, surrounded by people frantically trying to both help the duke and find the assassin. Realizing what was happening, Katherine and her sister-in-law went to pieces. 'Such screechings and such distractions I never heard nor saw, and I hope I shall never to see the like again', said a shaken eyewitness. Had Felton really wanted to get away, he might have been able to do so in the great commotion. However, he actually chose to identify himself, wanting to ensure that people would know who had slain the hated Buckingham. He later had a change of heart. When at trial, he argued that the murder he had committed was wrong instead of justified, pleaded guilty, and was speedily hanged on 29 November.[5]

While the general population received the news of Buckingham's death with glee and celebrations, those close to him were inconsolable. A servant whispered the news to King Charles while he was attending religious services. A testament to

Charles's ability to control his emotions, he continued to sit quietly until the ceremony had ended, rather than cause a disruption. Then, he 'suddenly departed to his chamber, and threw himself upon his bed, lamenting with much passion and with abundance of tears the loss [. . .] and he continued in this melancholic . . . discomposure of mind many days'.[6] Buckingham's mother, siblings, and other relatives shared the heartbreak and shock. Their grief was magnified by the loss not only of a beloved family member, but also of their main source of money, prestige, and power.

What did Frances think when the astounding news of Buckingham's murder reached her hiding place in Shropshire? Considering how Buckingham had hounded her over the last few years, it is hard to imagine her wasting many tears on him, although she in all likelihood found the manner of his demise shocking. She would have to consider how his death would affect her constantly challenged financial situation. Since Buckingham had taken control of John's affairs during his illnesses, he had been the one paying the one thousand mark annual allowance to Frances, finally agreed upon after Frances's angry pressing of the reluctant Buckingham in the early 1620s. Buckingham had not been very orderly in the running of either his own or John's finances, so after his death, his confused widow and her advisers tried to figure out his byzantine accounts. The vast debts and numerous financial obligations that Buckingham had taken on made the task rather depressing for the grieving Katherine. She recognized that while Buckingham had been paying Frances, he was doing so on behalf of his brother, even though her husband unfortunately might have arranged it in such a way that it seemed to have become his legal responsibility. Now that he was dead, the responsibility should rightfully revert back to John, or John's current caretaker, she argued, rather than devolve on her young son George, Buckingham's heir. Since John was staying with his mother, Katherine suggested that her mother-in-law now make the payments to Frances on John's behalf, reminding the older lady that she had previously promised she would do so. In order to subtly convince her, Katherine suggested that it would be very difficult to honour the annuity Buckingham had wanted to give to his mother if the estate was still burdened with the payments to Frances. The old countess was not pleased at all at this suggestion and mild threat, reminding Katherine that not only was she still in deep mourning for her dear departed son, but also that John could not pay Frances's annuity, since the death of his brother had left him 'without means'. She would not and could not pay it. The countess also intimated that if it had been up to her, Frances would not have received the annuity in the first place, because she did not think she deserved it. She did agree to send her daughter Susan, Countess of Denbigh, to lobby the king to release Buckingham's estate from the responsibility of the annuity.[7] The flurry of letters do not reveal how this particular dispute ended and who, if anyone, actually paid the annuity. The particulars of Frances's financial arrangements after Buckingham's death remain uncertain.

While Frances continued to hide away in Shropshire, other members of Buckingham's family soon followed him into the grave, thinning the herd of Frances's enemies. Buckingham's younger brother Kit, the man who had taken over the High Commission prosecution of Frances in 1625, died on 3 April 1630. Kit, Earl of Anglesey, did not die by an assassin's hand, however, but instead fell victim to disease. He was buried in St George's Chapel at Windsor. Two years later, on 19 April 1632, Frances's formidable mother-in-law, the Countess of Buckingham, also passed away. The lady, in her early sixties when she died, had made a remarkable career for herself. She had survived three husbands, presided over the incredible rise of her son, and forcefully manoeuvred all her children into wealthy marriages. She had become powerful, wealthy, and a member of the nobility in her own right, regularly participating in court life in James's reign and receiving an official appointment in Queen Henrietta Maria's household, even though the reluctant queen initially had to be forced by Buckingham and Charles to accept her. She had been very ambitious and largely successful in her goals. The death of two of her sons before her own was doubtless a sorrow: she was left with only the deficient John, from whom she did not expect much at this point. Her daughter Susan was safely married to the Earl of Denbigh and had given her grandchildren. The death of Buckingham was softened slightly by the fact that he left behind three children, to whom the countess seemed genuinely attached, referring to two of them by their nicknames. Buckingham's oldest daughter Mary was called Mall, and little baby Francis, born seven months after the death of his father, went by Frank. George was still just George, a name too precious to change.[8]

Frances's husband John, saddened by the loss of his family members, mostly retired from court after Buckingham's death. He had held no formal position at court after Charles's ascension: it was largely his connection to Buckingham which had kept him in the royal palaces. With his brother gone, John's own influence—certainly lessened by his mental illness—diminished even further. He remained the titular Keeper of Denmark House, but others performed the regular tasks required to maintain that palace. John's participation in the Parliaments of the 1620s had already been sporadic, to say the least, but since Charles ruled throughout the 1630s without calling Parliament at all, that reason for attending the capital was removed as well.[9]

Although John was no longer present at court, King Charles continued to be concerned about the health of his former servant and the brother of his great friend and favourite. Charles took over the role of John's protector. The king ordered for his care when he was reportedly suffering from 'distemper and weakness' again in 1631. The king was especially concerned that he be kept away from harmful foods and practices, to prevent 'such ill accidents as often accompany such distempers'.[10] During this period, Frances and John appear to have been completely estranged from each other: no records of communication between them exist. The news of the many Villiers deaths and John's illness probably made Frances hope that her husband might join them in the afterlife. If only John were gone, she could marry Howard. John, weak in mind, turned out to be strong in body. He stubbornly refused to die, and Frances and Howard had to continue waiting.

According to a later charge in the mid-1630s, Frances and Howard had several more children while living together in Clun. It was impossible for Frances to claim that any children she gave birth to while in Shropshire could have been her husband's, so her options to care for such children were limited. She could have given them up, or sent them to be raised by others. However, the charge is probably not true. Frances may have been pregnant, and she may have given birth to a child or children who did not survive, of course, but there exists no other evidence of Robert having any brothers or sister. No one else mentions additional children born to the couple, and the lengths to which Frances would later go to establish her son Robert in life suggests that she was not likely simply to have abandoned any putative younger siblings.[11]

Frances followed the events in the capital from afar, but did not herself figure in any gossip until she was mentioned in a disturbing and violent tale in 1632. In a letter to his mother in April of that year, Sir Thomas Barrington mentioned Frances and Howard. Thomas Barrington's father, Sir Francis Barrington, had been a member of the committee who had investigated the High Commission's violation of Howard's privileges in 1626.[12] After relating two sensational stories of spousal murders by poison in London, Barrington added a juicy story of how Frances had fled to the city for 'cure' after Howard had cut her face with a knife while they were fighting. Barrington wrote:

> Sir Robert Howard hath converted his extremity of loving lust into a foule a disguise of inhumanity as he hath putt upon his long kept mistress the Lady Purbeck her fayre face [...] as many crosses upon with his unkind knife as he could find attractive beautyes in her severall features.

Barrington was horrified at the 'unheard of ferocity', which he found 'most unmanly' and savage. While he argued Frances might have brought such divine punishment on herself as a result of her sinful living, Barrington still believed that Howard, who was 'the cause of all her shame and sufferings', should not be the one to offer her violence in addition to the dishonour of making her his mistress. Luckily for Frances, it seems the incident was only a rumour, as in a later letter, Barrington briefly added that 'Sir Robert Howard sayth he never did cut my Lady Purbeck's nose'.[13] Later sources never mention any facial disfigurement or scars of any sort, but rather continue to extol Frances's beauty. The two lovers may have fought or had a falling out, without bloodshed. The type of violence described in the rumour is telling: marking the face, specifically cutting the nose, constituted a traditional punishment for prostitutes and for female sexual offenders. Barrington and others who found Frances's adultery sinful could easily imagine her a victim of the kind of violence reserved for women who had illicit sex.[14]

Frances, with her nose intact, left Clun and Shropshire behind in the summer of 1632 and chose to live with her retired and elderly father at Stoke until his death two years later.[15] Stoke Manor, about twenty miles west of London, just to the north of Windsor, was within easy reach of the city but still a tranquil country retreat. After a long career, with many run-ins with both King James and King Charles, Sir Edward Coke had retired from public life, keeping himself busy with the final volumes of his magnum opus, *The Institutes of the Lawes of England*. Coke had often interpreted the law in favour of common law, which the kings, especially Charles, saw as threatening the royal jurisdiction. In fact, Charles was so concerned about Coke's writing that he at one point ordered all of his papers confiscated, so that anything problematic could be removed and censored.[16] Coincidence, perhaps, but in the gallery of Coke's manor hung a portrait of the highly principled Sir Thomas More, the man who rather lost his head than swear the oath recognizing King Henry VIII as the head of the English Church.[17]

At first, settling in Stoke with her father seems an unlikely move: Frances had not enjoyed a good relationship with her father since her contentious and forced marriage fifteen years earlier. Her father had not helped her at all during her legal troubles, leaving her to fight his old colleagues on her own. Her departure suggests a temporary falling out with Howard earlier that year, as Thomas Barrington reported, and that she needed a new place to stay. While at Stoke, it is not likely that Frances saw much of Howard, if at all. Even if the couple remained on good terms, Coke probably would not have been too welcoming towards the lover of his adulterous daughter.

In the past, Frances had relied on assistance from her mother when she was in trouble, living and travelling with her when her husband was ill. If Frances either needed or wanted to leave Clun in 1632, that option was less attractive. Her mother mostly lived in London, and Frances was probably not quite ready to brave a move back to the capital. More significantly, Frances may not have been welcome in Hatton House at the time.[18] Throughout the 1620s legal proceedings, Frances had steadfastly argued that she and Howard were only friends and that baby Robert was her husband's child. While not many were convinced by Frances's denials, Lady Hatton had dutifully supported her daughter during this time. But when Frances actually went to live with her lover in Clun in 1628, her earlier claims of innocence rang very hollow. Anyone, including her mother, who had wanted to believe or pretend to believe that Frances had not committed adultery, could no longer do so. In another interesting twist, Lady Hatton reportedly became very friendly with Frances's sister-in-law Susan Villiers Fielding, Countess of Denbigh, during the summer of 1628, just after Frances had left for Shropshire. The Earl of Clare reported that the two ladies 'ar becum all one, shee [Denbigh] hath been once or twyse eating creame at Hatton house, and sum traffike there is between them besyds good morrows twyse or thryse the week'.[19] Clare called the friendship a 'wonderment:' if Lady Hatton was on such good terms with one of the Villiers family so soon after Frances's conviction and failed petition in the House of Lords, it probably means that she was not on very good terms with her daughter.

Frances, as the youngest daughter, may have also felt compelled to perform her filial duty and keep her aged father company during his last years. Coke led a retired life at Stoke, but he was a spry octogenarian (Fig. 7.3). Every morning, he rode his horse to exercise and 'to take the air'. In May of 1632, Coke had an accident: his horse stumbled and both horse and rider fell. By an extreme measure of good luck, or through God's providence, which was how Coke chose to interpret it, he was not hurt, although his head landed dangerously near some sharp stones and the heavy horse rolled on top of him.[20] The incident proved that the old man needed attending, and Frances complied.

Even though Coke was not seriously hurt from the riding accident, the years eventually caught up with him. By 1633 and 1634, he had weakened significantly. When a friend generously sent him doctors to 'regulate his health', Coke dismissed them and responded that he 'had never taken physic since he was born, and would not now begin'. Medical treatments were rather pointless, he argued, since 'he had now upon him a disease which all the drugs of Asia, the gold of Africa, nor all the doctors of Europe could cure—old age'.[21] On Wednesday, 3 September 1634, between eleven and twelve o'clock at night, old age finally won. Frances's father died peacefully in his sleep. According to his good friend Sir Julius Caesar, he went to his eternity 'like a lambe, without any groans or outward signs of sickness, but only spent by age'.[22] A good death, according to the standards of the time.

Fig. 7.3. Sir Edward Coke. Coke was about seventy-seven years old in this picture. John Payne, after unknown artist, 1628–9. National Portrait Gallery, London.

News of Coke's weakening and death sparked a flurry of activities. On 1 September, two days before Coke's actual passing, the king's secretary issued a warrant to search his house and to confiscate any potentially seditious or troublesome writings. Sergeants at arms swiftly rode to Stoke and proceeded to carry out their orders, before Coke had even had time to die. So, while Coke was expiring peacefully in his bedchamber, the king's men were busy rifling through the papers in his study, taking with them manuscripts as well as many other documents. The king also had Coke's room in the Temple Inn in London searched and confiscated further papers and possessions there.[23]

Other people impatiently waiting for Coke's demise included those who hoped to profit from it financially. Despite not being able to hold on to royal favour for extended periods of time, Coke had managed to amass a great fortune, part of which he acquired through his marriage to Lady Hatton. His sons from his first marriage had done their best to whittle it down by racking up huge debts, which Coke paid, if not always willingly. According to one report in 1623, Coke was nearly 'crackt, his brains being overburthened with a surcharge of his childrens debts that arise to 26,000 li besides 10,000 li of his owne'.[24] Nonetheless, at the time of his death, he owned more than sixty manor houses and estates and many other forms of incomes, in addition to furniture, plate, jewels, and other valuables. The estate constituted a big prize. Considering the constant battles over property and income between Lady Hatton and Coke throughout their tumultuous marriage, it is hardly surprising that she would fight her step-sons to maximize her portion of the inheritance. She had impatiently waited for her elderly husband to die for several years. At one point during the summer of 1634, Lady Hatton heard what proved to be a false rumour that Coke had already died. She brought her brother Edward Cecil, Viscount Wimbledon, with her for male support and hurried down towards Stoke with the intention of taking possession of the estate before any of Coke's sons could arrive. Half-way there, she received the disappointing news that Coke was still very much alive, indeed that he had improved significantly and was now healthier than ever. Downcast, Lady Hatton turned around and went back to London, forced to bide her time a little longer.[25]

A few months later, when the reports were actually true, Lady Hatton sprang into action again. There was some confusion at first, because no one could find Coke's will. It turns out that it had been among the confiscated papers and it was eventually probated several months later, on 7 February 1635. In the meantime, Lady Hatton quickly took possession of the manor at Stoke and petitioned the king for redress for the financial difficulties Coke had caused her. Coke and Lady Hatton had lived apart since Frances's marriage, but she had not received any maintenance from her husband during that whole time. As a result, she had accumulated significant debts. When she tried to sell some of her lands to raise funds, he refused to agree to it. Since wives could not sell property without the approval of their husbands, Lady Hatton had applied to the king to be recognized as a *femme sole* (a legally independent woman) in this particular instance. The king had allowed it as long as she paid a fine, but Coke was still preventing the sale. Ultimately, she did get Coke's approval, but she had to buy it from him by giving him £1,000 in gold and a manor in Norfolk called Fakenham. Now, Lady Hatton wanted an equitable solution.[26]

The king also received a petition from Sir Maurice Berkeley, the husband of Frances's elder sister Elizabeth. Poor Elizabeth, already long dead at this point, had reaped precious few benefits from her wealthy parents. Married years after her beautiful younger sister, Elizabeth's dowry was much smaller than Frances's, and Coke did not even pay all of it. Berkeley was now hoping to get some justice for little Frances, the daughter to whom Elizabeth had given birth shortly before she died. Berkeley claimed that Coke had promised to pay £4,000 to Berkeley's father, and that he would settle £1,000 per year on Berkeley himself, as part of the marriage agreement. However, Coke had only paid £3,500 to Berkeley's father, so that the son felt obliged to take out a loan in order to pay his father the difference. He had now been paying off that loan with interest for ten years. Furthermore, Coke had convinced Elizabeth to forgo a portion of her inheritance, although he had settled even more money on her sister Frances, Buckingham having pushed him to do so. Berkeley argued that Coke had refused to approve the sale of Lady Hatton's lands, because he was concerned that she was in effect disinheriting her daughters. He also said that Coke had assured him that the Fakenham manor, now claimed by Lady Hatton, should be given to little Frances Berkeley, along with £1,000, presumably the same sum of money Lady Hatton had been forced to give to Coke earlier. Berkeley was hoping that the king would ensure justice for his daughter, 'it being reasonable', he argued, 'that if reliefe be given to the Lady Hatton upon agreem'nte for the benifitt of her and her Children, that the Lady Berkeley and her Child (who are in effect disinherited by both, and without any demerit) should be considered'.[27]

The will eventually materialized, but it still did not provide very clear directions to Coke's heirs. Coke had written the will more than ten years earlier. It turned out to be surprisingly simple, clearly meant to complement other, more complex, legal agreements. Coke directed his executors (his friends Sir Thomas Coventry, the king's Lord Keeper—who had been involved in the investigation and prosecution of Frances in 1625—and Sir John Walter) to carry out his 'indentures and conveyances' in the interest of his 'offspring linage and posterity'. He mentions none of his family members by name in the main text of the will and the only specific bequests he made were £30 in plate to each of his executors and to Sir Ranulphe Crewe (also one of the men who had investigated Frances). In an added codicil to the will, Coke stated that he wanted to be buried next to his 'firste good wife', meaning Bridget Paston. He did not want to have anything further to do with Lady Hatton after his demise.[28]

Although not mentioned in the will, Lady Hatton was legally entitled to receive her jointure, the widow's share, from Coke's estate. She wanted more. Appealing again to the king and Privy Council, Lady Hatton listed the many wrongs Coke had offered her. If he had better remembered her in his will, she insisted, she would not have said anything about her mistreatments at his hands. She was a modest woman, and would have put up with them rather than publish them and have the world find out about her horrible husband. Modesty and discretion were not among Lady Hatton's qualities: she had never been reluctant to let the world know about Coke's wrongdoings. She recounted their early clashes, and Coke's previous violent behaviour, both in connection with the unsanctioned marriage of her gentlewoman to Coke's ward, as well as Frances's marriage.[29] Lady Hatton's appeals worked. She was able to get both Stoke and Fakenham. As a widow, she was now able to control her own wealth, finally free from the constant arguing and fighting with Coke. In contrast, Berkeley was not successful in his bid for his daughter: Fakenham would be Lady Hatton's, and she in turn bequeathed it to her grandson Robert, Frances's son and Frances Berkeley's cousin. Young Frances, like her mother, continued to be neglected by her mother's family. Our Frances, already provided for through her large dowry—although she was not able to enjoy it—did not receive anything else from her father. Generally, when a family had both sons and daughters, the daughters received their share of the family wealth through their dowries rather than inheritance, whereas sons had to wait and get their shares when their father died.

After Coke's death, Frances hoped that her old sins finally had been forgiven or at least forgotten. While her husband was still very much alive, her main persecutors—Buckingham, Kit Villiers, and their mother the Countess of Buckingham—were all dead. Frances was also under the impression that she had regained some measure of King Charles's goodwill. In a later letter to Secretary of State Sir Francis Windebank, Frances referred to a 'little seruice I had the happiness then to have lately done his Ma:ty' and to the king's expressed 'good opinion of me in my owne particular'. Perhaps the service she was referring to was connected to the king's confiscation of her father's papers. Frances seems to have truly believed that her troubles were over. She even met Secretary Windebank in person on one occasion, and he did not indicate that she should expect any further problems with the king. Finally, after six years of involuntary exile, she felt confident enough to leave the tediousness of country living behind and move back to the excitement of London during the winter of 1634–5.[30]

In London, Howard was waiting for her. Any possible rift between them had now healed and the two reunited. The pair were simply unable to stay away from each other, against their better judgements. Howard arranged lodgings for Frances in Westminster, very close to Whitehall Palace and right across the river from Lambeth Palace, the main London seat of the Archbishop of Canterbury, William Laud. For the sake of discretion, the two did not live together. Howard, as was his habit when in London, was mostly staying with his older brother at Suffolk House in Charing Cross, although he could now often visit Frances. As Archbishop Laud noted, the choice of location for Frances's abode was unfortunate, as it 'was so near the Court and in so open a view; that the King and the Lords [of the Privy Council] took notice of it, as a thing full of Impudence, that they [Frances and Robert] should so publically adventure to outface the justice of the Realm, in so fowl a business'. Charles told Laud that it was his duty to deal with this 'impudence', considering he was now the highest church official in England. Laud explained that he had not acted in the matter previously, because Frances was the wife of a nobleman and could therefore not be arrested without the king's express commands. Now, when Laud knew his master's mind, he promised to deal with the 'impudence' immediately (Fig. 7.4). A secretary drew up a royal warrant for the arrest of both Frances and Howard on 14 March 1635. Laud's sergeants were able to find both of them the very

Fig. 7.4. William Laud, Archbishop of Canterbury. Along with King Charles, Laud insisted that Frances and Howard be brought to heel, and properly punished for their sexual sins. After Anthony van Dyck, c.1635. National Portrait Gallery, London.

next day and promptly arrested them, no doubt aware of the difficulties of detaining the slippery viscountess in the past. Frances soon found herself in the Gatehouse Prison near Westminster Abbey and Howard was sent to the Fleet Prison.[31] Laud did not entrust the pair to the 'honorable' house arrest at the London aldermen: straight to prison they went, as if to underscore that this time there would be no leniency and no respite.

Eight years after her adultery conviction, Frances now had to face the High Commission court and the penance yet again. She was 'much troubled at it', said Laud, in a grave understatement. As before, she was determined not to give in to the Lords of the Commission, but her situation in prison at first seemed rather hopeless. Not only was she separated from Howard, but Laud had also ordered that they both be kept 'close prisoners'. They were to be isolated from other prisoners, no visitors were allowed to see them, and they were denied access to ink and paper, thus making it near impossible to communicate with people on the outside. Seventeenth-century prisons were dreadful places: cold, draughty, overcrowded, and rife with vermin and diseases. Generally, prisoners also had to pay for their involuntary lodging and the meagre food. As was true everywhere else in society, people who had money could have a more tolerable experience. Upper-class prisoners were not thrown in a dungeon: they were generally given a separate chamber in the higher floors of the buildings, often with a window. In some cases, they were allowed to have their own furnishings and bed linen brought in, wall-hangings to keep the cold out, and their own food, sometimes prepared by a private cook. Long-term upper-class prisoners were also allowed to walk in the prison yard or roof to take the air occasionally, and to receive visitors and visit with other inmates. Frances and Howard did not have those privileges, since they were close kept.[32]

Charles and Archbishop Laud had their separate reasons for prosecuting Frances again after so many years. Laud was primarily concerned with upholding the integrity and the authority of the Court of High Commission. As Bishop of Bath and Wells, he had been part of the Commission which had found Frances guilty in 1627. He had voted for her conviction, convinced that she was guilty of the crime of adultery and that she deserved the punishment meted out to her. The fact that he owed much of his rise and success under the new reign to his close association with Buckingham probably also helped convince him. By the time of the 1635 proceedings, Laud held the highest position in the Anglican Church, subordinate only to the sovereign. By the 1630s, the High Commission court was increasingly unpopular with many Puritan-leaning English subjects, who viewed it as a tool of oppression against those not favouring Laud's rather conservative interpretation of Protestantism.

As a result, Laud was especially keen to ensure that the rulings of the High Commission should be enforced. However, as he himself said, he was also acting on the orders of King Charles, without which he would not have been able to arrest Frances.

The king had multiple reasons to force the stubborn Frances to submit once and for all. First, Charles found Frances's adultery distasteful. He had expressed his dislike with Frances as early as 1625, when the birth of her son and her affair with Howard had become public knowledge. Influenced by the ire of his friend Buckingham, no doubt, Charles had wanted Frances removed from her rooms at his princely London palace, Denmark House, so that he would not be seen as in any way approving of her behaviour or her person.[33]

In fact, Charles disliked premarital and extramarital sex more generally. He had no such proclivities himself, and heartily disapproved of them in others. Charles never took a mistress, although court factions attempted to get his attention by putting forward potential candidates who they thought might please him when he was a young man. Some courtiers thought he might be especially susceptible to the temptation during the first, troubled years of his marriage to Henrietta Maria, but they were wrong. When Buckingham died in 1628, Charles transferred his affections for his best friend and favourite wholly to his wife, which she at that point was happy to receive and reciprocate, after years in the margins of her husband's life. It was a drastic shift. An initially sour union turned into a love story. England had not witnessed such a happily married and stable royal couple and family for quite some time. Charles and Henrietta Maria became fully devoted to each other, remaining untouched by sexual scandals during their marriage. One writer has suggested that Charles II was actually the son of Henrietta Maria's devoted Master of Horse, Sir Henry Jermyn, but the evidence is highly circumstantial and mostly promulgated in anti-royalist camps during the Civil War and its aftermath. Charles, a highly principled man, habitually unable or unwilling to see others' points of view, had even less tolerance for philandering courtiers after experiencing a happy marriage himself.[34]

Ironically, Charles made an exception for Buckingham, the notorious ladies' man. In addition to more casual couplings and affairs, the beautiful and politically astute Lucy Percy, wife of James Hay, Earl of Carlisle, was Buckingham's mistress for many years. In all likelihood, Charles knew about the relationship, and still insisted that she become part of his wife's household. Initially, the pious queen did not want Lady Carlisle as a lady-in-waiting because she thought she was immoral. The queen's dislike was probably also influenced by the fact that she resented Buckingham's influence with her husband. She wanted neither Buckingham's mistress nor his female relatives in her household, as it would only increase his influence. Eventually, the charming Lady Carlisle managed to change the queen's mind, becoming a close confidante.[35]

By the 1630s, Charles and Henrietta Maria also worked to remake the court into a virtuous space full of matrimonial and platonic love, void of illicit sexual relationships and encounters. Charles displayed an incredible ability to control his emotions, and he equated passions and emotions, especially those ignited by extramarital sexual desires, with chaos and trouble. He wanted an orderly court, where everyone knew their role and position and where his own orderly and loving family with himself as the unquestioned paterfamilias, could serve as a model for his subjects and for the larger state. The laxer and more casual behaviour at his father's court would not continue. Charles introduced a strict court protocol to ensure that access to the royal persons was limited, and to inspire proper respect and awe of their majesty. The art sponsored by, and created for, the royal family also reflected this matrimonial ideal: court entertainments, like the masques in which the queen herself sometimes participated, tended to display marital bliss and emphasize spiritual rather than physical love. Painters, most famously the Dutch artist Anthony Van Dyck, produced several portraits displaying the happy—and growing—royal family (see Fig. 7.5). Charles encouraged courtiers to marry when he thought it appropriate, disliked when he heard of disputes between spouses, and above all, did not tolerate sexual missteps, which could invite disorder. His courtiers were keenly aware that they had to either avoid or conceal sexual escapades. As one courtier wryly noted: 'We keep all our virginities at court still, at least we lose them not advowedly.'[36] Charles interpreted Frances's adultery, and her continued relationship with Howard, as an affront to the good moral order he worked hard to establish.

Ensuring that Frances was punished for her misdeeds was also a way for Charles to remain loyal to his dead friend and favourite Buckingham, including the duke's family. After Buckingham's murder, Charles declared himself 'a father to the Dukes children, a husband to his duches, and a frend and master to his frends and seruants, a sonne to his mother, a brother to his brother and sister'.[37] Charles made good on his promise and favoured all of Buckingham's family members while they lived. Even the disappointing drunkard Kit Villiers received the keepership of Hampton Court Palace a few months after Buckingham's murder.[38] Since Buckingham had very much wanted Frances punished for cuckolding his brother, Charles also respected Buckingham's wishes even after his death. If Frances had remained tucked away in the countryside somewhere, Charles might not have acted. Her presence in London proved too much of a reminder of her transgressions against Buckingham

Fig. 7.5. King Charles I, Queen Henrietta Maria, and their children, the future King Charles II and Princess Mary. Engraving by Bernard Baron (1741), after Antony van Dyck, 1632. National Portrait Gallery, London.

and his brother for Charles to simply forget about it: now her old offences came to light again and thus could not be ignored.

Charles's continued allegiance to the Villiers and his dislike of sexual improprieties were evident in his reactions to another affair, which unfolded two years before the renewed charges against Frances and Howard. In 1633, Eleanor Villiers, one of the queen's maids-of-honour, found herself pregnant. Eleanor was Buckingham's niece, the daughter of his elder half-brother. When Eleanor was examined about her pregnancy, she said that Sir Henry Jermyn, the queen's Vice-Chamberlain, was the child's father. Jermyn readily admitted to having sex with Eleanor, but refused to marry her when that was broached as the solution to the dilemma. Jermyn argued that he had never promised her marriage in the first place, and moreover, that he had no intentions of marrying her now, since he considered her a dishonourable woman. Jermyn believed that Eleanor was 'no fit wife' for a prominent and ambitious courtier, precisely because she had been willing to have sex with him without the promise of marriage, and also because he claimed she had sex with two other men besides himself. Jermyn, himself guilty of having sex with no intentions of marriage, rejected Eleanor for doing the same. After having told Charles of Eleanor's other sexual relationships, Jermyn hoped that 'this will suffice to keep your Majesty in your justice from propounding this gentlewoman to me for a wife', and charitably added 'I do conceal many things that would much more than all this conduce to my discharge and the accusation of others'.[39]

The Villiers family was outraged by Jermyn's aspersions on Eleanor's character. They demanded that he marry her in order to restore her now sullied honour, and even offered a sizeable dowry of £8,000 to entice the reluctant man. King Charles agreed with them and ordered Jermyn imprisoned for several months, hoping that it would help persuade him. It did not. Finally, the king gave an ultimatum: Jermyn had to either marry Eleanor or leave the court and the country altogether. Jermyn, hell-bent on not marrying his mistress, choose exile in France. Charles would have been happy to get rid of Jermyn, but at the earnest request of Henrietta Maria, the king relented and allowed him to return to England and to the queen's service two years later. Jermyn remained a bachelor and the queen's devoted servant, which later earned him high appointments and eventually an earldom. Eleanor's court career, however, ended for good. She gave birth to a girl around the New Year, at which time she continued to insist that Jermyn was the child's father and that 'never any other man had to do with her'. Making unmarried mothers give an oath regarding the paternity right before the birth was a common method to establish fatherhood. People believed that a woman suffering from the pains of childbirth would tell the truth. In addition, any assistance with the birth should be withheld until the desperate woman gave the solemn oath. Consequently, a Dr Harris, who was present for the birth, took careful notes of Eleanor's oath and statements and dutifully showed them to the king. The exiled Jermyn made no attempt to recognize his child, although his father felt bad enough about his son's cavalier treatment of Eleanor that he paid for and sent her a midwife to help her with the birth. Eleanor remained unmarried for the rest of her life, forever marked by her illicit relationship.[40]

Jermyn's stubbornness frustrated Charles. His refusal to obey direct royal commands was not just a personal irritant, but also a larger political problem. The same dilemma characterized Frances's case, although her challenge to the royal authority was even more problematic for the king. Frances had thwarted the king's authority in her earlier escape from the penance. Urged on by Buckingham, King James had ordered that the case be investigated in the first place and Charles had continued to support Buckingham's bringing the case to the High Commission. The end of the trial and the conviction took place during Charles's early reign, when the young king was also trying to establish his own newly acquired power in the face of recalcitrant Parliaments looking for redress. When commentators recounted the story of the officers chasing the wrong person through the city, with Frances cleverly slipping away, they were retelling and spreading the story of one woman's defying royal authority. To the king, this was an outrage. Charles viewed himself as a divine right monarch, whom God had placed on the throne, and who therefore did not have to answer to his subjects. His stubborn insistence on his absolute royal powers would eventually put him in open war against his Parliament in the 1640s.[41]

In early April 1635, both Howard and Frances were duly summoned to appear in front of the High Commission, which was also working to include new charges of adultery as the couple had been living together after the 1627 conviction. Howard appeared first, on 2 April. This time, he swore the ex officio oath immediately. Since 1635 was in the middle of Charles's personal rule, when the king ruled without Parliament for a full eleven years, Howard could not claim Parliamentary privilege as he had done in 1625. This time, he was allowed to go free, paying a bond of £1,500 to ensure that he would appear in court again when ordered to do so. Two weeks later, he was back in court, but his answers were not considered sufficiently forthcoming. Commissioners ordered him to attend at the next court day, when they would decide any possible new charges against him.[42]

While Howard appeared in court and did what was asked of him, albeit reluctantly and tersely, Frances stalled and resisted. She was ordered to appear in court on 16 April, but the keeper of Gatehouse Prison informed the frustrated commissioners that Lady Purbeck simply refused to come, since she 'wanted clothes fitting for her to come abroad in'. Frances was able and willing to use her noble position: the prison keeper would have been reluctant to use physical force against a woman of her status. In her absence, the commission read the old sentence against her and announced that she would be doing the penance at the church of St Clement Danes a week from the coming Sunday. The king's advocate would also bring new charges of adultery against her, which then might bring further punishments. On 25 April, Howard appeared again, but Frances still did not come. The case was put off until the next court day. Frances never would appear before the High Commission, however, because before the keeper could bring her to do the penance, she escaped from prison. Howard managed to engage a friend to bribe Akila Weeks, the Gatehouse Prison keeper, to assist the imprisoned viscountess. The friend also brought new clothes for Frances: doublet, hose, and a large overcoat, so that she could disguise herself as a man. Just like her dramatic escape from the penance in 1628, a cross-dressed Frances slipped away from her persecutors. As she walked out of her cell, the bribed guard closed and locked the door behind her in order to delay the discovery and give her more time to get away.[43]

While Frances escaped, Howard did not. The court ordered Howard to bring forth Frances, but he refused. As Mr G. Garrard reported to the Earl of Stafford, Howard was 'like to pay dear for his unlawful pleasures'. The commission promptly threw Howard back into Fleet Prison and ordered that he be kept 'close prisoner' again. Akila Weeks, the Gatehouse Prison keeper, also had to face the consequences of his actions, as it was immediately clear to Laud that Frances had inside help. She 'got out of her prison, leaving the doors locked. Yet I do not think she got out of the keyhole', Laud observed drily. After a lengthy examination, the Privy Council removed Weeks from his position and he joined Howard at the Fleet Prison, finding himself on the more unpleasant side of the locked doors. Hopefully, the bribe that Howard had funnelled to Weeks was substantial enough to make his role in Frances's escape worthwhile.[44]

Howard remained in the Fleet Prison for about two months, until the king ordered him released in early June. The High Commission agreed to free him, but in order to keep the authority of the court intact, they argued that some sort of punishment was a must, since he was clearly guilty of the charges of adultery. Thus, the commission 'admonished Sir Robert not in future to come or remain in her [Frances's] company'. He had to enter a £2,000 bond payable to the king: should he not keep his promise, he would forfeit that money. In addition, he had to enter an additional £1,500 bond with a proctor, which he would forfeit if he did not appear in front of the court in a timely fashion if called again. The earlier 'rustie sword' of excommunication in 1625 clearly had not been a sufficient deterrent to keep

Howard away from his beloved Frances. The commissioners hoped that the prospect of losing £3,500 would do the trick.[45]

Meanwhile, Frances had decided to put some more distance between herself, the High Commission court, and the Gatehouse Prison. Knowing that her second escape from the penance and from the authority of the king and High Commission would not soon be forgotten, she believed she was no longer safe in England. Still in the disguise of male clothing, she travelled south and made her way across the English Channel to Guernsey, where a relative of hers, the Earl of Danby, served as governor. Officially, Danby claimed to have no knowledge of her whereabouts in his territory. From the Channel Island, she later made the brief trip to St Malo on the French mainland, and later resurfaced in Paris.[46] The escape plan and execution had been made very hastily, in order for Frances to avoid the dreaded penance. The result of the escape dragged on, however, as her exile lasted years. Frances did not set foot on English soil again for almost six years.

CHAPTER 8

FRANCES IN FRANCE

Frances arrived in mainland France during the summer of 1635, no doubt feeling relieved at having escaped the dreadful imprisonment, the pending penance, and Laud and Charles's clutches, but also devastated to leave Howard behind. True to form, she continued to resist King Charles's attempts to assert his authority over her. This required making new allies, whom she hoped could help her return to England without having to be subjected to the humiliating penance. When it came to protecting her honour, Frances proved to be even more stubborn and unyielding than the increasingly rigid King Charles.

The king was furious with Frances's disappearance. By late July he sent a messenger to France 'with a Privy Seal from his Majesty to summon her into England within six Weeks after the Receipt thereof, which if she do not obey, she is to be proceeded against according unto the Laws of this Kingdom'.[1] Charles only knew that Frances had escaped to France, but he did not know her exact whereabouts. This first messenger probably did not even find Frances in order to deliver the king's commands, but if he did, Frances promptly ignored the royal orders. She knew that she was out of reach of Charles's control: he could order her around all he wanted, but safely in France, she could simply ignore His Majesty. The strong arm of the sovereign reached only to the shores of Dover.

Early the following year, the king made a renewed attempt to get Frances back to England. On 8 February 1636, the Secretary of State John Coke recorded another warrant 'whereby His Majesty commands her [Frances] upon her allegiance to repair into England immediately upon receipt thereof'.[2] A month later, Secretary Coke informed John, Lord Scudamore, English ambassador to France, of the king's writ and the arrival in Paris of a special messenger to deliver it. The secretary also reminded the ambassador that Lady Purbeck was an escaped prisoner, implying that he should not treat her with kid gloves. Coke ordered Scudamore to 'procure information of her abode' as it was believed that she 'lurketh in Paris or not far from thence'.[3] In other words, Scudamore was tasked with finding her.

By that time, Frances had rented a house in Paris for herself and a small staff of servants. According to Scudamore, she had moved into the house in late February, living alone. She lived openly, or 'publickly', as Scudamore put it. The house stood in the same neighbourhood as the ambassador's own Paris abode, so Frances must have felt relatively secure. In order to ensure that the writ bearing the heavy royal privy seal was properly delivered to the right person, and that Frances would not attempt to claim that she had never received it, the messenger had orders to give the writ to Frances in person. At this point, Frances had already heard news of the coming of the special messenger and was devising ways to avoid him altogether. She instructed her servants not to open the door to anyone they did not know. The messenger failed multiple times to find her in the house as the servants could easily pre-screen visitors through a small grate in the door and refused to allow him in or even to open the door. In order to get around these difficulties, Scudamore and the messenger constructed a clever alternative plan for the delivery. They put the writ in a box and the messenger managed to get it inside Frances's house by throwing it through an open second-storey window, into Frances's dining room. At this point, the messenger initially thought that he had done his duty, but Scudamore reminded him that he had to make sure that Lady Purbeck had actually been in the house when he threw in the writ. The two then enlisted the assistance of a sister of one of Frances's servants, undoubtedly rewarded with a tempting payment. The sister went to Frances's house and knocked on the door. Since Frances knew the woman, she cracked the door open herself to speak with her. The woman then gave a pretext of wanting to see her sister, and Frances, not suspecting anything untoward at the time, promised that her sister would be allowed to go home to her family that very night. The messenger, hiding nearby, could clearly both see and hear Frances through the slightly opened door. Therefore, he concluded, he had ensured that Frances was personally present when the writ was served and he was content that all the legalities had been observed.[4]

Temporarily outwitted, but never outmanoeuvred, Frances soon discovered the box with the writ in her dining room, but she continued to ignore the king's orders. She now had other support besides her own iron will. Cardinal Richelieu, King Louis XIII's trusted and very powerful chief minister, had taken up her cause. Frances had somehow managed to receive Richelieu's promise of protection, perhaps by presenting him with a written petition explaining her predicament, a method she had learned from her mother, or perhaps by having persuaded him of her plight in person. The English messenger had arrived in March, right after the busiest social season in Paris. During the months of January and February, the court put on a series of splendid entertainments, the most spectacular of which was the *ballet de cour*, or court ballet, which had nobles and royals participating in the highly scripted performance. In February and March of that year, the Duke of Parma was also visiting, and the royals provided extra entertainments in his honour. Frances, a beautiful foreigner with a scandalous and dramatic past, a well-practised court lady, and a woman who was getting quite skilled at attracting men and women who could help her cause, might have participated in the entertainments and managed to get the attention of both the royal couple as well as Richelieu.[5]

The morning after the delivery of the royal writ, Richelieu's eyes and ears in Paris had informed him of Charles's special messenger, sent to summon Frances home. Although the relationship between England and France was not as strained in the 1630s as it had been in the years of the quasi-war between the two countries in the late 1620s, the cardinal was still not pleased that the English king was thus openly challenging the jurisdiction of the King of France in his own capital, harassing a person who was now under French protection. In order to send a clear message of disapproval, Richelieu dispatched officers with a large company of fifty archers into the streets of Paris. They were tasked with finding Frances, and to offer her protection against Charles's messenger. When Ambassador Scudamore heard about Richelieu's move, he found it prudent to 'hasten the messenger out of the way' so that he would not have to try to explain himself to the cardinal's archers.[6]

Frances also made a new friend and strong ally in Sir Kenelm Digby, an Englishman living in Paris. Digby was an eccentric character to say the least, with wildly varied careers as a courtier, diplomat, philosopher, scientist, alchemist, amateur theologian, gentleman traveller, and Mediterranean privateer. His father, Sir Everard Digby, had been hanged, drawn, and quartered in 1606 for his role in the thwarted, Catholic-led, Gunpowder Plot. The plotters planned to kill King James by blowing up the House of Lords while the king was present. Digby grew up Catholic, but converted briefly to Anglicanism. In 1635, having re-converted to Catholicism, Digby left England and went to live in Paris. At this point in his life, he was still grieving over the mysterious death of his beloved wife, the beautiful Venetia Stanley, in 1633. Venetia inexplicably passed away in her sleep without any sign of serious illness, only thirty-three years old. Some suspected foul play and the authorities ordered an autopsy, although the doctors found nothing conclusive. In the absence of a satisfactory explanation, rumours abounded and some believed that Digby had a hand in his wife's demise, perhaps as a result of jealousy, as Venetia had many suitors before she married, and, possibly, while she was married as well. Digby grieved very deeply for his wife, semi-retiring from the world for two years. He had plasters made of the dead Venetia's face, hands, and feet, and also asked his artist friend Anthony Van Dyck to paint a portrait of the dead woman. In Van Dyck's portrait, Venetia is lying in her bed and appears to be just sleeping, resting her head in one of her hands. Supposedly, that is exactly how her maidservant found her the morning after she had died. Digby took the portrait with him even when he travelled, so that he could more easily contemplate the image of his dead wife. Normally a smart dresser, he started wearing simple, voluminous dark mourning clothes, and also refused to shave, resulting in a long, scraggly, and rather wild-looking beard. When he walked about in Paris, dark robes flapping in his wake, he was also usually accompanied by his favourite dog, an enormous English mastiff. Frances befriended this odd character, who quickly gathered a reputation as a learned eccentric and romantic hero in Paris.[7]

Digby had an eye for beauty, particularly for beautiful women. In letters to friends, he sometimes indulged in long, flowery, and intricately detailed descriptions of beauties he had encountered and by whom he had been captivated, although unfortunately none survives describing Frances.[8] By all accounts, Frances was lovely to look at, so the interest of an eccentric aesthete is easy to imagine. Her dramatic life-story was an added attraction, as Digby, no stranger to drama himself, believed that Frances's suffering had 'polished, refined, and heightened what nature gave her'.[9]

Physical attractions aside, Digby also found in Frances a potential convert. The new friends became deeply involved in spiritual and philosophical discussions. They spent hours talking about religion, as Digby laboured to convince Frances that Catholicism was the only true form of Christianity. Since others in Frances's surroundings had converted, or considered converting, to Catholicism, most notably her husband, her mother-in-law, and her sister-in-law, the Duchess of Buckingham, undoubtedly she had been exposed to similar theological discussions in the past. While Frances had not been the contemplative kind previously, her years of relative retirement and solitude in Shropshire and at Stoke perhaps pushed her towards a greater concern with matters spiritual and intellectual. The relationship with Howard may have caused her religious concern as well, since adultery, especially the adultery of a woman, was a grievous sin. At the behest of Frances, Digby wrote down his arguments for Catholicism so that she could reflect at greater leisure on the matter at hand. His main argument was a conventional one, consisting of the view that the Catholic Church was the only Christian church which had kept the direct teachings of Christ himself intact, through the organized and orderly transfer of knowledge and doctrine from generation to generation in an uninterrupted line, whereas Protestants introduced novelties and individual, and thus unreliable, interpretations of God's teachings. Digby also placed a great deal of emphasis on the importance of getting one's spiritual affairs in order during this life, because he believed that whatever state the soul was in at the time of the death of the body, would be the state of the soul for all eternity. Digby told Frances that to be 'happy in the next life, one must not settle their [sic] predominant affections upon any creature whatsoeuer, or any good that we can attayne to the knowledge of in this life'. To love someone or something too much was thus problematic, because 'what natural good soeuer we loue or enioy here, we must by death be diuorced from' and 'that separation will cause perpetuall sorrow, because the affections remaine unchangeable' in the soul even after death.[10] Perhaps Digby was trying to resolve his great love for his dead wife, and perhaps Frances found this argument compelling as well, trying to find a way to reconcile and get over her love for Howard in order to have a more peaceful and joyful eternal life. In any case, the two wounded souls reached the same conclusion: Frances did decide to convert. Two years later, Digby's work was published with the title *A Conference with a Lady about Choice of Religion*. While he was certainly happy with Frances's decision, Digby was not just focusing on converting this one lady: he honed in on other potential targets as well, prompting the Earl of Leicester to view Digby as a theological predator, complaining that 'Sir Kenelm is busy in seducing the King's subjects in these parts from the Church of England'.[11]

In addition to her spiritual life, Digby also sought to improve Frances's temporal situation by trying to influence the king and the lords at home to change their minds about her. In 1636, Digby wrote a lengthy letter to Edward, Lord Conway, one of the Privy Councillors, in which he advocated for a pardon for Frances, so that she could safely return to England. Comparing Frances to her maternal uncle, Edward Cecil, Viscount Wimbledon, the poetic Digby found Wimbledon woefully wanting and Frances the shining star of her family:

> Here is a Lady that he [Wimbledon] hath reason to detest aboue all persons in the worlde, if robbing a man of all the portion of witt, courage, generousnesse, and of heroicall partes due to him, do merit such a nation of the minde towards them that haue thus bereaued them. For surely the Genius that governeth that family, and that distributed to each of them their shares of natures guiftes, was either asleep or mistook (or somewhat else was the cause) when he gave my lady of Purbecke a dubble proportion of these and all other noble endowments, and left her poore Uncle so naked and unfurnished.

Pleased with his own wittiness, Digby then emphasized that Frances's greatness was not part of the joke, but most real:

> Truly my Lord to speak seriously, I haue not seene more Prudence, sweetnesse, goodnesse, honor, and brauery shewed by any woman that I know, then this unfortunate lady sheweth she hath rich stocke of. Besides her natural endowments, doubtlessly her afflictions adde much, or rather haue polished, refined, and heightened what nature gave her you know vexatio dat intellectum [harassment gives greater understanding].

Digby next argued that to force the praiseworthy Frances to live in exile was a great dishonour, and that those who could fix the problem should be ashamed of not having done so sooner:

> Is it not a shame for you Peeres (and neere about the king) that you will let so braue a lady liue as she doth in distresse and banishment, when her exile serueth strangers but to conceive scandalously of our nation, that we will not permit those to liue among us who haue so much worth and goodnesse as this lady giveth shew of?[12]

Following Frances's own tactics, Digby completely ignored her offences, choosing to highlight what he considered her supremely positive sides instead. Frances was blameless: in this situation, it was the peers of England who were guilty for allowing the further suffering of 'so braue a lady' to continue. Indeed, *their* behaviour was a blot on England's honour, because those who knew Frances in France believed that the English king and peers must not be capable of appreciating true virtue. Digby also wrote letters to other members of the council, hoping to thus sway them in Frances's favour, as he argued that if she were not allowed to return to England, she 'does resolve to put herself into some monestary'. Digby's impassioned intervention may not have been working to Frances's advantage, however. One of the London letter-writers snickered at what he felt was Digby's exaggeration of Frances's virtues and also reported that 'his majesty does utterly dislike that the lady is so much directed by Sir Kenelm Digby, and that she fares nothing better for it'.[13]

While Charles may not have been happy with the Catholic Digby's enthusiasm for Frances's virtues, Frances's conversion did open up new doors for her in Catholic France. It made her more likeable to the French king and queen, for example. By March and April 1636, Louis XIII and his queen, Anne, resolved to take up her cause with King Charles, asking him to give Frances a pardon. King Louis and Richelieu instructed the extraordinary ambassador to England to lay the groundwork and the ambassador was 'very zealous in the business'.[14] Perhaps King Louis still remembered the insult that Buckingham had offered him by openly courting his queen during his visit to accompany Henrietta Maria to England years earlier. It may have given the French king some small joy to help a woman who had resisted Buckingham's attempts to punish her.

Frances was also working hard herself, writing letters to various people in England, in hopes that they could intercede on her behalf. First was a long letter to Queen Henrietta Maria: it took up a full three sheets of paper. Frances explained the circumstances of her life, describing it 'from her childhood to her conversion', hoping that the queen would take pity on her and ask the king for her pardon. Emphasizing the conversion to Catholicism as an integral part of her life's story was, naturally, a calculated move to gain the Queen's favour. Henrietta Maria was a very devout Catholic who viewed the better treatment of Catholics and the furthering of the Catholic cause in England as one of her life's major projects. In addition, like her brother Louis, Henrietta Maria was never fond of Buckingham. Her marriage had been unhappy during the early years when Buckingham was the focus of Charles's affections, so Frances probably hoped that the queen would feel some affinity for a woman who also had been brought low by their shared nemesis. Since Charles was now so much in love with his wife, perhaps she would be able to persuade her husband to forgive Frances? As their love grew, Henrietta Maria's influence with the king had increased, resulting in the king sometimes granting his beloved small favours. Unfortunately, Frances's letter to the queen has not survived. However, it is likely to be similar to her 1641 petition to the House of Lords. In the petition, Frances highlighted the wrongs she had to endure, which she argued should excuse her evading the High Commission, while she mostly avoided discussing the adultery and her son Robert's paternity. Frances also wrote letters to her widowed sister-in-law (now remarried to the Earl of Antrim), and to 'some other of the great ladies', hoping to get them to 'take off my Lord's Grace of Canterbury', meaning Archbishop Laud.[15] These letters have not survived either. Frances knew that if only Laud and Charles could be persuaded to forgive her, or at least to leave off actively prosecuting her, she would be in the clear to return to England.

Among the flurry of letters, Frances also wrote to the royal secretary Sir Francis Windebank, asking him to 'second the sute I haue made to his Ma:ty by the Queene'. Here, Frances said she thought that the King had had a good opinion of her before her 'last unfortunate trobles' (referring to the High Commission trial the previous spring) and that she could not understand why the king was so upset with her, 'seeing I haue done nothing since that time to draw this new displeasure upon me'. She requested that 'his Ma:ty will be gratiously pleased to take off his further indignation against me, and accept of my humble casting my self att his royall feet to ask pardon for anything I may haue bin so unfortunate as to offendd him in'.[16] Frances was playing the wounded and naive innocent here: she knew why the king was angry, of course. She had time and again flaunted her disobedience, both of the orders of the High Commission and of the direct commandments of the king for her to return to England.

Frances also tried to make Windebank feel guilty about her plight. She argued that before her arrest the previous year, Windebank had given her no inkling that 'any of the former violent proceedings agaynst me could have bin this renewed to procure my ruine'. Rather, Windebank had been sent 'by his Ma:ty in a message of grace', thanking Frances for a service she had done the king. Thus, having lulled her into a false sense of security and having given her no prior warning about the coming arrest, she implied that Windebank certainly owed her a favour at this point. She closed the letter by pointedly asking him to 'perform such for me as the place you hold neere his Ma[jes]ty may iustify you to do' and hoping that God would inspire him to do 'what may become you in my behalf'.[17]

If any of the people Frances wrote to during this hectic spring actually interceded with the king on her behalf, they were unsuccessful. No pardon was forthcoming. By the summer of 1636, Frances had, as Digby predicted, moved into a Parisian convent. The convent, located in the south-western suburb of St Marceau (between the 5th and 13th arrondissements), had been established just a few years earlier by English Augustinian nuns. Since convents and monasteries had been closed in England as a result of the Protestant Reformation, English Catholics who wished to live a religious life in monastic settings had to go abroad to do so. The English convent in Paris quickly became a place of refuge and education for English Catholic women, and soon moved into larger, more permanent housing in Rue Des Fosses St Victor.[18] Frances had several reasons for moving into the convent in St Marceau. First, she was making a show of pious living, as a way to retreat from the world that she felt was treating her badly. She had no plans to take the veil permanently. Instead, she followed a common practice of using convents as a temporary refuge. Living a simple, more religiously focused life in the convent could also signal to others that if Frances had committed sins earlier in her life, she was now atoning for them and thus ready to receive forgiveness. In addition, Frances needed to economize: even the small household she was keeping in France was costly and Frances had limited resources. Cardinal Richelieu had helped her with an introduction into the convent and Digby might have encouraged this move as well, part of his persistent campaign of convincing Parisian ladies of the great spiritual benefits of monastic living.[19]

Frances's stay in the convent proved brief. She was used to living with greater freedom of movement and more luxuries than the convent allowed, even for a guest. She still had strong ties to the world, and did not feel comfortable among the more devoted nuns. Ambassador Scudamore, previously bemused by Frances's professed piety, gleefully reported to Secretary Windebank the reasons behind Frances's leaving the convent. The 'lady abbess being from home', related Scudamore, 'somebody forgot to provide Lady Purbeck her dinner and to leave the room open where she used to dine. At night expostulating with the abbess, they agreed to part fairly, which the abbess was the more willing unto in regard Lady Purbeck did not live according to that strictness which was expected.'[20]

At the end of the same letter, Scudamore also warned Windebank that Frances expected Howard to come to Paris any day to visit her. The promise of seeing Howard again also hastened Frances's departure from the convent: the abbess would in all likelihood not have been pleased to have a lover come visit a boarder within the convent walls. A full year had passed since the two had seen each other. It had been an abrupt break: they had only had time to be together for a few months in between the death of Frances's father and their arrests and imprisonments. The terms of their imprisonment had prevented them from seeing anyone, least of all each other. The escape from prison had to be arranged very quickly, in order to avoid the scheduled penance. While Howard had orchestrated the whole thing, he had asked a friend to arrange the actual payment to the prison keeper. If the two had time to meet before Frances set off for Guernsey in her disguise, it would have been a brief meeting at most. Cut off from so many familiar faces in her exile, Frances relished the thought of Howard's arrival in Paris.

Scudamore asked Windebank to ensure that Laud knew about Howard's potential plans so that he could either prevent him from going, or, more satisfactorily for Laud, catch him in the act. Howard was spending a suspicious amount of time in the busy port-town of Dover, where his brother Theophilus, Earl of Suffolk, was overseeing the ports in his position as Lord Warden of the Cinque Ports. From Dover, only about twenty miles of sea separated England from Calais in France. In good weather, a ship could cross over in a matter of a few hours. The Privy Council tasked Suffolk with investigating his brother's movements during the summer. Suffolk assured the lords that Howard had been in England the whole time and that while in Dover, he had not 'so much as one night lodged forth of the castle [Dover Castle], in which respect there is an impossibility of his going into France'.[21] Theophilus had to make a similar proclamation to the council in late December of the same year, when Howard, at Dover then as well, was rumoured to have gone to France once more.[22] The councillors also asked Scudamore to quietly investigate and gather any information or rumour that Howard had indeed been visiting Frances.[23]

Despite Theophilus's assurances to the contrary, Laud was convinced that Howard had been in France at some point and he was determined to prove it. The council asked Howard's other brother, Edward Howard, Baron Escrick, as well as his brother-in-law Edward, Lord Vaux, to vouch for Howard's movements. Still unsatisfied, the council ordered Howard to appear before them in person to explain himself.[24] Howard declared his innocence, but left Dover for London nonetheless. He arrived a bit too quickly for Laud, who had not had time to collect all his proofs for full questioning. When palace guards brought word to Laud that Howard was waiting outside, King Charles happened to be in the same room. Laud, worried that Charles thought he was pushing his persecution of Howard a bit too far, hurriedly explained to the king that 'he honoured that family [the Howards], but was zealous to prevent that living in such a train as Sir Robert Howard and my Lady Purbeck had been accused for'. He also assured the king 'that though his proofs were not ready at present, yet he doubted not but he would prove that Sir Robert Howard and my Lady Purbeck had met privately together this summer'. Laud also 'did reprove Sir Robert Howard's living so much at Dover Castle, which was too near to France', and told him to live at a more safe distance in Audley End instead, until 'he had more leisure for questioning him for breaking his bonds'.[25]

Laud did not continue his investigation into Howard's travels to France. The matter simply vanished. As Laud's nervous reassurance to the king that he 'honoured that family' implied, Charles's appetite for focusing on Howard had always been rather weak. For Charles, it was Frances who was the main offender, the one that mattered. Frances had cuckolded his dearest friend's brother, Frances was trying to pass off her bastard as the legitimate heir to her husband's noble title, and Frances was an adulterer. Howard had certainly committed a sexual sin, but his crime was less problematic for Charles, because he was unmarried, did not hold an important position at court, did not regularly interact with the king, and his powerful family seemed to support and back him. It was Charles who had ordered Laud and the High Commission to release Howard from prison two months after Frances's prison escape, for example, and Laud had to comply, against his own wishes. While the royal power, first in the guise of James and then Charles, always remained more reluctant to punish Howard, Laud, representing the power of the Church, was more interested in making Howard pay dearly for his sinful sexual transgressions. Laud believed that Howard's sins were as egregious as Frances's, and he regularly mentioned the two living in sin together as a joint 'impiety'.

By April that same year, Howard joined Frances in her new religion as well. He was not alone: an increasing number of Englishmen and -women converted to Catholicism in the 1620s and 1630s, some clearly inspired by their Catholic queen, and others simply returning openly to their old family faith.[26] George Garrard, a friend of Howard's, reported the news of the conversion to the Earl of Stafford, and said he was sorry to see his friend defect in such a way. Garrard argued that Howard had now doubled his sins, and that Frances was the cause of it: 'My Lady Purbeck left her Country and Religion both together, and since he [Howard] will not leave thinking of her, but live in that detestable sin still, let him go to their Church for Absolution, for Comfort he can find none in ours.'[27] Garrard believed that the Catholic notion of confessing and performing some form of works as penance for sins committed in order to receive divine forgiveness might be attractive to what he considered to be a habitual sinner like Howard.

During Frances's time in exile, none of the contemporary sources mention a word about her son Robert. In fact, since the dramatic diversionary high-speed chase through the streets of London and Frances's flight from the penance in 1628, young Robert did not feature at all in discussions, notes, letters, court records, or other sources about Frances, Howard, Lady Hatton, Sir Edward Coke, or any of the Villiers. No one mentions what happened to Robert when his mother was imprisoned in the Gatehouse, or when she escaped both prison and England dressed in male clothing. No one mentions Robert's presence in France during the late 1630s either. Since his mother's adultery conviction, Robert had been legally established as an illegitimate child, and the whereabouts of a bastard was not all that important to the news writers, diplomats, politicians, and gossips of the time. Frances and her transgression were their main targets. The silence surrounding the boy during this time is frustrating, but as a young man, Robert actually gives us a small clue. At one point during the 1640s, Robert briefly mentioned that he had 'been taken beyond the seas when only nine years old'.[28] Technically, since Robert was born in October of 1624, he would have been ten and a half in the spring of 1635 when Frances fled to France. However, early modern people did not always keep a very close count of their ages, so he may have simply been a year or two off. The clue is scant, but a clue nonetheless: it appears that his mother brought young Robert with her to France.

In the first few years of her exile, Frances no doubt believed that she would be able to re-cross the Channel and return rather promptly, as soon as she could get that much-desired pardon from the king. Months stretched into years, with no pardon forthcoming. The French royal effort to help a disgraced English lady cooled when success in convincing the stubborn Charles to change his mind proved so elusive. King Louis and Richelieu had bigger concerns than Frances. In 1635, France entered the Thirty Years War, fighting against the Holy Roman Empire and Spain. While France was eventually successful in that war, it would last for two more decades (the Thirty Years War ended in 1648, but France and Spain continued to fight until 1659). Neither Louis nor Richelieu lived to see the end of that war. In the late 1630s, English news writers filled their letters with other news and gossip. Frances, living quietly in France, no longer caught their attention. English officials communicating with their agents in France were also more concerned with other business, although they kept up with the movements of Frances and other English Catholics as a matter of course. In March 1638, almost three years after Frances had arrived in France, the English diplomatic agent René Augier wrote in code from Paris to an unknown recipient in England and reported that he met and spoke with Lady Purbeck regularly, and—although more seldom—also her friend Sir Kenelm Digby. Frances and Digby, fellow Catholics now since her conversion, were using the same chapel for their worship, and Digby had rented a large house in the Paris suburb of St Germaine, Augier relayed.[29]

Back in England, the temporary and deceptively peaceful lull of the 1630s was broken by a worsening political and religious crisis. Charles's constant financial problems had caused him to have to call Parliament three times during the late 1620s, but those Parliaments became contentious, as Charles refused to address the grievances of the MPs (including Buckingham's near monopoly on royal favour and disastrous foreign policies), and the MPs refused to grant him sufficient funds. Charles, firmly convinced of his divine right to rule with minimum interference from his subjects, determined to rule without Parliaments. The king and his advisers devised alternative ways to raise money for the royal coffers, such as forced loans and inventive extensions on a tax called 'ship money', traditionally levied without the need for Parliamentary approval. Throughout the 1630s, those methods were becoming increasingly unpopular, especially since the absence of Parliament meant an absence of the traditional forum to air and discuss grievances. In addition, the perception that the court was becoming a centre of Catholicism worried staunch Protestants, especially Puritans. By the late 1630s, when Charles tried to impose a new Anglican prayer book on his Presbyterian-minded Scottish subjects, they had had enough and rebelled, leading to the first of two Scottish wars, the so-called Bishops' Wars of 1639 and 1640. The first of these conflicts ended in a stalemate, and Charles, in desperate need of money, decided to end the eleven years of personal rule and called Parliament in 1640. The first 1640 Parliament, known as the Short Parliament, refused to cooperate with Charles's demands for money, presenting him instead with a long list of grievances. Charles, exasperated, dismissed the Parliament after it had met for only three weeks. The lack of funds and multiple tactical mistakes led to Charles's loss in the second war with the Scottish in 1640. Charles, now in an even weaker position than before, had to call Parliament again. This new Parliament, beginning in November 1640, would become the Long Parliament, the body which refused to be dismissed and which ultimately declared open war against their own king in 1642.[30] The rapid political changes taking place in an England hurtling towards civil war would work in Frances's favour and finally allow her to return to her home country.

The developing political crisis meant that many of those individuals who had been instrumental in Frances's prosecution and in insisting on enforcing the rule of the High Commission would either not be interested in continuing it, or not in a position to do so. The king himself was busy with other—obviously much more

151

pressing—matters and could no longer afford the luxury of concerning himself with the whereabouts or deeds of his long-dead favourite's adulterous sister-in-law. In addition, Parliament charged Archbishop Laud, the most dogged of Frances's and Howard's persecutors, with a whole bevy of crimes late in 1640. Laud was not just an archbishop, but also an integral part of Charles's Privy Council. Having moved in the highest circles of both secular and religious power for over a decade, Laud now fell fast and hard: Parliament promptly sent him to the Tower and although he did not know it yet, he would not leave there alive. King Charles was increasingly unable to rescue or protect his former advisers against an outraged and empowered Parliament. Sir Francis Windebank, the king's secretary who had neglected to help Frances in her quest for a pardon, had to flee England in a panic when the increasingly Puritan Parliament discovered that he had signed letters of grace to English Catholics and Jesuit priests operating in England. Like Frances, Windebank now was forced to experience exile in France: he was never able to return and died in Paris in 1646.[31]

Laud's fall had the greatest effect on both Frances's and Howard's lives. Among the many other charges Parliament levied against Laud, they found that he was guilty of having illegally imprisoned and otherwise unfairly treated several persons, including Sir Robert Howard. Howard introduced a petition to the House of Lords in December 1640, arguing that his 1635 imprisonment and forced bonds had in fact been illegal and outside the scope of the High Commission, that the bonds should therefore be returned to him and that he should be compensated for the expenses he incurred as a result of his imprisonment. The Lords formed a committee and tasked them with addressing the petition. The committee, 'after serious Consideration thereof', decided that Howard was in the right. They ordered that the bonds totalling £3,500 should be repaid to him and furthermore that he should have £1,000 in damages. Half of the damages should be paid by Laud himself, whereas the payment of the other half was divided between two of the lawyers who had served the High Commission and who had been instrumental in the 1635 case.[32] Howard was no doubt delighted at this welcome and profitable turn of events. Laud was not. He grudgingly paid Howard the money and argued bitterly that he was innocent of the charges, but had he somehow overlooked following the letter of the law exactly 'yet somewhat was to be indulged, in regard I did it to vindicate such a crying Impiety'. While he implied that he could say much more about the Howard and Lady Purbeck saga, he restrained himself, stating that he would 'blast no Family of Honour [the House of Howards] for one Man's fault'.[33] Laud's own saga did not end happily. He lingered on in prison until 1645, when Parliament finally decided to bring him to trial, swiftly found him guilty of treason, and executed him on 10 January 1645.

The dismissal of Howard's bonds ensured that he no longer had to fear legal and financial retribution if he spent time with Frances again. The imprisonment of Laud meant that Frances could also finally feel safer from the penance and further imprisonment. She had been gone for more than five years, without any clear idea of when, or even if, she might return. And yet Howard, ever patient, had waited, and even converted to Frances's new religion. By early 1641, her long exile finally ended: Frances returned to England and began the arduous process of trying to re-establish herself and her son in English society. Unfortunately, while the rise of Parliament and the failures of the king made it possible for her to return, the coming of the Civil War would make her much-longed-for homecoming less sweet and create new reasons for divisions in her already dysfunctional family.

CHAPTER 9

ENDINGS

H aving heard of Laud's fall and her lover's new fortunes, Frances must have had high expectations as she re-crossed the English Channel. It seemed as if the threat of having to do the penance and being imprisoned had diminished. She would be back in familiar surroundings, with people she loved. Perhaps she could now enjoy a more peaceful and carefree existence after her difficult years of exiles, legal uncertainties, and financial difficulties. When Frances set foot on English soil again, the political crisis was brewing, but the outbreak of civil war was still more than a year and a half away. Her optimism was unwarranted. The Civil War would impose a whole new slew of hardships on her, her family, and her lover. Choosing sides in the conflict was a tricky business, and trying to hold on to alliances and friendships, or have access to property and income, depended much on being on the 'right' side.

Once back in England, Frances was hoping that she would be able to replicate Howard's retribution against the discredited Laud and the High Commission. She needed to situate herself and her son for a prosperous future in England. She wanted to guarantee both of them an income, to protect herself from further legal troubles, and she wanted to see her enemies suffer as she had. In order to accomplish all of those objectives, Frances again appealed to the peers of the realm and promptly petitioned the House of Lords in early February, 1641.

In her petition, Frances delivered a very cleaned-up version of her life and troubles. In this telling, as before, the Villiers were the greedy villains, and Frances the wounded and wronged heroine. She argued that her in-laws had separated her from her husband against both of their wishes in order to be able to control his money and property, most of which she had brought into the marriage. Buckingham had made an agreement with her father to purchase lands for Frances and any children of the marriage with parts of her dowry, but he had not done so. After having taken control over John's property, the Villiers worked to discredit and dishonour Frances, causing her to be illegally imprisoned, charged, and falsely found guilty of adultery. In the end, all of these troubles had forced her to flee the country. Now she was back, and requesting that the Lords 'in the Care of her and her posterity to take order for the safe Custody of the Evidences of her owne Lands and disposeing the said £10,000 according to the said Agreement which hitherto is not done'.[1] She was determined to recuperate some of the wealth she had brought into her marriage and lost to Buckingham.

Frances also wanted to resolve her legal troubles once and for all. Laud may have been rendered harmless, but since she had not received any royal pardon for her offences before returning to England, her legal standing remained tenuous. She was an escapee twice over and a convicted adulteress who had not yet performed her penance. Arguing that her conviction was illegal to begin with, that the High Commission had not the right to try her, and that she had been found guilty based on 'negative proofs', she asked the Lord's 'honorable and favorable interpretacion' of her actions and that they intercede with 'her gracious Soveraigne for his Royall pardon'. If she had a pardon, she would not have to worry about either prison or penance anymore.

Additionally, Frances sought revenge. In her petition, she wanted those who had been involved in what she termed 'illegal Proceedings' against her 'be called to answer' for what they had done and 'receive punishment according to their Demerits'. Specifically, she mentioned William Alcocke, administrator of the late Buckingham's property, her sister-in-law Susan Fielding, the Countess of Denbigh 'and such others as pretend title to the Lord Purbeck's lands', Archbishop Laud, Sir Henry Marten (Dean of Arches and lawyer in the High Commission), and others who had been 'Agents and Instruments' in the legal cases against her.[2] Considering that the Commons had already fined and censured Laud and Marten for their role in the imprisonment of Howard, Frances may reasonably have thought that the Lords would be willing to do the same in her case.

Another main goal of Frances's petition was to establish Robert as her husband's child, rather than her lover's. If Robert could be accepted as the legitimate son of a nobleman, instead of the bastard of a knight without many prospects, Frances must have believed that her only child would have a much better chance in life. Declaring Robert legitimate would have double benefits: Frances would show that her High Commission conviction was wrong, and Robert would profit both economically and socially, inheriting the Purbeck title. To that end, Robert had already started using the last name Villiers, previously going either by his earlier alias Wright, or his father's name, Howard. Before Frances presented her petition to the Lords in February, a note in the House of Commons Journal from 10 January 1641, states that 'Mr. *John Ashe* further reported a Paper, containing the whole State of the Case of *Robert Villers* Esquire, Son and Heir-apparent to the Lord Viscount *Purbeck*: Which was read; and nothing done upon it.'[3]

In her own follow-up February petition, Frances held that Robert was indeed her husband's son and went to great lengths to explain away some of the most damning evidence presented against her so many years ago. The main pieces of evidence that led to a conviction in her adultery trial included the fact that Frances had been separated from her husband at the time when she became pregnant, the great secrecy surrounding her pregnancy and the birth, the hiding away of baby Robert, and then, of course, her many intimate meetings with Howard. Now, Frances argued that even though the Villiers had been trying to keep her separated from her husband, the spouses had managed to meet behind their backs a few times. Without actually stating it, Frances implied that Robert had been conceived during one of those visits. Knowing that the English law favoured considering children conceived by a married woman legitimate if at all possible, Frances knew that it was enough for her to make people think that she may have been in her husband's presence. She did not have to prove that they had sex, or even discuss the matter. Frances explained that the secrecy of their meetings had been necessary, because the annual mainten-ance agreement that Buckingham had offered her spelled out that she would only receive her annuity as long as she was *not* cohabiting with her husband. Afraid to lose her only financial support, Frances had thus been forced to secret meetings, even with her own husband. Furthermore, the circumstances surrounding Robert's secretive birth were also the fault of the Villiers. Late in her pregnancy, her mother-in-law with many others had burst into her room in the middle of the night, 'barbarously haled her out of bed, and Sir Edward Villiers Knt [Buckingham's half-brother] being one of the company most unhumanely held her by force upon pretence that midwives and others should search her whether she were with child or not to the danger of her self and the like of her Child'. It was this danger that caused Frances to 'withdraw herself to a private place unknown to her adversaries until her delivery and to take upon her a feigned name both for herself and the sonne borne of her body'.[4]

Frances's 1641 version of events does not quite square with the evidence from the examinations of witnesses in 1625, of course. Those witnesses, including Frances's own gentlewoman attendants, said that Frances remained at Denmark House right up until the day of the birth. In addition, Frances's petition does not mention Howard at all, no doubt realizing that she could not explain away the many witness depositions about their regular romantic and passionate meetings. Better to stay silent on the matter, and not remind people of evidence she could not refute. Conveniently for Frances, all the Villiers who had been involved in the alleged nightly visit and in the details of her trial were dead by 1641 and could thus not be brought as witnesses against her. She could rearrange the story to fit her current needs.

The Lords certainly intended to hear Frances's cause, but they never made any final decisions: Frances's case was repeatedly tabled, as the Parliament was slogging its way towards civil war. They first heard the petition on 8 February, and by 22 February, they granted warrants to Frances to send for witnesses. After that, the case kept bumping into delays. On 12 May, the Lords appointed 21 May as the day to hear the case, but that day passed without any hearing. They made two more tries on 15 June and 30 June, but each time, nothing happened. In the last attempt on 30 June the Lords appointed 5 July as the time for a hearing, but that day the king decided to attend Parliament, which threw off the schedule. There is no further mention of the petition or the cause in the records of the House of Lords. At this point, Parliament had discovered the king's attempts to bring a large share of the royal army to London to 'protect' the sovereign, and that was the uppermost issue in the minds of both king and Parliament. Considering that Parliament had not met for such a long time, the volume of business, especially of private petitions, was very great. On 6 July, the Lords declared that they would consider no further private petitions, and that public business would have precedence over private affairs. Those petitions which already had dates set for their hearings would proceed as scheduled, but those who had no particular dates set yet would not be heard until the next session of Parliament. While Frances's case had been scheduled multiple times but never heard, it did not receive a new date.[5] Ultimately, her petition failed to get the results she wanted.

Although Parliament never heard her case, it was indirectly immensely helpful. The opposition to the arbitrary power of the High Commission had been growing throughout the 1620s and 1630s, and by the time of the Long Parliament, MPs felt emboldened to act. Having debated the issue throughout the spring of 1641 in both the Commons and the Lords, in July of 1641, Parliament formally abolished the High Commission altogether. Although Frances's adultery conviction was never overturned, the court whose punishment she had escaped twice now no longer existed. The same act that abolished the High Commission also made it illegal for any church official to 'impose or inflict any pain, penalty, fine, amerce-ment, imprisonment or other corporal punishment upon any of the King's sub-jects for any contempt, misdemeanour, crime, offence, matter or thing whatsoever belonging to spiritual or ecclesiastical cognizance or jurisdiction'. With or without a royal pardon, Frances no longer had to worry about the threat of imprisonment or penance hanging over her.[6]

During the period of her wrangling with Parliament, Frances gives no clue regarding where she was living when she first returned to England. She probably did not live with Howard during the first year or so, at least not openly: that would have made it difficult for her to establish Robert as her husband's son. However, they may have met discreetly and spent time together.[7] She did not go back to her husband. John was not well in 1640, again having episodes of the same mental affliction that he had suffered from during earlier years. In April, when the king finally called Parliament, John was excused because he was 'not well but proxy shall be sent'. He did not attend any of the days in April or May.[8] In August, and again in October, King Charles, still concerned about the health of his favourite Buckingham's brother, made arrangements for his care. He ordered that his servants 'take special care to keep him from all things that may increase his distemper, not suffering him to fall into excess of wine, tobacco, or any other thing that may be hurtful to him'.[9] Again in November, John was too ill to attend the new Parliament, sending a proxy instead.[10] John's illness would certainly make it highly unlikely that Frances would have chosen to go back to her husband, considering that it was his illness which had been the catalyst for their separation so many years ago.

John's vulnerability and mental instability did work in Frances's favour when it came to the rehabilitation of her son, however. Without the active protection and intervention of Buckingham and their mother, and with Charles preoccupied with his increasingly severe clashes with his Parliament, John was now much more receptive to Frances's persuasions. The viscount told his friends that 'his Lady was a very good woman' and that he regretted having treated her badly in the past, 'declaring it was occasioned only by his Mother the Countess of Buckingham'. Frances managed temporarily to convince him to accept Robert as his son. As a result, John became very friendly with Robert during the early 1640s, openly calling him 'his son', frequently exchanging visits and gifts, as well as having financial dealings with him. John and Robert joined in the sale of some lands, and the documents described Robert as Robert Villiers, 'Son and Heir Apparent of John Lord Viscount Purbeck'. In addition, John 'expressed great affection' to Robert, 'often drank to him by the name of Son Robert; many times declared great anger against any person that should but question whether he were his son or not'.[11] John's friends and servants were probably concerned about this turn of events, trying to tell John that he was being duped, but he refused to listen. In 1640, before Frances's and Robert's return, King Charles had been concerned about the effect John's reoccurring disease may have on his estate and commanded a servant to 'use your best endeavors to dissuade him from all his exorbitancy in his expenses and from disposing of any part of his estate without the consent of his friends'.[12] John was only too willing to go along with Frances's plan, and resisted his friends' attempts to protect him from his own emotions.

Frances's mother and Robert's grandmother, Lady Hatton, certainly participated heartily in the project of making Robert legitimate. Lady Hatton had been dismayed and troubled by Frances's adultery, and she had disapproved of her continued relationship with Howard. Now when her only surviving daughter was finally back home after her long exile, Lady Hatton must have been relieved that Frances was working to remake her life-story and to establish Robert as a person who could hopefully be reintroduced to English high society without the stigma of illegitimacy. Until her death, Lady Hatton referred to her grandson as Robert Villiers, son of Viscount Purbeck, and she left him a sizeable portion of her estate.[13] Had not so many other events intervened, perhaps Frances really would have been successful in remaking Robert into John's son.

After a royal plan to surprise and arrest the most prominent oppositional Parliamentary leaders was foiled in January of 1642, the king and his court left the capital, deeming it no longer safe to remain. Queen Henrietta Maria left the country altogether in February, travelling to The Hague in the Netherlands. There, she worked hard to raise both support and money for her husband's cause, selling and pawning off crown jewels so that her husband could pay for an army to turn on his own rebellious subjects. Throughout the spring and summer, both sides began their preparations for an armed conflict. King Charles finally raised his banner at Nottingham in August, and on 23 October, the first major battle of the Civil War took place at Edgehill.

Like so many other noble houses, Frances's family ended up on different sides in the conflict, although at least initially the majority of them were royalists. Despite the fact that King Charles's dislike of her and her actions had caused her so much trouble, Frances firmly sided with the king. She, like so many others at the time, believed in the king's right to rule, and could not support a Parliament who openly rebelled against royal power. Howard likewise supported the king and became a Cavalier, as the followers of the king were called. He became a colonel of a company of dragoons in Shropshire, and he was in Hopesay in August of 1642, dealing with the nascent military business there.[14] Howard and Frances's son first served in the king's army when he turned eighteen in 1642, although he later switched sides. Frances's half-brothers were also royalists, as was Sir Maurice Berkeley, the husband of Frances's dead sister Elizabeth and the father of Frances's niece and name-sake.

The position of Frances's husband is a bit more ambiguous and difficult to pin down. After 1641, the Long Parliament House of Lords excused John from his duties. The Lords' Journal does not say why, but one would assume it had some-thing to do with suspecting him of royalist leanings. In 1646, he tried to regain his seat, arguing that his recent presence in the royalist garrison of Newark had been against his will, but he was unsuccessful.[15] Suspicions of his royalist leanings aside, Parliament nonetheless acted in John's favour on several occasions. In 1643, the House of Lords ordered that 'the Lady *Boddenham* shall have a Protection for her House in *Rutlandshire*, where the Earl of *Purbecke* [sic] lives with her'. Two years later, the Lords ordered that John leave the Villiers estate Burley on the Hill and go stay with his Parliamentarian nephew, the new Earl of Denbigh, instead (John's brother-in-law, the first Earl of Denbigh, was a royalist who died in a battle where his son was among the enemy). And yet another year after that, they gave John a 'Pass, to go and come from *London*, to his House at Stoke, in the County of Buck[inghamshire], and also a Protection for his quiet living and inhabiting there'. (By 1646, John had inherited Stoke from Lady Hatton.)[16] In 1643 and 1644, Parliament also attempted to ensure that John received some of his regular income (discussed later in this chapter). In 1647, the then captured king was even allowed to visit John at Stoke.[17] Perhaps John's established history of intermittent illnesses ensured that Parliament did not view him as a particularly threatening person.

Lady Hatton, on the other hand, became a staunch supporter of Parliament, a Roundhead. Perhaps being married to Sir Edward Coke, who had challenged the royal prerogative on several occasions and who had always supported the rights of Parliament, had rubbed off on her, even though she tended to disagree with her husband on most matters as a sort of automatic reflex after their many years of fighting. Lady Hatton became an active politician, and her manor at Stoke turned into a meeting place for leaders of the Parliamentary forces, many of them her close friends. Her opposition to the king would end up temporarily costing her control of Stoke. At one point, Prince Rupert, the nephew of King Charles and the young hero of the Cavaliers, took control of the manor, forcing Lady Hatton to vacate it and leave for Hatton House in London instead. Lady Hatton left a letter for Rupert, the son of Elizabeth of Bohemia and the Palatinate whose exiled court in the Netherlands Lady Hatton and Frances had visited in the early 1620s, trying to convince him of the necessity to support Parliament:

> The Parliament is the only firm Foundation of the greatest Establishment the King or his Posterity can wish and attain, and therefore if you should persist in the unhappinesse to support any Advice to break the Parliament upon any Pretence whatsoever, you shall concur to destroy the best Groundwork for his Majesty's prosperity.[18]

Lady Hatton's advice notwithstanding, Prince Rupert never wavered in his support of his uncle. However, Rupert's younger brother Prince Charles did disagree with his brother and expressed his support for Parliament, which also earned him Lady Hatton's approval in the form of a $500 bequest for him in her will.[19]

Young Robert started out as a royalist, but switched sides in the middle of the conflict and became an even more ardent Roundhead than his grandmother. According to Robert himself, his mother's influence, coupled with the fact that he had spent such a long time of his formative years overseas and thus had become 'a stranger to the constitution' led him to join King Charles's forces initially. He had risen quickly in the ranks, starting as a private at age eighteen in 1642, and became a colonel just two years later. But, he argued, once he learned more about 'the constitution and cause [sic] of this kingdom', he quickly left the royalist camp and 'submitted to Parliament'. Robert was careful to point out that he had switched sides while it still looked as if King Charles might be successful, so that he would not be thought to be a turncoat, but rather a person led by his own mature convictions. Furthermore, he brought witnesses to prove that he was a Protestant. The Catholicism of his mother, his father, as well as his pretended father John, no doubt made him extra suspicious to an increasingly Puritan Parliament. Parliament fined Robert for his royal service, but he managed to convince them of his new allegiance. His adherence to Parliament was quite sincere, and it must have severely disrupted his relationship with his mother, but perhaps drawn him closer to his grandmother. Robert was taking the first step in asserting himself as an independent young adult, and beginning the process of distancing himself entirely from his mother and the Villiers.[20]

With her mother and her son on the opposite side in the war, Frances now had to seek out other family members for support. During the summer of 1644, Frances stayed with her royalist half-brother, Sir Robert Coke, at his estate in Kingston. It must have felt strange to be back at Kingston, where her father had stashed her to keep her out of her mother's reach during the contentious marriage negotiations twenty-seven years earlier. It certainly would have made for some curious reminiscences between the siblings: how might they have remembered their father and his actions, knowing how his plans had been foiled so spectacularly since that fateful marriage, and how troubled Frances's life had been? Frances's brother, like so many other royalists, now also had his own problems. He had refused to pay fees, sequestrations, and other requirements to Parliament, and Parliamentary committees brought up his offences again and again, trying to make him pay up. They were also concerned about the company he kept, his royalist sister included. During the spring of 1645, when Parliament questioned Sir Robert about his activities, he confessed that 'the Lady Purbeck was at his House all the Summer [1644], but is gone since his Coming to London'.[21]

Sir Robert Coke's royalist stance also caused financial trouble for Frances's husband. In 1643, John petitioned Parliament because he had not received rents from Coke properties, which he had been assured by Frances's father as long as Lady Hatton lived. Sir Robert had inherited the lands from his father, and he had dutifully delivered the rents to John twice a year ever since 1634. However, with the Coke lands now sequestered, Sir Robert was both unable and unwilling to pay John what he owed. John argued that these funds were his only means of support, and Parliament decided in his favour, arguing that the Committee of Sequestration should pay him out of the money they had taken from Sir Robert. Apparently, the business was still not settled over a year later, when it showed up again in the House of Lords. The Lords again reiterated that John's annuity should be paid.[22]

By late October 1644, Parliament also seized some of Frances's goods. In this instance, it was not an issue of any land holdings, rents, or anything else to do with real estate, but rather some of Frances's movables that they had managed to confiscate, through the diligent work of a Colonel Berrowe. Promptly evaluated and sold, the items brought an additional £42 into the Parliamentary coffers, with Frances so much the poorer.[23]

Leaving her brother at Kingston, Frances travelled to Oxford, which had rapidly developed into the royalist headquarters. The relocation of the king's court had transformed the seat of learning into a very crowded temporary seat of government. The king also called a rival Parliament in Oxford, which sat in two sessions, one from January to April 1644, and a second from October 1644 to March 1645. Howard, at first a member of the Long Parliament but unseated there in 1642 because of his active support for the royalist cause ('for being very active to advance and put in Execution the Commission of Array, after it was declared by both Houses to be illegal'), in all likelihood sat in the Oxford Parliament.[24] Howard and Frances were thus staying in the same city again, although there is no way of knowing for sure if they were sharing quarters. The war brought so much uncertainty and many hardships, but perhaps the fact that they were close again was of some comfort. Any joy would be brief, as their time together was running very short.

Lady Anne Fanshawe, who lived in Oxford from 1643 until May of 1645, later wrote a memoir about her wartime experiences. She described the conditions in the small city as very crowded, the food as meagre, and the many temporary inhabitants, even the 'high' ones, as chronically poor and wanting even the basic necessities. Fanshawe further remembered: 'We had the perpetual discourse of losing and gaining towns and men; at the windows the sad spectacle of war, sometimes plague, sometimes sicknesses of other kinds, by reason of so many people being packed together, as I believe there never was before of that quality; always want; yet I must needs say that most bore it with a martyr-like cheerfulness.'[25]

In May 1645, the king and a portion of the army were away campaigning, when the Parliament's New Model Army arrived at the gates of Oxford. The Parliamentarian army laid siege to the city for three weeks, but left abruptly in order to engage the king at Naseby in Northamptonshire. Lady Fanshawe made it out of the city just before the siege began, but Frances did not. She was stuck in the besieged city, with the enemy army closing in. Food and medicine were scarce and an already weakened population was in poor shape to battle the infections and fevers, which spread rapidly. The overcrowded conditions made the contagions even more rampant, and Frances fell ill along with so many others. She had survived much during her very eventful life, including parental kidnappings, a disastrous marriage, a sexual scandal, prison and exile, economic hardships, and even a dangerous bout of smallpox. Yet this time, she could not fight her enemy effectively, she could not file a petition, she could not flee, and she could not find an ally able to help her out of her troubles. She was just short of forty-three years old when she breathed her last. She slipped away very quietly, leaving few traces of her last illness and death. Other than a very brief mention of her burial in the parish records, no one really paid any attention to the passing of yet another temporary Oxford resident, whose role in the politics of the heated Civil War era was minimal. It did not elicit any commentaries from the gossips and news writers, who had found her scandals so intriguing and titillating in previous decades. She was buried in the chancel of the church of St Mary the Virgin on 4 June 1645 (see Fig. 9.1). The church is wedged between All Souls and Brasenose Colleges, facing the High Street on one side. According to a late nineteenth-century description, the pavement in the chancel still had the initials engraved of those interred there, and among the list was 'Fraunces, viscountess Purbeck'.[26] The stone is no longer there, a fitting symbol of Frances's momentarily visible, but later largely forgotten, life.

When Frances died, she no longer had the support of her two closest family members: her son and her mother, both of whom were on the side of the enemy. Lacking sources, there is no way of knowing if Howard was still in Oxford when Frances died, and if he was not, when and how he found out about the death of the woman who had played such a large role in his life. The royal Oxford Parliament had been dismissed by March of 1645. Howard may have stayed in Oxford for some time, or he may have gone to back to his post as governor of the royalist forces at Bridgnorth Castle, some thirty miles north-east of his Clun estate in Shropshire.

Only about half a year after Frances's death, her mother, the indomitable Lady Hatton, passed away in Hatton House in London. Lady Hatton died at age sixty-seven on 3 January 1646, having outlived two husbands and both of her children. Neither Frances nor her mother lived to see the outcome of the Civil War. Frances

Fig. 9.1. St Mary the Virgin, University Church in Oxford. Frances was buried here after she died in 1645. Photo: Richard Semik/Shutterstock.

died just before the royalist forces lost a decisive encounter with Parliament at the Battle of Naseby on 14 June 1645. After Naseby, the royalists' downhill trajectory began, as their campaign slouched from one defeat to another. While the Parliamentarian army lifted the siege of Oxford without taking it in the summer of 1645, a year later, they marched in and took control of the city. By 1647, they had captured King Charles, and although he managed to escape and briefly fight again, by 1648, he was recaptured, put on trial for treason, convicted, and finally beheaded on 30 January 1649. After the death of the king, England was ruled without a king for little over a decade, a period known as the Interregnum. Parliament, headed by Puritan Lord Protector Oliver Cromwell, ruled the country in a largely failed, and promptly terminated, experiment.

Even though the tide turned in favour of Parliament by the summer of 1645, Howard continued to fight for the king. By spring of 1646, he was at Bridgnorth in Shropshire, directing the defences of the castle. In April, a Parliamentarian army surrounded the castle and laid a multi-week siege to it. The Parliamentarian forces were ultimately successful and took control of the garrison. Together with other royalist officers, Howard was forced to sign an agreement. Considering the brutality of the war, the terms of the agreement were rather lenient: he had two months to go to his home and decide if he wanted to submit to Parliament and 'compound for delinquencies', that is, pay a portion of what his estates were worth to Parliament, in addition to fines and fees for not having paid his dues in the past few years. The other options included exile abroad or going to another one of the king's garrisons. Howard clearly had no taste for leaving England, and he appeared done with the fighting. He chose to remain at home in Shropshire and deal with the reality of the situation. Once Howard's fine was set, which took two full years, he was slow in paying it, arguing that he did not have all the proofs he needed to show the various charges on his estate. Over the course of the next few years, he petitioned for a lowering of his fine multiple times, and the Committee for Compounding actually did so twice. Then Howard petitioned for extensions to pay his fine, which he also received twice. By the early 1650s, he was petitioning Parliament for the right to sell property in order to be able to pay the remainder of his fine.[27]

By early 1646, Howard had lost both the war and the woman he loved. Throughout at least the last twenty-two years, Howard had been loyal to Frances. Even though they had been separated for years at a time, they kept coming back to each other. This loyalty and persistence was something that others greatly admired in Howard, even those who did not agree with their relationship at all. He was from a large, powerful family, and even though he was a younger son, he had inherited the Shropshire estate and could thus have made his prospects greater by making a politic marriage, perhaps to an heiress with some land of her own. Instead, he remained unmarried for as long as Frances lived, as long as there was still a chance for them to be together in a legitimate way. The couple had hoped that Frances's husband would follow his younger brothers into the grave as quickly as possible so that they could quietly marry. John was not forthcoming: he stubbornly outlived them both, ensuring that marriage always remained an impossible dream.

Three years after Frances's death, Howard, by now in his late middle age, did finally take a wife. With Frances gone, he finally started to consider his posterity. In 1648, he married the much younger Katherine Neville, daughter of Henry Neville, Baron Abergavenny. Howard may have come to know Katherine through his brother-in-law, Edward, Lord Vaux, who was Katherine's maternal uncle. Vaux had married Howard's sister Elizabeth in 1632, only a few weeks after the death of her first husband, William Knollys, Earl of Banbury. Elizabeth had married the significantly older Knollys in 1605, when she was only nineteen and he a mature sixty-one. The marriage was childless until 1627, when Elizabeth gave birth to a son, followed by another son in 1631, when Knollys was eighty-three and eighty-seven years old respectively. It was generally assumed that the sons were not Knollys's, but rather fathered by Elizabeth's lover Lord Vaux, who later also settled some property on the one surviving boy. Similarly to Howard and Frances's son Robert's name shifts, both boys also sometimes used the surname Vaux as well as Knollys. Unlike her unlucky brother, Elizabeth did get to marry her lover when her old husband died, although she had to wait quite a while before the long-lived Knollys finally gave up the ghost.[28]

Howard lived for five years as a married man and had three sons with his wife in rapid succession: Henry, Edward, and another Robert. On 22 April 1653, he died. He was buried in the church of St George in Clun, which still has a brass plaque commemorating him on the east wall.[29] Howard's will only made provisions for his legitimate children.[30] Maybe he thought that the young man, now twenty-nine years old and a married man, was already taken care of by his grandmother's will, or that John still claimed him at this point. Maybe he was also angry because his first-born had switched sides during the war. He may also have chosen to ignore Robert after he married and had younger, unquestionably legitimate sons. Howard's estate, like so many others, was severely diminished as a result of the wars. His wife still struggled with the debts he left behind in the 1660s.[31] She remarried, taking Robert Berry of Ludlow as her second husband. At one point, her new husband was in a legal dispute with her son Henry over property that she claimed was part of her jointure, but which Henry claimed was part of his inheritance from his father.[32]

Frances, Howard, and Lady Hatton were thus all dead by the mid-1650s. Buckingham, the Countess of Buckingham, Kit Villiers, King Charles, Archbishop

Laud, and Sir Edward Coke were also gone. Only the sickly John was still alive. Apparently, his disastrous first experience with marriage did not deter him from trying it again: after Frances's death, he married Elizabeth Slingsby, daughter of Sir William Slingsby of Kippax. When Sir William had died in 1638, he left a £2,000 marriage portion for his daughter Elizabeth.[33] It was nothing as spectacular as Frances's juicy dowry, but John was probably happy to have it nonetheless. It would be a rather brave woman to marry John at this point. We know he could be kind and caring, of course, but the prospect of marrying an ageing man (he was in his sixties) with a clear record of troubling mental illness must have been rather daunting to many women. He no longer had the added attraction of his closeness to his powerful brother Buckingham or of the now dead and discredited King Charles, and not a great deal of wealth left either. He still had his title, of course, giving him something of a lure. It is not entirely clear when they married, but it must have been sometime before 29 August 1655, which is when John wrote his will, the first mention of his new wife. The marriage was childless and when he finally died in 1658 John gave everything he had, 'all [his] Estate reall and personal whatsoeuer', to his 'most deare and loving Wife, the Ladie Elizabeth Viscountess Purbeck'. He also appointed his wife as the sole executrix of his will. Frances may have persuaded John to consider Robert his legitimate son temporarily, but he had clearly changed his mind before he died. The will does not mention Robert at all.[34] Perhaps it was John's new wife who convinced her husband to give up the charade, as she certainly profited from that decision.

Young Robert, the product of Frances's and Howard's relationship, had a rather eventful life himself. After the death of his grandmother Lady Hatton, Robert received an inheritance which he claimed 'he looked not for'.[35] In fact, although Lady Hatton spread her bounty to several persons, Robert was the main recipient of his grandmother's estates. He received the manor of Fakenham, and holdings at Stoke Poges and Farnham Royal, as well as the use of Hatton House until the death of Viscount Purbeck, when he would receive the manor at Stoke as part the inheritance from his mother. Furthermore, he received all of Lady Hatton's 'plate, household stuffe, utensils, goods & chattels at her house at Stoke', as well as her 'ora'ge tawny Sparva of velvet & Damask' and her 'twoe best Chests of Lynnen the one of Beddlynnen the other of fine Damaske'.[36] For this bounty, he had to pay, however: the zealous Parliamentary Committee for Compounding went back and forth with Robert over the next ten years regarding what he should properly contribute based on the worth on his various estates, including ones which he received or purchased with the dowry from his bride.[37]

Robert's cousin Frances Berkeley, Lady Hatton's only other grandchild, was not mentioned at all in her will. In the 1650s, when she was in her early thirties, she was still unmarried. Her father provided for her in his will, but her life clearly did not turn out as grandly as might have been expected considering her wealthy grandparents. In his will, Sir Maurice ensured that she would get £100 outright the year following his death, in addition to a £30 annuity. In a codicil to his will, he added a stipulation that on the deaths of three other beneficiaries (a patroness of the family, his wife, and his father), his daughter's annual income would increase up to £60 per year. Furthermore, she was to receive a trunk full of clothes.[38]

On 23 November 1648, the same year that his father Howard married, the now twenty-four-year-old Robert also took a wife. He chose the nineteen-year-old Elizabeth, daughter of Sir John Danvers. Danvers was Lady Hatton's first cousin, and had served as one of the executors of her will. Fortunately, his marriage seems to have been a happier one than that of his mother. It was definitely more fruitful: Robert and his wife ended up having two sons and three daughters together.

Robert's father-in-law was also a firm Parliamentarian. In fact, he was chosen to be on the committee which tried, convicted, and signed the death warrant of King Charles in 1649, and would thus be one of those termed 'regicide' or 'murtherer of the king' after the restoration of the monarchy in 1660. No doubt his father-in-law helped to establish Robert's credentials as a Parliamentarian. By the 1650s, Robert also decided to take his wife's last name, instead of keeping Villiers, which came with so many complications. Part of the reason for the name change seems to have been Robert's desire to erase his brief past as a royalist. In the Parliament of 1658, his loyalties questioned, he defended himself in the following way: 'I wonder that I should be accused of being a Cavalier or bearing the armes for Charles Stuart which I never did for I protest I so much hated him & his cause that because those of the name Villiers did all side with him and assist him therefore I hated the name also & changed it for Danvers.'[39] Robert was not quite truthful here, considering his early career within the ranks of the royalists. Additionally, by the 1650s, his mother, his father, and his grandmother were all dead, and John no longer claimed him as his son. Perhaps Robert was also trying to create a new sense of belonging, a new family, with his in-laws. Considering the dysfunction and problematic relationships in his own family, who could blame him?

When the exiled son of the dead king was invited back to England in 1660 to restore monarchy and become recognized as Charles II, those who had supported the Cromwellian regime during the Interregnum often found themselves in trouble. That included Robert Danvers alias Villiers. In 1660, Robert was called to explain his statements in previous years. In addition to the above statement about hating Charles Stuart, Robert had also proclaimed 'that rather then the late King should want one to cut of[f] his Head, he [. . .] would do it himself'. To make matters worse, he was also accused of religious irregularities, having in 1649 'scoffed at Judgement to come' and 'with Blasphemous words dared God to maintain his owne Quarrell'. Robert found himself in prison for about three months over the issue.[40] He tried to evoke Parliamentary privilege, as he was elected as a member of the House of Commons for the new Parliament of 1660. That action began a whole new set of complications, because the House of Lords decided to call Robert to sit there as Viscount Purbeck, the rightful heir of John Villiers.

So once more, Robert found himself in a sort of limbo, squeezed between his roles as a son of two men. He had made up his mind at this point, though: he did not want the title, and he wanted to remain simply Robert Danvers. He told the Lords that the 'honor was but a shadow without substance', and that his 'small estate was unfit to maintain any such honor', and, most importantly, that the 'Noble Family he comes off neuer Owned him neither hath he any estate from them'. Ultimately, he paid a fine to the new King Charles in order to give up any claim to the title completely, and he was henceforth known as Robert Danvers, usually with an addition of 'alias Villiers' but he was not called to the House of Lords again.[41]

Robert continued to adhere to his anti-royalist ideas, to his detriment. In 1661, Thomas Venner, a Fifth Monarchist, led a small group of men in a rebellion against the king in London. The Fifth Monarchist was one of the many unorthodox religious groups that had developed during the Interregnum period: they believed the end of the world was near and sought to establish godly rule in England. The rebellion only lasted a few days and failed completely. In the aftermath, someone remembered that they had overheard Robert say that 'the Anabaptists would prevail, and he should adhere to his former principles, absolutely disliking monarchy'. Robert soon found himself in the Tower. In July the following year, his wife was allowed to visit him there. Transferred to York, he managed to repeat his mother's feat and escape prison. He did not stay free for very long, however, because he was later imprisoned in the Isle of Wight. By 1668, he was at liberty again, but only to be beset by creditors in place of jailors. Desperate, he now crossed over the English Channel, landing at Calais, where he stayed until his death in 1674, at fifty years old. He was buried in the Catholic church of Notre Dame in Calais, suggesting that he had also converted while in France.[42] From the time of his birth, Robert's very existence had been problematic and scandalous, and a large portion of his life was determined by his mother's actions and others' reactions to her. Once he became an adult and made his own decisions, his political and religious convictions eventually led him into trouble with the new royal order, and ironically, his struggles with imprisonments, exile, and conversion mirrored his mother's difficult life.

EPILOGUE

E ven after the death of her only son, the tales of the adultery and the brazen escapes of the Viscountess Purbeck were not laid to rest. Frances's life and actions echoed, and were re-hashed in the latter decades of the seventeenth century by the daughter-in-law and grandson she had never met. Although Robert Wright/ Howard/Villiers/Danvers had vehemently rejected his mother's attempt to make him a Villiers and the noble position it offered, his widow believed that she might do better as the dowager Viscountess Purbeck rather than just the widow of plain Mr Danvers. Like Frances, she also thought that it was the best way to ensure a better life for her children, especially considering the troubles her husband—and by extension, his family—had suffered as a result of his anti-royalist political convictions. Consequently, she began to lobby that her eldest son, also named Robert, claim the title of Viscount Purbeck.[1]

The Danvers family, who now took on the name Villiers instead, brought the issue to Parliament in 1675, petitioning the House of Lords to allow the young Viscount Purbeck his rightful position as a nobleman of the realm.[2] The House of Lords now had to take yet another stand about Frances's behaviour and the status of her son. In making their case, the Danvers/Villiers family largely ignored Frances's adultery conviction and the evidence that led to it. When they addressed it at all, they pointed to Frances's cleaned-up version in the 1641 petition. Instead, they felt they could make their strongest case by focusing on the law regarding legitimacy: John had been in England when the child was conceived, the couple had been lawfully married, so that should be enough to make Robert John's legal son. They also emphasized that John had owned him as a son, although they ignored that that was only a temporary situation in the 1640s. When Robert had rejected the call to sit in the House of Lords in the 1660s, and paid a fine to the king to ensure that his name was stricken from the lists of those eligible, his descendants now argued that such an action had not negated his nobility. They emphasized that a noble title could not be removed simply by paying a fine, as it was inherent in the blood. Therefore, even though Robert himself did not want to use the title, he could not get rid of it. His descendants, who shared his blood, also shared his nobility.[3] The Danvers/Villiers argument was rather inconsistent: Robert's descendants focused on the inherent nobility of the blood at the same time as they were rather vague on precisely whose blood coursed through Robert's veins, since they insisted that he should be considered John's son based on a rather liberal interpretation of English law.

The case stretched on for years, often halted and delayed by the second Duke of Buckingham, the eldest surviving son of the murdered Buckingham, as well as his first cousin the Earl of Denbigh, son to the first Buckingham's beloved sister Susan. Hence these sons of the dead Villiers were now working against the dead Frances's grandson, mirroring the same family divisions and struggles that had developed during Frances's lifetime. The nobles in the Lords agreed with the point that nobility could not be ended by a fine. They worried that it would give nobility a very uncertain status. Although the case caused plenty of debate, many Lords still opposed the Villiers/Danvers claim to the Purbeck title. They argued that the adultery conviction, and the evidence on which it was based, was the key to the case. Since Robert was clearly not John's son, all other arguments, what he had said or done afterwards, or whether or not John had accepted him as his son at some point, did not much matter. Since Robert had not, in fact, been the son of John, Viscount Purbeck, his descendants therefore could not claim the title, nor a seat in the House of Lords.[4] Although the majority of the Lords held that Danvers/Villiers claim to the title was not valid, they did not come to a final conclusion in the House. Instead, for reasons not entirely clear, they referred the matter to King Charles II, petitioning him to suggest the introduction of a bill in the House of Commons, which if passed, would make it illegal for Robert Danvers/Villiers to claim the Purbeck title in the future. The king, son of the stubborn Charles I, told the Lords he would consider their petition, but ultimately made no suggestion of such a bill. The Danvers/Villiers were kept out of the lists of the House of Lord's membership. Although thus defeated, Robert's descendants persisted in using the Purbeck title, and after the death of the second Duke of Buckingham in 1687 without an heir, they claimed that title as well, albeit equally as unsuccessfully. Officially, the Buckingham title became extinct (it was resurrected in a new creation in the early eighteenth century, when John Sheffield received it from Queen Anne). In the end, the dead George Villiers, first Duke of Buckingham, did indeed manage to ensure that Frances's bastard did not gain his title, or the title of his brother. Had she not died prematurely, perhaps Frances could have told her grandchildren and great-grandchildren that being a Villiers was not worth the trouble, as heartache and endless struggles surely followed.[5]

FAMILY TREES

What follows are simplified family trees of the Coke, Cecil, Villiers, and Howard families, as well as the royal House of Stuart. I use the abbreviation 'm' to denote a marriage, followed by a number if the person married multiple times.

The Coke Family

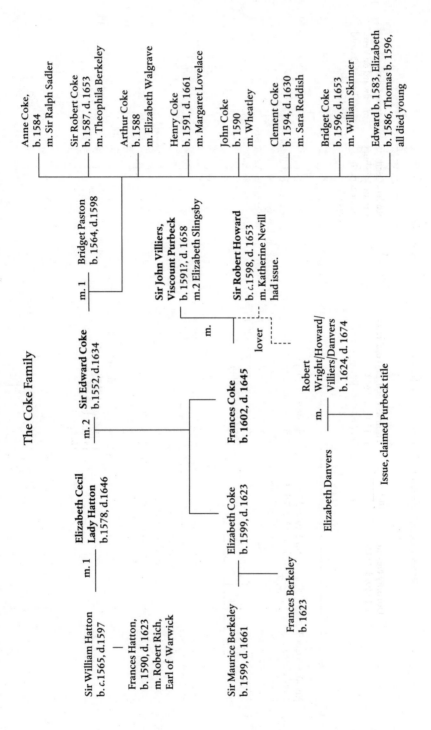

The Cecil Family

William Cecil, Lord Burghley, Queen Elizabeth's Secretary of State. b. 1520, d. 1598

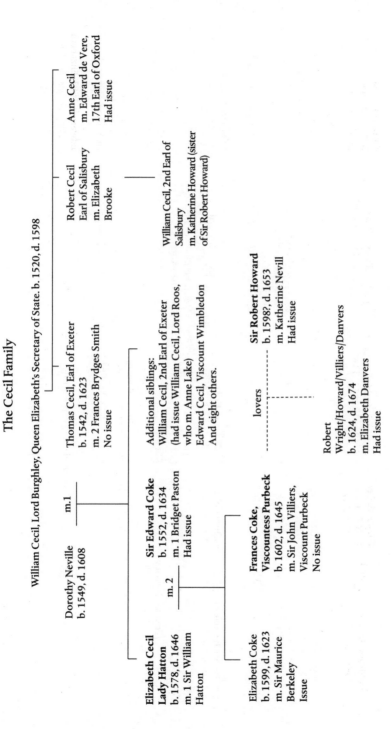

Dorothy Neville
b. 1549, d. 1608

m.1

Thomas Cecil, Earl of Exeter
b. 1542, d. 1623
m. 2 Frances Brydges Smith
No issue

Robert Cecil
Earl of Salisbury
m. Elizabeth
Brooke

Anne Cecil
m. Edward de Vere,
17th Earl of Oxford
Had issue

William Cecil, 2nd Earl of
Salisbury
m. Katherine Howard (sister
of Sir Robert Howard)

Sir Edward Coke
b. 1552, d. 1634
m. 1 Bridget Paston
Had issue

Additional siblings:
William Cecil, 2nd Earl of Exeter
(had issue William Cecil, Lord Roos,
who m. Anne Lake)
Edward Cecil, Viscount Wimbledon
And eight others.

Sir Robert Howard
b. 1598?, d. 1653
m. Katherine Nevill
Had issue

lovers

Robert
Wright/Howard/Villiers/Danvers
b. 1624, d. 1674
m. Elizabeth Danvers
Had issue

Elizabeth Cecil
Lady Hatton
b. 1578, d. 1646
m. 1 Sir William
Hatton

m. 2

Frances Coke,
Viscountess Purbeck
b. 1602, d. 1645
m. Sir John Villiers,
Viscount Purbeck
No issue

Elizabeth Coke
b. 1599, d. 1623
m. Sir Maurice
Berkeley
Issue

The Villiers Family

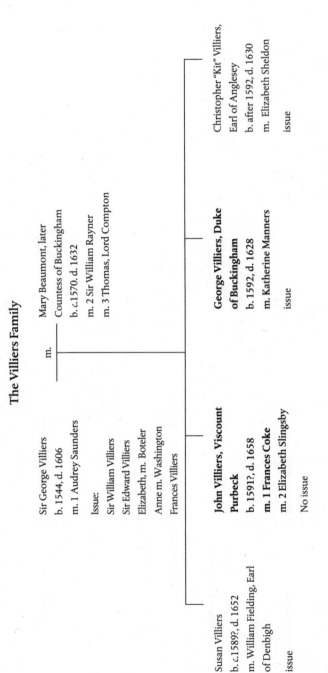

Sir George Villiers
b. 1544, d. 1606
m. 1 Audrey Saunders

Issue:
Sir William Villiers
Sir Edward Villiers
Elizabeth, m. Boteler
Anne m. Washington
Frances Villiers

m.

Mary Beaumont, later
Countess of Buckingham
b. c.1570. d. 1632
m. 2 Sir William Rayner
m. 3 Thomas, Lord Compton

Susan Villiers
b. c.1589?, d. 1652
m. William Fielding, Earl
of Denbigh

issue

John Villiers, Viscount
Purbeck
b. 1591?, d. 1658
m. 1 Frances Coke
m. 2 Elizabeth Slingsby

No issue

George Villiers, Duke
of Buckingham
b. 1592, d. 1628
m. Katherine Manners

issue

Christopher "Kit" Villiers,
Earl of Anglesey
b. after 1592, d. 1630
m. Elizabeth Sheldon

issue

The Howard Family

Thomas Howard, 1st Earl of Suffolk
b. 1561, d. 1626

m.

Katherine Knyvet, Countess of Suffolk
b. 1564, d. 1633

Theophilus Howard
2nd Earl of Suffolk
b. 1582, d. 1640
m. Elizabeth Hume
Had issue

Frances Howard
b. 1590, d. 1632
m. 1 Robert Devereux,
Earl of Essex (annulled)
No issue
m. 2 Robert Carr, Earl of
Somerset
Had issue

Elizabeth Howard
b. 1583, d. 1658
m. 1 William Knollys, Earl
of Banbury
No issue
m. 2 Edward, Lord Vaux
Had issue, born during
first marriage

Sir Robert Howard
b. 1598?, d. 1653
m. Katherine Nevill
Had issue

Thomas Howard,
Earl of Berkshire
b. 1587, d. 1669
m. Elizabeth Cecil
Had issue

Frances Coke
Viscountess Purbeck
b. 1602, d. 1645
m. John Villiers, Viscount
Purbeck
No issue

lovers

Robert Wright/Howard/Villiers/Danvers
b. 1624, d. 1674
m. Elizabeth Danvers
Had issue

Catherine Howard
b. c.1588, d. 1673
m. William Cecil,
Earl of Salisbury
Had issue

Additional siblings:
Gertrude Howard
Sir William Howard
Emily Howard, died young
Sir Charles Howard
Henry Howard
John Howard, died young
Edward Howard
Margaret Howard, died young

The Royal House of Stuart

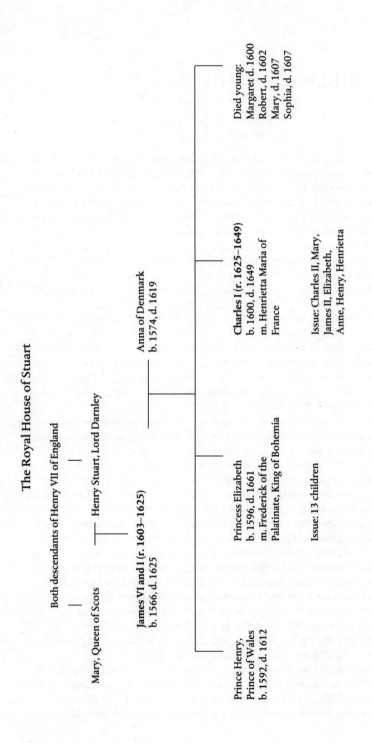

Both descendants of Henry VII of England

Mary, Queen of Scots

Henry Stuart, Lord Darnley

James VI and I (r. 1603–1625)
b. 1566, d. 1625

Anna of Denmark
b. 1574, d. 1619

Prince Henry,
Prince of Wales
b. 1592, d. 1612

Princess Elizabeth
b. 1596, d. 1661
m. Frederick of the
Palatinate, King of Bohemia

Issue: 13 children

Charles I (r. 1625–1649)
b. 1600, d. 1649
m. Henrietta Maria of
France

Issue: Charles II, Mary,
James II, Elizabeth,
Anne, Henry, Henrietta

Died young:
Margaret d. 1600
Robert, d. 1602
Mary, d. 1607
Sophia, d. 1607

BIBLIOGRAPHIC ESSAY

Thus far, historians have not paid much attention to Frances, because she did not herself hold a significant position or have the ear of royalty. However, many of the people whose lives were intertwined with Frances's were heavily involved in the political, social, and religious activities of the courts of James I and Charles I. As a result, scholars have written numerous studies focusing on the kings, their queens, Buckingham, William Laud, Sir Edward Coke, and so on. Sometimes, these writers have added brief discussions about the scandal caused by Frances's adultery, often presented as an amusing anecdote, or a juicy, gossipy titbit. Thomas Longueville was the first person to write a longer account of Frances's life. His *The Curious Case of Lady Purbeck: A Scandal of the XVIIth Century* was published in 1909, and, as the title suggests, focuses mostly on the scandal produced by Frances's contentious marriage and adultery. His account is heavily influenced by the restrictive sexual mores of late Victorian and early Edwardian England: Longueville found Frances's adultery problematic, but also fateful and tragic. In 1936, Laura Norsworthy's biography of Frances's mother Lady Elizabeth Hatton, *The Lady of the Bleeding Heart Yard*, included substantial material about Frances, but suffered from a few omissions, anachronistic interpretations, and chronological mistakes. For example, Norsworthy appears to have mistaken many of the key dates, as she was not figuring in the Old Style dating when reading crucial sources (the English began the year on 25 March instead of 1 January until 1752). In recent years, literary scholar Emily Ross has written a dissertation and two articles about the events and gossip surrounding Frances's contested marriage, exploring questions about authorship and distribution of gossip and information in early seventeenth-century England, but she does not focus on the entirety of Frances's life.[1]

Frances's dramatic life has inspired novelists to write fictional accounts as well. In 1961, Hilda Lewis wrote a novel entitled *Call Lady Purbeck*, based on Frances's life. The novel largely follows Norsworthy's narrative, but does not cover Frances's last years. In 2006, Natalie Hodgson published a slim volume entitled *Fateful Beauty: The Story of Frances Coke 1602–1642*. The publisher categorizes the book as historical biography. It follows the basic outline of Frances's life, but has numerous mistakes and omissions, such as the wrong date of her death. It also takes significant liberties with entirely invented events and dialogue, does not provide any sources, and would therefore more appropriately be classified as historical fiction rather than biography. Frances has also been the subject of Midi Berry's self-published novel *Nights of the Road* (2015), which intertwines the lives of seventeenth-century Frances and a twenty-first-century woman in the genre of "time-slip." These three writers, for reasons of character developments and plots that rightfully belong to novelists' tool box, tend to portray Frances as an entirely blameless victim, and the Villiers as the undisputed villains, leading to a rather black and white picture, lacking the nuance of the messier realities.[2]

My own relationship with Frances began many years ago, while I was writing a book about Tudor and Stuart nobility and illicit sex (*Love, Lust, and License in Early Modern England: Illicit Sex and the Nobility*, Ashgate, 2008). I then explored Frances's court case and its aftermath in a chapter entitled 'Preserving Honor: Frances Coke and Robert Howard'. Frances's fascinating story intrigued me and I quickly became convinced that it needed a book to do it full justice. As is often the case, other projects and work duties intervened, but Frances was always in the back of my mind, until I finally resolved to go ahead and write her first full biography.

In contrast to Longueville and Norsworthy, I live in a time period when many source collections, like the State Papers, other letter collections, and Parliamentary records and journals, have been calendared, printed, and in some cases digitized. As a result, I have been able to do more systematic searches, and find further sources than was practically possible for my predecessors. I can thus correct mistakes in earlier works, and recreate Frances's life in greater detail, especially the court cases, interactions with Parliaments, and her later years. Significantly, the earlier works were published long before the great wealth of women's and gender history produced in the last few decades even existed. We know so much more about the female experience in early modern England today than we did in the early to mid-twentieth century, especially within the fields of sex and marriage. As a historian specializing in women's and gender history, I use current knowledge of the history of love, sex, marriage, and power when interpreting and recreating Frances's life, which allows me to present a more nuanced view of Frances and the people around her.

NOTES

Prologue

1. Diane Purkiss, *The English Civil War: Papists, Gentlewomen, Soldiers, and Witchfinders in the Birth of Modern Britain* (New York: Basic Books, 2006), 266–78; Michael Braddick, *God's Fury, England's Fire: A New History of the English Civil Wars* (New York: Allen Lane, 2008), 374–6; Andrew Clark, ed., *Survey of the Antiquities in the City of Oxford composed in 1661–6 by Anthony Wood* (Oxford: Clarendon Press, 1899), 115, 246.

Chapter 1

1. Elizabeth Goldring, Faith Eales, Elizabeth Clarke, and Jayne Elisabeth Archer, eds., *John Nichols's The Progresses and Public Processions of Queen Elizabeth I: A New Edition of the Early Modern Sources* (Oxford: Oxford University Press, 2014), v. 4, 62–3; Allen Boyer, *Sir Edward Coke and the Elizabeth Age* (Stanford: Stanford University Press, 2003), 213; Catherine Drinker Bowen, *The Lion and the Throne: The Life and Times of Sir Edward Coke (1552–1634)* (Boston: Little, Brown and Company, 1956), 122; John Campbell, *The Lives of the Chief Justices of England* (London: Murray, 1849), v. 1, 254–5.
2. *ODNB*, 'Elizabeth Cecil', 'Thomas Cecil', 'Sir William Newport alias Hatton'; Laura Norsworthy, *The Lady of the Bleeding Heart Yard: Lady Elizabeth Hatton, 1578–1646* (New York: Harcourt Brace and Co., 1936), 2–4.
3. Campbell, v. 1, 240–1.
4. *ODNB*, 'Sir Edward Coke'; Campbell, v. 1, 240–1, 246; Drinker Bowen, chaps. 5, 9, 10.
5. PROB 11/200/312. The fact that Frances had a step-sister with the same name has caused some confusion for historians and antiquarians who sometimes have mixed up the step-sisters. For example, Catherine Drinker Bowen believed Frances Hatton was Lady Hatton's daughter from her first marriage (Drinker Bowen, 117).
6. Boyer, 207–13; Campbell, v. 1, 253; Drinker Bowen, 115; Humphrey Woolrych, *The Life of the Right Honourable Sir Edward Coke, Knt., Lord Chief Justice of the King's Bench* (South Hackensack: Rothman Reprints, 1972; orig. 1826), 39.
7. Boyer, 211; Drinker Bowen, 115–16.
8. SP 12/268/90, 15 Sept. 1598, Tobie Matthew to Dudley Carleton; Michael G. Brennan, Noel Kinnamon, and Margaret P. Hannay, eds., *The Letters of Rowland Whyte (1595–1608)* (Philadelphia: American Philosophical Society, 2013), 285–6, 2 Feb. 1598, Rowland Whyte to Sir Robert Sidney.
9. Quoted in Drinker Bowen, 79.
10. Campbell, v. 1, 254.
11. David Loyd, *State-worthies, or the Statesmen and Favourites of England, from the Reformation to the Revolution* (London: J. Robson, 1766), v. 2, 112.
12. Campbell, v. 1, 39, 242–3.

13. On Lady Hatton's general character, see Norsworthy, 2–3. On Lady Hatton's court career, see D. J. H. Clifford, ed., *The Diaries of Anne Clifford* (Stroud: Alan Sutton, 1990), 24; Leeds Barroll, *Anna of Denmark, Queen of England: A Cultural Biography* (Philadelphia: University of Pennsylvania Press, 2001), 48, 91–2, 94; Norsworthy, 17. On Lady Hatton's arguments with her husband over money and property, see her petitions; printed in Pierre Bayle, *A General Dictionary Historical and Critical* (London: Bettenham, 1736), v. 4, 388; Elizabeth Hatton's petition to King Charles, SP 16/280/12, undated, filed under 1634. On Lady Hatton's flair for the dramatic, see John Chamberlain's comparison between her and the contemporary actor Richard Burbage. Norman Egbert McClure, ed., *The Letters of John Chamberlain* (Philadelphia: American Philosophical Society, 1939), v. 2, 77, 24 May 1617, Chamberlain to Carleton.

14. For more on the laws of marriage in early modern England, see Thomas Ridley, *A View of the Civile and Ecclesiastical Law: and Wherein the Practice of them is Streitened and May be Relieved Within this Land* (4th ed., Oxford, 1676); R. B. Outhwaite, *Clandestine Marriage in England, 1500–1850* (London: Hambledon Press, 1995); Diana O'Hara, *Courtship and Constraint: Rethinking the Making of Marriage in Early Modern England* (Manchester: Manchester University Press, 2000); James Brundage, *Law, Sex and Christian Society in Medieval Europe* (Chicago: University of Chicago Press, 1987); Frederick Pedersen, *Marriage Disputes in Medieval England* (London: Hambledon Press, 2000); Conor McCarthy, *Marriage in Medieval England: Law, Literature, and Practice* (Rochester, NY: Boydell Press, 2004); Richard Adair, *Courtship, Illegitimacy and Marriage in Early Modern England* (Manchester: Manchester University Press, 1996); Henry Swinburne, *A Treatise of Spousals or Marriage Contracts* (London: Printed by S. Roycroft for Robert Clavell, 1686); Reginald Haw, *The State of Matrimony: An Investigation of the Relationship between Ecclesiastical and Civil Marriage in England after the Reformation with a Consideration of the Laws Relating Thereto* (London: SPCK, 1952); Charles Donahue, *Law, Marriage and Society in the Later Middle Ages: Arguments About Marriage in Five Courts* (New York: Cambridge University Press, 2007).

15. Campbell, v. 1, 255; Norsworthy, 11–12; Woolrych, 40–1.

16. John Strype, ed., *The Life and Acts of John Whitgift* (Oxford: Clarendon Press, 1822), v. 2, 400–1; Bayle, v. 4, 382; Campbell, v. 1, 256.

17. McClure, v. 1, 54, 22 Nov. 1598, John Chamberlain to Dudley Carleton.

18. SP 12/270/177, 30 April 1599, Affidavit of Mary Berham; John Aubrey, *Brief Lives* (Oxford: Clarendon Press, 1898), v. 2, 67–8. The spelling of Coke's name is actually misleading: his name was and is pronounced 'Cook', and during the sixteenth and early seventeenth century, before the standardization of spelling, it was often spelled 'Cooke' or 'Cook', in addition to 'Coke'. Campbell, v. 1, 240.

19. Coke's *Vade Mecum* or Memoranda Book, printed in Frederic Madden, Bulkeley Bandinel, and John Gough Nichols, eds., *Collectanea Topographica et Genealogica* (London: J. B. Nichols, 1840), v. 4, 108–22; LMA, St Andrew Holborn, Register of baptisms, 1558–1623, P82/AND2/A/001/MS06667, Item 001; McClure, v. 1, 84–5, 23 Aug. 1599, Chamberlain to Carleton; Goldring et al., v. 4, 79.

20. LMA, St Andrew Holborn, Register of baptisms, 1558–1623, P82/AND2/A/001/MS06667, Item 001. The date of Frances's birth was long unknown: Longueville and Norsworthy were guessing, as have most other writers. The only previous person to get her birth date correct was Frances Hodgson, in *Fateful Beauty: The Story of Frances Coke, 1602–1642* (London: Eye Books, 2006), but she does not refer to a source, and she is also three years off on the death date.

21. Coke's *Vade Mecum* in Madden et al., v. 4, 108–22.

22. See for example the case of Penelope Rich and Charles Blount, Earl of Devonshire, in Johanna Rickman, *Love, Lust, and License in Early Modern England* (Aldershot: Ashgate, 2008), 134–8; Amy Louise Erickson, 'Common Law, Common Practice: The Use of Marriage Settlements in Early Modern England', *Economic History Review*, v. 43 (1990), 21–39.
23. Coke's complaints and Lady Hatton's response printed in Bayle, v. 4, 388.
24. Coke's complaints and Lady Hatton's response printed in Bayle, v. 4, 388; Woolrych, 145–6. Campbell suggests that Lady Hatton refused to change her name because she did not want to be demoted from being Lady Hatton to simply Mistress Coke, since Coke had not yet been knighted when they married. While that might have figured in to her decision, it would not have been an issue after 1603, when King James knighted Coke and she could have been Lady Coke had she so wished. She did not wish so, of course. Campbell, v. 1, 256.
25. SP 16/280/16, undated, calendared for 1634, Lady Hatton's petition; *ODNB*, 'Walter Aston'.
26. SP 16/280/16, undated, calendared for 1634, Lady Hatton's petition; Lady Hatton's answer to Coke's charges in 1617, printed in *Bayle*, v. 4, 388. On the ideals of early modern marriage, see for example Elizabeth Foyster, *Meanings of Manhood in Early Modern England* (New York: Oxford University Press, 2003), chap. 3, which analyses sixteenth- and seventeenth-century conduct books.
27. McClure, v. 1, 131, 19 Sept. 1601, Chamberlain to Carleton.
28. *CSP Domestic, James I (1603–1610)*, 152, 25 Sept. 1604, unknown to Justice Gawdy; McClure, v. 1, 204, 15 Feb. 1605, John Chamberlain to Ralph Winwood; Andrew Thrush and John P. Ferris, *The History of Parliament: The House of Commons 1604–1629* (Cambridge: Cambridge University Press, 2010), v. 3, 556–60, 597–8, 619–20; Thrush and Ferris, v. 6, 45–9; *ODNB*, 'Francis Gawdy'; Coke's *Vade Mecum*, in Madden et al., v. 4, 108–22.
29. Clifford, 24; Barroll, 48, 91–2, 94; Norsworthy, 17.
30. Campbell, v. 1, 257–76; Drinker Bowen, 182, 278–82, 340–1.
31. Lady Newdigate-Newdegate, *Gossip from a Muniment Room* (London, 1897), 20, undated, William Knollys to Anne Newdigate.
32. Naomi Miller and Naomi Yavnew, eds., *Gender and Early Modern Constructions of Childhood* (Aldershot: Ashgate, 2011), 4; Rachel Trubowitz, '"But Blood Whitened": Nursing Mothers and Others in Early Modern Britain', in Miller and Yavneh, eds., *Maternal Measures: Figuring Caregiving in the Early Modern Period* (Aldershot: Ashgate, 2000), 82–104.
33. Norsworthy, 5–7.
34. William Page, ed., *A History of the County of Buckingham* (London: Victoria County History, 1925), v. 3, 302–13; Drinker Bowen, 525–7.
35. George Banks, *The Story of Corfe Castle* (London: John Murray, 1853), 1–98.
36. SP 14/92/227, 22 July 1617, George Gerrard to Carleton. For a good overview of the historiography, see the introduction in Hugh Cunningham, *Children and Childhood in Western Society Since 1500* (New York: Pearson Longman, 2005) and Albrecht Classen, 'Philippe Ariès and the Consequential History of Childhood, Family Relations, and Personal Emotions: Where Do We Stand Today?' in Classen, ed., *Childhood in the Middle Ages and the Renaissance: The Results of a Paradigm Shift in the History of Mentality* (Berlin: Walter de Gruyter, 2005), 1–65. See also Patricia Phillippy, 'A Comfortable Farewell: Child Loss and Funeral Monuments in Early Modern England', Carol Levin, 'Parents, Children, and Responses to Death in Dream Structures in Early Modern England', and Jane Couchman, '"Our Little Darlings": Huguenot Children and Child-Rearing in the Letters of Louise de Coligny', in Miller and Yavneh, *Gender and Early Modern Constructions of Childhood*, 17–38, 39–50, 101–16.

37. Phillip Yorke, ed., *Letters to and from Sir Dudley Carleton during his Embassy to the Netherlands* (London, 1775), 26–7, 14 May 1616, Ralph Winwood to Dudley Carleton, and 30 May 1616, Carleton to Winwood; SP 84/72/242, 18 May 1616, William More to Carleton; Maurice Lee, *Dudley Carleton to John Chamberlain 1603–1624: Jacobean Letters* (New Brunswick: Rutgers University Press), 202.

38. Allison Coudert, 'Educating Girls in Early Modern Europe and America', in Classen, 389–413; Cunningham, 79–110.

39. Baldassare Castiglione, *The Book of the Courtier*, trans. Thomas Hoby (London, 1561), Book Three.

40. *CSP Venice (1617–1619)*, v. 15, 108–26, 24 Jan. 1618, report to Doge at Venice; Margaret Hannay, *Mary Sidney, Lady Wroth* (Aldershot: Ashgate, 2010), 43, 65, 72–4.

41. Hannay, 76–7, 84.

42. SP 14/92/234, 24 July 1617, John Finet to Carleton.

Chapter 2

1. W. D. McCray, ed., *Beaumont Papers: Letters Relating to the Beaumont Family, of Whitley, Yorkshire, from the Fifteenth to the Seventeenth Centuries* (London: Nichols and Sons, 1848), 34–5, 22 Nov. 1617, Thomas Paulyn to Sir Richard Beaumont.

2. Roger Lockyer, *Buckingham: The Life and Political Career of George Villiers, First Duke of Buckingham 1592–1628* (New York: Longman, 1981), 3–24.

3. Lockyer, *Buckingham*, 28, 43.

4. Cynthia Herrup, *A House in Gross Disorder: Sex, Law, and the 2nd Earl of Castlehaven* (Oxford: Oxford University Press, 1999), 26–38.

5. Alastair Bellany and Thomas Cogswell, *The Murder of King James* (New Haven: Yale University Press, 2015), 8–9; Michael Young, *James VI and I and the History of Homosexuality* (Basingstoke: Macmillan, 2000), chap. 2. It is also entirely possible that James, a rather accomplished legal and theological scholar, did not at all interpret his relationships with his favourites as the crime of sodomy. Legally, the act had to involve anal penetration in order constitute sodomy. Men who stood accused of sodomy sometimes defended themselves by arguing that although there had been physical contact, there had been no actual penetration. The accused in the much publicized rape and sodomy trial of the Earl of Castlehaven in 1631 made that particular argument, for example. Herrup, 29, 46.

6. Lockyear, *Buckingham*, 33–4; Bellany and Cogswell, 10–18. Sir Thomas Monson tried and failed to replace Buckingham in 1618. McClure, v. 2, 151, 27 March 1618, John Chamberlain to Dudley Carleton; ibid., 156, 10 April 1618, same to same.

7. Lockyer, *Buckingham*, 34, 38; McClure, v. 2, 52, 8 Feb. 1617, Chamberlain to Carleton; *CSP Domestic, James I (1611–1618)*, 9 Aug. 1618, Abraham Williams to Carleton.

8. E. A. Wrigley, R. S. Davies, J. E. Oeppen, and R. S. Schofield, *English Population History from Family Reconstitution 1580–1837* (New York: Cambridge University Press, 1997), 122–6; Peter Laslett, *The World We Have Lost, Further Explored*, 3rd ed. (London: Routledge, 2000), 81–121; Alan Macfarlane, *Marriage and Love in England: Modes of Reproduction 1300–1840* (Oxford: Blackwell, 1986), 119–47; Mary Abbott, *Family Ties: English Families 1540–1920* (New York: Routledge, 1993), 6–10.

9. *CSP Domestic, James I (1611–1618)*, 6 Nov. 1616, Sir John Throckmorton to Carleton; McClure, v. 2, 32–3, 9 Nov. 1616, Chamberlain to Carleton.

10. SP 14/88/3, 3 July 1616, Alex Williams to Carleton; SP 14/88/22, 13 July 1616, Sir Ralph Winwood to Carleton; McClure, v. 2, 11, 22 June 1616, Chamberlain to Carleton; ibid., 14, 6 July 1616, same to same; Drinker Bowen, 370–90; Bayle, v. 4, 283–386.

11. McClure, v. 2, 38, 23 Nov. 1616, Chamberlain to Carleton; ibid., 45, 21 Dec 1616, same to same; SP 14/89/124, 7 Dec. 1616, Edward Sherburn to Carleton; SP 14/89/141, 14 Dec. 1616, same to same.

12. McClure, v. 2, 64, 15 March 1617, Chamberlain to Carleton; SP 14/90/205, 11 March 1617, Sir William Lovelace to Carlton.

13. McClure, v. 2, 64, 15 March 1616, Chamberlain to Carleton.

14. McClure, v. 2, 11, 22 June 1616, Chamberlain to Carleton.

15. Coke and Lady Hatton's 1617 petitions, printed in Bayle, v. 4, 387–8.

16. McClure, v. 2, 38–9, 23 Nov. 1616, Chamberlain to Carleton; ibid., 41, 7 Dec. 1616, same to same.

17. McClure, v. 2, 38–9, 23 Nov. 1616, Chamberlain to Carleton; ibid., 41, 7 Dec. 1616, same to same; Coke and Lady Hatton's 1617 petitions, printed in Bayle, v. 4, 387–8.

18. McClure, v. 2, 77, 24 May 1617, Chamberlain to Carleton; SP 14/92/134, 25? May 1617, Edward Sherburn to Carleton; SP 14/92/162, 4 June 1617, George Gerrard to Carleton.

19. McClure, v. 2, 79–80, 4 June 1617, Chamberlain to Carleton; APC, v. 35, 1616–17, 274–6.

20. P. R. Seddon, ed., *Letters of John Holles, 1587–1637* (Nottingham: Thoroton Society, 1975), v. 2, 172–4, 17 July 1617, John Holles to Buckingham.

21. McClure, v. 2, 14, 6 July 1616, Chamberlain to Carleton; SP 14/88/12, 11 July 1616, Edward Sherburn to Carlton.

22. June 1617, Secretary Winwood to Edward Coke, quoted in Hastings Lyon and Leon Block, *Edward Coke: Oracle of the Law* (New York: Houghton Mifflin, 1929), 247.

23. June 1617, Secretary Winwood to Edward Coke, quoted in Lyon and Block, 247.

24. Withipole had married one of Lady Hatton's first cousins, Frances Cornwallis. McClure, v. 2, 88–90, 19 July 1617, Chamberlain to Carleton; SP 14/92 f. 227, 22 July 1617, George Gerrard to Carleton; SP 14/92/230, 24 July 1617, Edward Sherburn to Carleton; letter to Anne Sadler from a relative, 26 July 1617, printed in 'Lord Bacon and Sir Edward Coke', *Athenaeum: Journal of Literature, Science, and Fine Art* (17 May 1862), 661–2.

25. Letter to Anne Sadler from a relative, 26 July 1617, *Athenaeum* (17 May 1862), 661–2. McClure, v. 2, 88–9, 19 July 1617, Chamberlain to Carleton; Lyon and Block, 249. Lyon and Block have mistakenly dated the warrant 12 January, although it should be 12 July 1617.

26. Letter to Anne Sadler from a relative, 26 July 1617, *Athenaeum* (17 May 1862), 661–2; McClure, v. 2, 89, 19 July 1617, Chamberlain to Carleton; SP 14/92/227, 22 July 1617, Gerrard to Carleton; 15 July 1617, Edward Coke to Buckingham, printed in Bayle, v. 4, 387.

27. Letter to Anne Sadler from a relative, 26 July 1617, *Athenaeum* (17 May 1862), 661–2; Lisa Jardine and Alan Stewart, *Hostage to Fortune: The Troubled Life of Francis Bacon* (London: Victor Gollancz, 1999), 402; Lyon and Block, 249.

28. The council met on Sunday 13 July. SP 14/92/227, George Gerrard to Carleton, 22 July 1617; Letter to Anne Sadler from a relative, 26 July 1617, *Athenaeum* (17 May 1862), 661–2; Lyon and Block, 252–3.

29. SP 14/92/227, George Gerrard to Carleton, 22 July 1617; Lyon and Block, 252–3.

30. *HMC Downshire*, v. 6, 236–7, 22 July 1617, John More to William Trumbull; Robert Stephens, ed., *Letters of Sir Francis Bacon, Baron of Verulam, Viscount St. Alban, and Lord High*

Chancellor of England. Written during the Reign of King James the First (London: Benjamin Tooke, 1702), 207–9, 12 July 1617, Bacon to Buckingham; Jardine and Stewart, 401–2.

31. Stephens, 210–16, 25 July 1617, Bacon to King James; ibid., 25 July 1617, Bacon to Buckingham; ibid., 31 July 1617, Bacon to King James; ibid., 23 Aug. 1617, Bacon to Buckingham.

32. 25 or 26 Aug. 1617, King James to Francis Bacon, quoted in Jardine and Stewart, 408–9.

33. Seddon, v. 2, 184–5, 5 Aug. 1617, Lady Hatton's petition to the king.

34. McClure, v. 2, 89, 19 July 1617, Chamberlain to Carleton; ibid., 91–2, 9 Aug. 1617, same to same; Seddon, v. 2, 188–9, 6 Aug. 1617, Lord Holles to Sir Thomas Lake; ibid., 191–3, 15 Aug. 1617; *HMC Downshire*, v. 6, 246–7, 1 Aug. 1617, John Castle to William Trumbull; Lady Hatton's petition to the Privy Council; Seddon, v. 2, 193–4, 15 Aug. 1617, Holles to Sir Thomas Lake. In March 1620, Buckingham's mother invited Katherine Manners to supper and had her stay the night, with Buckingham also present in the house at the same time. Katherine's father, the Earl of Rutland, argued that his daughter's virtue had been compromised and would not receive her back in his house until she was wed to Buckingham. The wedding took place in May of 1620. Lockyer, *Buckingham*, 58–60.

35. Letter to Anne Sadler from a relative, 26 July 1617, *Athenaeum* (17 May 1862), 661–2; Seddon, v. 2, 193–4, 15 Aug. 1617, Holles to Sir Thomas Lake; Lady Hatton to Buckingham, printed in Woolrych, 133–4.

36. SP 14/93/28, 18 Aug. 1617, George Gerrard to Carleton (Gerrard included a copy of Frances's letter); another copy of the letter is in the Cecil Papers, printed in *HMC Salisbury*, v. 22, 52.

37. McClure, v. 2, 100–1, 11 Oct. 1617, Chamberlain to Carleton; *CSP Domestic (James 1611–1618)*, 482–3, 22 Aug. 1617, Sir Arthur Tyringham to Carleton; *HMC Downshire*, v. 6, 261–2, 21 Aug. 1617, Tobie Mathews to George Gage (who was at Brussels). Oxford later married another of Lady Hatton's relatives, Lady Diana Cecil, in 1624.

38. McClure, v. 2, 91–2, 9 Aug. 1617, Chamberlain to Carleton; ibid., 98, 27 Aug. 1617, same to same.

39. *HMC Salisbury*, v. 22, 52, before 19 Sept. 1617, Frances Coke to Lady Hatton.

40. Yelverton to Bacon, 3 Sept. 1617, quoted in Lyon and Block, 257.

41. Seddon, v. 2, 200–1, 10 Sept. 1617, Lady Hatton's petition to King James.

42. BL Additional 5834, f. 10.

43. Joseph Foster, ed., *London Marriage Licenses 1521–1869* (London: Bernard Quaritch, 1887), 1388. The licence says that John was twenty-five and Frances sixteen, but it seems it is slightly mistaken. John was probably twenty-six and Frances was about to turn fifteen. *HMC Downshire*, v. 6, 290–1, 18 September 1617, John Castle to William Trumbull; ibid., 295, 26 Sept. 1617, Viscount Lisle to William Trumbull.

44. *HMC Downshire*, v. 6, 290–1, 18 September 1617, John Castle to William Trumbull; SP 14/93/156, 6 Oct. 1617, Sir Gerard Herbert to Carleton; SP 14/94/5, 492, 4 Nov. 1617, King James to Sir William Craven.

45. McClure, v. 2, 100–1, 11 Oct. 1617, Chamberlain to Carleton; *HMC Downshire*, v. 6, 290–1, 18 Sept. 1617, John Castle to William Trumbull.

46. Edmund Sawyer, ed. *Memorials of Affairs of State in the Reigns of Q. Elizabeth and K. James I* (London: T. Ward, 1725), v. 2, 43, Jan. 1604, Dudley Carleton to Ralph Winwood; McClure, v. 1, 495–7, 30 Dec. 1613, Chamberlain to Alice Carleton; ibid., v. 1, 497–9, 5 Jan. 1614, Chamberlain to Carleton; ibid., v. 1, 512, 17 Feb. 1614, Chamberlain to Alice Carleton; SP 14/95/14, 12 Jan. 1618, Sir Gerard Herbert to Dudley Carleton.

47. *HMC Downshire*, v. 6, 299–300, 2 Oct. 1617, John Castle to William Trumbull; McCray, 34–5, 22 Nov. 1617, Thomas Paulyn to Sir Richard Beaumont; Emily Ross, 'The Case of the Crying Bride: Gossip Letters about the Wedding of Frances Coke', *Comitatus: A Journal of Medieval and Renaissance Studies*, v. 40 (2009), 231–47.

48. SP 14/93/156, 6 Oct. 1617, Gerrard Herbert to Dudley Carleton; McClure, v. 2, 100–1, 11 Oct. 1617, Chamberlain to Carleton; McCray, 34–5, 22 Nov. 1617, Thomas Paulyn to Sir Richard Beaumont.

49. For more on early modern food, see Joan Thirsk, *Food in Early Modern England: Phases, Fads, and Fashions 1500–1760* (New York: Continuum Books, 2006); Stuart Peachy, *The Book of Pies, 1580–1660, volume I: Pastry and Meat Pies* (Bristol: Historical Management Associates, 1995); Alison Sim, *Food and Feast in Tudor England* (New York: St. Martin's Press, 1997).

50. SP 14/93/156, 6 Oct. 1617, Gerrard Herbert to Dudley Carleton; McClure, v. 2, 100–1, 11 Oct. 1617, Chamberlain to Carleton; McCray, 34–5, 22 Nov. 1617, Thomas Paulyn to Sir Richard Beaumont.

51. McClure, v. 1, 424, 18 Feb. 1613, John Chamberlain to Alice Carleton. Similarly, James also visited his early favourite Philip Herbert, Earl of Montgomery, and his new bride Susan de Vere after their court wedding in 1604. Sawyer, v. 2, 43, Jan. 1604, Dudley Carleton to Ralph Winwood.

52. SP 14/93/156, 6 Oct. 1617, Gerrard Herbert to Dudley Carleton.

53. McClure, v. 1, 495–7, 30 Dec. 1617, Chamberlain to Alice Carleton. *HMC Dudley*, v. 5, 414, 27 Sept. 1617, Robert Sidney to Barbara Sidney.

Chapter 3

1. McClure, v. 2, 11 Oct. 1617, Chamberlain to Carleton. The king also thanked Lord Craven for his service in keeping Lady Hatton in his custody. SP 14/154/5, 4 Nov. 1617, King James to Craven.

2. Petition quoted in Bayle, v. 1, 387–8.

3. *CSP Domestic (James 1611–1618)*, 493, 4 Nov. 1617, Gerard Herbert to Carleton; McClure, v. 2, 110, 31 Oct. 1617, Chamberlain to Carleton.

4. McClure, v. 2, 113–14, 8 Nov. 1617, Chamberlain to Carleton.

5. SP 14/154/15, 8 Nov. 1617, John Pory to Carleton; SP 14/154/23, Nov. 1617, John Peyton to Carleton; SP 14/154/24, Nov. 1617, Sir Horace Vere to Carleton; McClure, v. 2, 117–18, 15 Nov. 1617, Chamberlain to Carleton.

6. SP 14/154/6b, 4 Nov. 1617, Gerard Herbert to Carleton; SP 14/154/29, 14 Nov. 1617, Nathaniel Brent to Carleton; SP 14/154/23, Nov. 1617, John Peyton to Carleton; SP 14/154/24, Nov. 1716, Sir Horace Vere to Carleton; SP 14/156/94, 30 March 1618, Nathaniel Brent to Carleton; McClure, v. 2, 101, 11 Oct. 1617, Chamberlain to Carleton; ibid., 114, 8 Nov. 1617, Chamberlain to Carleton; ibid., 126, 3 Jan. 1618, Chamberlain to Carleton; ibid., 110, 31 Oct. 1617, Chamberlain to Carleton; ibid., 113–14, 8 Nov. 1617, Chamberlain to Carleton.

7. Stephen White, *Sir Edward Coke and the Grievances of the Commonwealth* (Manchester: Manchester University Press, 1979), 9; Thrush and Ferris, v. 3, 560–97; Drinker Bowen, 435–57.

8. McClure, v. 2, 141, 14 Feb. 1618, Chamberlain to Carleton.

9. I have written about the Lake–Exeter feud in a previous book. See Rickman, 81–3, 86–8, 90.

10. BL Additional MS 5834, fol. 4, 5; Robert Johnston's *Historia Rerum Britannicarum* (Amsterdam, 1655); Arthur Wilson, *The History of Great Britain, being the Life and Reign of King James I* (London, 1653), 147.

11. Twentieth-century writers have tended to be a little more nuanced in their assessment, although they all agree that John was a not a good match for Frances. Thomas Longueville, who first wrote about Frances's story in 1909, was the most tempered and said that John was 'unattractive and much older' than Frances. In her 1936 biography of Lady Hatton, Norsworthy stated that John was 'a dismal knight a good deal older' than Frances and that he was 'repugnant to her'. Novelist Hilda Lewis described John as an old fool, with 'melancholy dog's eyes', a 'weak chin', and a 'thin beard'. Primarily, these earlier authors tend to focus on making John seem as unattractive as possible in order to be better able to 'justify' Frances's later adultery. The more horrible John was, the easier to forgive Frances's transgressions. Thomas Longueville, *The Curious Case of Lady Purbeck: A Scandal of the XVIIth Century* (London: Longman, Green, and Co., 1909), 23, 80–1; Hilda Lewis, *Call Lady Purbeck* (New York: St. Martin's Press, 1961), 27; Norsworthy, 37, 117.

12. If he had been twenty-five, he would have been born in 1592. However, according to Lockyer's biography, Buckingham was born in August of 1592, which, if true, must mean that John was born the year before, in 1591, or potentially in 1590. Lockyer, *Buckingham*, 3.

13. Lockyer, *Buckingham*, 33–4; Thomas Birch, ed., *The Court and Times of James the First; Illustrated by Authentic and Confidential Letters from Various Public and Private Collections* (London: Henry Colburn, 1849), v. 2, 78–9, 30 June 1618, Thomas Lorkin to Sir Thomas Puckering.

14. McClure, v. 2, 239–41, 31 May 1619, Chamberlain to Carleton; ibid., 243, 19 June 1619, Chamberlain to Carleton; ibid., 248–9, 26 June 1619, Chamberlain to Carleton.

15. J. B. Nichols, *The Progresses, Processions, and Magnificent Festivities of King James the First* (London: J. B. Nichols, 1828), v. 3, 176; Lockyer, *Buckingham*, 38.

16. SP 14/112/20, 18 Jan. 1620, Francis Nethersole to Carleton.

17. McClure v. 2, 254, 31 July 1619, Chamberlain to Carleton.

18. McClure, v. 2, 239–41, 31 May 1619, Chamberlain to Carleton; ibid., 248–9, 26 June 1619, Chamberlain to Carleton.

19. The *Secret History of James I* (John Phillips, 1690s) says Purbeck 'had more wit and honesty than all the kindred beside and did keep him in some bounds of honesty and modesty, whilst he lived about him, & would speake plaine English to him', quoted in Longueville, *The Curious Case of Lady Purbeck*, 64; Lockyer, *Buckingham*, 42–4.

20. McClure, v. 2, 279, 1 Jan. 1620, Chamberlain to Carleton.

21. *CSP Venetian*, v. 16 (1619–1621), 108–9, 10 Jan. 1620, Girolamo Lando to Doge and Senate; ibid., 120, 12 Jan. 1620, Lando to Doge and Senate.

22. McClure, v. 2, 282, 8 Jan. 1620, Chamberlain to Carleton.

23. McClure, v. 2, 279, 1 Jan. 1620, Chamberlain to Carleton.

24. McClure, v. 2, 413, 1 Dec. 1621, Chamberlain to Carleton; ibid., 419–20, 4 Jan. 1622, Chamberlain to Carleton.

25. McClure, v. 2, 100, 11 Oct. 1617, Chamberlain to Carleton.

26. Seddon, v. 2, 180–1, 26 July 1617, John Holles to Thomas Lake (in Scotland at the time); ibid., 181, 1 Aug. 1617, John Holles to Duke of Lennox; ibid., 189, 6 Aug. 1617, Holles to Thomas Lake.

27. Seddon, v. 2, 181, 1 Aug. 1617, John Holles to Duke of Lennox.

28. McClure, v. 2, 119–20, 29 Nov. 1617, Chamberlain to Carleton; *HMC Downshire*, v. 6, 357, 27 Dec. 1617, John Castle to William Trumbull.

29. McClure, v. 2, 319, 16 Sept. 1620, Chamberlain to Carleton; BL Additional 5834 F. 5.

30. *LJ*, v. 3, 5–201; McClure, v. 2, 402, 20 Oct. 1621, Chamberlain to Carleton; Page, v. 4, 462–6.
31. SP 14/151/116, 30? Aug. 1623, Katherine, Duchess of Buckingham to Secretary Conway.
32. Lockyer, *Buckingham*, 58–60.
33. The masque is reprinted in Nichols, *James*, v. 4, 673–709.
34. While the actors are not specifically named, clues within the play suggest that Buckingham led the band of gypsies and that John was among them as well. Nichols, *James*, v. 4, 683, n.2.
35. Nichols, *James*, v. 4, 673.
36. Lockyer, *Buckingham*, 115; John Lawson Parker, *The Life and Times of William Laud, Lord Archbishop of Canterbury* (London: C. J. G and F. Rivington, 1829), v. 1, 217–24; William Laud, *The Works of the Most Revered Father in God, William Laud D.D., sometime Archbishop of Canterbury* (Oxford: John Henry Press, 1853–7), v. 3, 138–9; Longueville, *The Curious Case of Lady Purbeck*, 67–8.
37. McClure, v. 2, 439, 8 June 1622, Chamberlain to Carleton.
38. *CJ*, v. 1, 705–6, 19 May 1624.
39. SP 14/152/9, 2 Sept. 1623, John Hippisley to Secretary Conway.
40. SP 14/152/16, 5 Sept. 1623, King James to Purbeck. The other letters: SP 14/214/42, 27 Aug. 1623, Secretary Conway to John Hippisley; SP 14/214/42, 2 Sept. 1623, Sir John Hippisley to Secretary Conway; SP 14/152/9, 2 Sept. 1623, John Hippisley to Secretary Conway; SP 14/214/43, 6 Sept. 1623, Secretary Conway to Lord Treasurer Middlesex.
41. *LJ*, v. 3, 205. John is not marked as attending any of the other days of Parliament during 1624.
42. McClure, v. 2, 573, 24 July 1624, Chamberlain to Carleton; *CSP Domestic (James 1623–1625)*, 322, 7 Aug. 1624, Secretary Conway to John Haughton.
43. SP 84/115/172, undated, calendared under 1623, Lady Hatton, Earl of Essex, and Lady Purbeck to Dudley Carleton.
44. Yorke, 307–8, 14 Sept. 1623, Carleton to Chamberlain.
45. John Smyth, *The Berkeley Manuscripts: The Lives of the Berkeleys* (Gloucester: John Bellows, 1883), v. 1, 256; Nichols, *James*, v. 4, 722; Thrush and Ferris, v. 3, 206–7.
46. SP 15/42/74, undated, but probably 1620.
47. Frances's 1641 petition printed in *A True State of the Proofs Offered at the Bar of the House of Lords, by Robert, son and heir of Robert, and grandson of John, late Lord Viscount Purbeck, to prove the legitimacy of Robert the father* (London, 1678).
48. *Cabala Sine Scrinia Sacra Mysteries of State and Government: In Letters of Illustrious Persons and Great Agents; in the Reign of Henry the Eight, Queen Elizabeth, K; James, and the Late King Charles* (London: G. Bede and T. Collins, 1654), v. 1, 313–14, undated, Lady Purbeck to the Duke of Buckingham.
49. McClure, v. 2, 439, 8 June 1622, Chamberlain to Carleton.
50. The petition in *A True State of the Proofs*.

Chapter 4

1. *ODNB*, 'Thomas Howard, Earl of Suffolk', 'Katherine Knyvett'.
2. Thrush and Ferris, v. 4, 814–15; H. Kent Staple Causton, *The Howard Papers, with a Biographical Pedigree and Criticism* (London: Henry Kent Causton and Son, 1862), 524. The *ODNB* gives 1584/5 as Howard's year of birth, but it is not correct. His parents married in 1583 and Howard's oldest brother Theophilus was born in 1584. Since Howard was the

fifth son, it would be impossible for him to be born only a year later. *ODNB*, 'Sir Robert Howard'.

3. *ODNB*, 'William Cecil, 2nd Earl Salisbury'; Lockyer, *Buckingham*, 56–7; McClure, v. 2, 533, 20 Dec. 1623, Chamberlain to Carleton.

4. McClure, v. 2, 474–5, 9 Sept. 1613, John Chamberlain to Dudley Carleton; T. B. Howell, ed., *A Complete Collection of State Trials and Proceedings for High treason and Other Crimes and Misdemeanors from the Earliest Period to the Year 1783* (London: T. C. Hansard, 1816), v. 2, 785–7; BL Additional 4129, f. 18.

5. *HMC Buccleuch*, v. 1, 140, 21 July 1613, Naunton to Secretary Winwood; McClure, v. 1, 469, 1 Aug. 1613, Chamberlain to Carleton; ibid., 478, 14 Oct. 1613, Chamberlain to Carleton; ibid., 495, 30 Dec. 1613, Chamberlain to Alice Carleton.

6. For full accounts and analysis of the murder, see Alastair Bellany, *The Politics of Court Scandal in Early Modern England* (New York: Cambridge University Press, 2002); David Lindley, *The Trials of Frances Howard: Fact and Fiction at the Court of King James* (New York: Routledge, 1993); Anne Somerset, *Unnatural Murder: Poison at the Court of King James* (London: Weidenfeld & Nicolson, 1997).

7. Nichols, *James*, v. 3, 215–20.

8. *CSP Domestic, James I (1619–1623)*, 13 Nov. 1618, Star Chamber Proceedings against Earl of Suffolk.

9. McClure, v. 2, Chamberlain's letters from Nov. 1618 to Oct. 1620: pp. 187, 199, 202, 204, 207, 225, 227–8, 238, 243, 263, 267–8, 272–5, 277–8, 281, 283–4, 313, 321. On the scandal, see also Linda Peck, *Court Patronage and Corruption in Early Stuart England* (Boston: Unwin Hyman, 1990), 181–4; SP 14/116/59, 3 Aug. 1620, John Woodford to Francis Nethersole.

10. Thomas became Earl of Berkshire, Edward became 1st Baron Howard of Escrick, Elizabeth married William Knollys, Earl of Banbury, Katherine married William Cecil, Earl of Salisbury, and Frances of course was a countess twice over, first as a result of her marriage to Robert Devereaux, Earl of Essex, and then, after the annulment, to Robert Carr, Earl of Somerset.

11. Thrush and Ferris, v. 4, 814–15; Causton, 510–11.

12. G. H. Gater and E. P. Wheeler, eds., *Survey of London: volume 18: St Martin-in-the-Fields II: The Strand* (London: London County Council, 1937) 10–20.

13. David Lindley, ed., *Court Masques: Jacobean and Caroline Entertainments, 1605–1640* (Oxford: Clarendon Press, 1995), 275, 277, 280; *ODNB*, 'Frances Howard'; Somerset, 35–6; Barroll, 91, 101–2.

14. McClure, v. 2, 88–90, 19 July, 1617, Chamberlain to Carleton.

15. McClure, v. 2, 199, 9 Jan. 1619, Chamberlain to Carleton; ibid., 533, 20 Dec. 1623, Chamberlain to Carleton; Lockyer, *Buckingham*, 60, 64–5; Nichols, *James*, v. 4, 946.

16. SP 14/183/50, Witness depositions in Frances's initial adultery investigation.

17. SP 14/183/50. The bed is now on display at the Victoria and Albert Museum in London: 'The Great Bed of Ware', Victoria and Albert Museum, accessed 1 July 2014, <http://www.vam.ac.uk/content/articles/t/the-great-bed-of-ware/>; 'The Great Bed of Ware', accessed 1 July 2014, <http://www.greatbedofware.org.uk/>.

18. Lauren Kassell, *Medicine and Magic in Elizabethan London: Simon Forman, Astrologer, Alchemist, and Physician* (Oxford: Clarendon Press, 2005), 1–2, 136, 210–25; Barbara Howard Traister, *The Notorious Astrological Physician of London: Works and Days of Simon Forman* (Chicago: University of Chicago Press, 2001), 3–30; A. L. Rowse, *Simon Forman: Sex and Society in Shakespeare's Age* (London: Weidenfeld & Nicolson, 1974), 192–215, 239–64.

19. Bellany, *The Politics of Court Scandal*, 144–8; Lindley, *Trials of Frances Howard*, 166–7, 176–80.
20. Alaistair Bellany, 'The Murder of John Lambe: Crowd Violence, Court Scandal and Popular Politics in Early Seventeenth-Century England', *Past & Present*, v. 200 (August, 2008), 37–76.
21. SP 14/183/50.
22. SP 14/183/50.
23. Bellany, 'The Murder of John Lambe', 37–9.
24. For an overview of the legal landscape of illicit sex in early modern England, see Rickman, 19–24.
25. Angus McClaren, *Reproductive Rituals: The Perception of Fertility in England from the Sixteenth Century to the Nineteenth Century* (New York: Methuen, 1984), 58–62.
26. Patricia Crawford, *Blood, Bodies and Families in Early Modern England* (Edinburgh: Pearson, 2004), 54–78; Maryanne Cline Horowitz, 'The Science of Embryology Before the Discovery of the Ovum', in Marilyn Boxer and Jean Quataert, eds., *Connecting Spheres: European Women in a Globalizing World, 1500 to the Present* (New York: Oxford University Press, 2000), 104–12.
27. Jennifer Evans, 'Gentle Purges corrected with hot Spices, whether they work or not, do vehemently provoke Venery: Menstrual Provocation and Procreation in Early Modern England', *Social History of Medicine*, v. 25 (2012), 2–19; Crawford, *Blood, Bodies, and Families*, 63–72; McClaren, 57–88.
28. Anne-Marie Kilday, *A History of Infanticide in Britain c.1600 to the Present* (New York: Palgrave Macmillan, 2015), 16–19, see also chap. 2 in the same book.
29. Richard Burns, *Ecclesiastical Law* (London: Stahan and Woodfall, 1788), v. 1, 110.
30. *HMC Hastings*, v. 2, 29, 29 March 1581, Francis Walsingham to Earl of Huntington; A. L. Rowse, *Sir Walter Raleigh: His Family and Private Life* (New York: Harper, 1962), 160.
31. Susan Vincent, *Dressing the Elite: Clothes in Early Modern England* (New York: Berg, 2003), 13–41; Anna Reynolds, *In Fine Style: The Art of Tudor and Stuart Fashion* (Royal Collection Trust, 2013), 33–77; Valerie Cumming, *A Visual History of Costume: The Seventeenth Century* (New York: Drama Books Publishers, 1984), 18–39.
32. The petition in *A True State of the Proofs*.
33. Adrian Wilson, *Ritual and Conflict: The Social Relations of Childbirth in Early Modern England* (Aldershot: Ashgate, 2013), chap. 4; Linda Pollock, 'Childbearing and Female Bonding in Early Modern England', *Social History*, v. 22 (1997), 286–306.
34. SP 14/183/50, 13 Feb. 1625, examinations sent to Buckingham from Solicitor General Heath. This source calls Elizabeth Ashley by the last name 'Ash', but other sources (*LJ* and *APC*) call her 'Mrs Ashley'. For the sake of consistency, I call her Elizabeth Ashley throughout. BL Additional MS 5834, f. 10; BL Additional 33896, note stating the entry in the church book of the baptism in Cripplegate.
35. Chamberlain remarked that it 'wold have done her more harm fortie yeares ago than they can do now' implying that the Countess's beauty had faded somewhat already, as had her court career, since her illness happened just as she and her husband's corruption scandal was under way. McClure, v. 2, 216–17, 20 Feb. 1619, Chamberlain to Carleton.
36. McClure, v. 2, 593, 18 Dec. 1624, Chamberlain to Carleton.

Chapter 5

1. McClure, v. 2, 599, 12 Feb. 1625, Chamberlain to Carleton.
2. Laud, v. 3, 156.

3. McClure, v. 2, 599, 12 Feb. 1625, Chamberlain to Carleton.

4. SP 14/183/41, 11 Feb. 1625, Buckingham to the Lord Chief Justice.

5. Bellany, *The Politics of Court Scandal*, 218–92, 231–2, 245–7; Roger Lockyer, *James IV and I* (New York; Longman, 1998), 35, 209; Alan Stewart, *The Cradle King: A Life of James VI and I* (London: Chatto & Windus, 2003), 146–7.

6. I discuss this history of adultery in Rickman, 22–4. See also Keith Thomas, 'The Puritans and Adultery: The Act of 1650 Reconsidered', in Donald Pennington and Keith Thomas, eds., *Puritans and Revolutionaries: Essays in Seventeenth-Century History Presented to Christopher Hill* (Oxford: Clarendon Press, 1978), 257–82; Robert Johnson and Maija Jansson Cole, eds., *Proceedings in Parliament 1628* (New Haven: Yale University Press, 1977), v. 2, 323, 329, 330–2; v. 3, 22, 26, 30, 34, 37; Simon D'Ewes, *A Compleate Journal of the Votes, Speeches and Debates, both of the House of Lords and House of Commons throughout the Whole Reign of Queen Elizabeth, of Glorious Memorie* (Wilmington, DE: Scholarly Resources, 1974), 641; Edward Cardwell, ed., *The Reformation of the Ecclesiastical Laws as Attempted in the Reigns of King Henry VIII, King Edward VI, and Queen Elizabeth* (Oxford: Oxford University Press, 1850), iii–v, 49–58.

7. Rickman, 19–22. See also Martin Ingram, *Church Courts, Sex, and Marriage in England, 1570–1640* (Cambridge: Cambridge University Press, 1987);Walter King, 'Punishment for Bastardy in Early Seventeenth-Century England', *Albion*, v. 10 (1978), 130–51; G. R. Quaife, *Wanton Wenches and Wayward Wives: Peasants and Illicit Sex in Early Seventeenth-Century England* (New Brunswick: Rutgers University Press, 1979); Richard Adair, *Courtship, Illegitimacy and Marriage in Early Modern England* (Manchester: Manchester University Press, 1996); Peter Laslett, Karla Oosterveen, and Richard Smith, eds., *Bastardy and Its Comparative History* (Cambridge, MA: Harvard University Press, 1980).

8. Johnson and Jansson Cole, v. 2, 329.

9. Rickman, chaps. 1 and 2. For the story of Mary Wroth and the Earl of Pembroke, see chap. 4.

10. SP 14/184/7, 19 Feb. 1625, Coventry and Heath to Buckingham.

11. SP 14/183/52, 13 Feb. 1625, Buckingham to Lord Chief Justice Sir Ranulphe Crewe.

12. Lockyer, *Buckingham*, 205–6.

13. SP 14/182/79, Jan. 1625, Sir John Coke to Buckingham.

14. SP 14/183/50, Notes on witness depositions; BL Additional 5834, f. 4 mentions that the midwife was questioned.

15. SP 14/183/50, Notes on witness depositions.

16. McClure, v. 2, 601, 26 Feb. 1625, Chamberlain to Carleton.

17. SP 14/184/7, 19 Feb. 1625, Innocent Lanier to Buckingham.

18. SP 14/183/50.

19. McClure, v. 2, 601, 26 Feb. 1625, Chamberlain to Carleton.

20. SP 16/26/176, June (?) 1626, Laud to Buckingham; Laud, v. 3, 154, 157.

21. For a good overview on early modern European witchcraft, see Bengt Ankarloo, Stuart Clark, and William Monter, *Witchcraft and Magic in Europe: The Period of the Witch Trials* (Philadelphia: University of Philadelphia Press, 2002). On the details of the sexual psychology of witchcraft, see for example Lyndal Roper, *Witch Craze: Terror and Fantasy in Baroque Germany* (New Haven: Yale University Press, 2004).

22. SP 14/188/50, 13 Feb. 1625, Buckingham to Coventry; SP 14/188/50, 16 Feb. 1625, Buckingham to Heath.

23. McClure, v. 2, 605, 12 March 1626, Chamberlain to Carleton.

24. SP 14/183/52, 13 Feb. 1625, Buckingham to the Lord Chief Justice.
25. *APC*, v. 39, 493–4.
26. SP 14/184/71, 19 Feb. 1625, Coventry and Heath to Buckingham; McClure, v. 2, 601, 26 Feb. 1625, Chamberlain to Carleton.
27. SP 14/183/52, 13 Feb. 1625, Buckingham to Lord Chief Justice. Buckingham expressed the same fear to Heath on 16 Feb.
28. McClure, v. 2, 619, 21 May 1625, Chamberlain to Carleton; William Bidwell and Maija Jansson, eds., *Proceedings in Parliament 1626* (New Haven: Yale University Press, 1991–6), v. 3, 102.
29. Lockyer, *Buckingham*, 285–6.
30. Roland Usher, *The Rise and Fall of the Court of High Commission* (Oxford: Clarendon Press, 1913), chaps. 1–3, 11–14; Bidwell and Jansson, v. 2, 330.
31. Usher, 367–71.
32. Frances's first appearance was on 5 March. *APC*, v. 39, 493–4; Laud, v. 3, 157.
33. Seddon, v. 2, 299, 2 March 1625, John, Lord Holles to Earl of Somerset. On William as Charles's servant: SP 14/214/9, 17 March 1623, and SP 14/214, 17 March 1623.
34. McClure, v. 2, 605, 12 March 1625, Chamberlain to Carleton; BL Additional 5834, f. 7; Bidwell and Jansson, v. 2, 327–8, 330.
35. Bidwell and Jansson, v. 2, 327–8, 330; *Cabala Sine Scrinia Sacra*, 103–4, 11 March 1625, Lord Keeper Williams to Buckingham; ibid., 13 March 1625, same to same.
36. Bidwell and Jansson, v. 2, 327–8, 330; McClure, v. 2, 607–8, 23 March 1625, Chamberlain to Carleton.
37. R. B. Outhwaite, *The Rise and Fall of the English Ecclesiastical Courts, 1500–1860* (Cambridge: Cambridge University Press), 12–13.
38. Thrush and Ferris, v. 4, 814–15.
39. BL Additional 5834, f. 5–7.
40. *Cabala Sine Scrinia Sacra*, 103–4, 11 March 1625, Lord Keeper Williams to Buckingham; ibid., 13 March 1625, same to same; McClure, v. 2, 601, 26 Feb. 1625, Chamberlain to Carleton.
41. McClure, v. 2, 599, 12 Feb. 1625, Chamberlain to Carleton.
42. McClure, v. 2, 599, 12 Feb. 1599, Chamberlain to Carleton; ibid., 605, 12 March 1625, same to same; ibid., 607, 23 March 1625, same to same; BL Additional 5834, f. 6–7; Frances's 1641 petition in *A True State of the Proofs*.
43. *Cabala Sine Scrinia Sacra*, 103–4, 11 March 1625, Lord Keeper Williams to Buckingham.
44. Anu Korhonen, 'Laughter, Sex, and Violence: Constructing Gender in Early Modern English Jestbooks', in Anna Foka and Jonas Liliequist, eds., *Laughter, Humor, and the (Un)making of Gender: Historical and Cultural Perspectives* (New York: Palgrave Macmillan, 2015), 133–50; Seddon, v. 2, 300–1, 4 March 1625, John Holles to George Holles; Johnson and Jansson, v. 2, 329; v. 3, 26, 30.
45. BL Additional 5834, f. 6–7.
46. McClure, v. 2, 607–8, 23 March 1625, Chamberlain to Carleton.
47. *Cabala Sine Scrinia Sacra*, 104, 13 March 1625, John Williams to Buckingham.
48. Bellany and Cogswell, 25–43; Nichols, *James*, v. 4, 1028–34; Stewart, 341–6; Lockyer, *Buckingham*, 233–4. Bellany and Cogswell's excellent book explores at great length the rumour—and the long life and meanings of that rumour—that Buckingham had poisoned James.
49. Outhwaite, *The Rise and Fall of the English Ecclesiastical Courts*, 10; Usher, 258–64.

Chapter 6

1. Nichols, *James*, v. 4, 1034–49; Bellany and Cogswell, 44–54.
2. Maurice Lee, *Great Britain's Solomon: King James VI and I in His Three Kingdoms* (Urbana: University of Illinois Press, 1990),264–93; Lockyer, *Buckingham*, 125–63; Stewart, 315–29.
3. Katie Whitaker, *A Royal Passion: The Turbulent Marriage of King Charles I of England and Henrietta Maria of France* (London: Norton, 2010), 32–43; Alison Plowden, *Henrietta Maria, Charles I's Indomitable Queen* (Phoenix Mill: Sutton Publishing, 2001), 16–21.
4. Quentin Bone, *Henrietta Maria, Queen of the Cavaliers* (Urbana: University of Illinois Press, 1972), 33–6; Ruth Kleinman, *Anne of Austria, Queen of France* (Columbus: Ohio State University Press, 1985), 62–9.
5. Kleinman, 62–9; Bone, 32–6; Whitaker, 45; Lockyer, *Buckingham*, 236–41.
6. Lita-Rose Betcherman, *Court Lady and Country Wife: Two Noble Sisters in Seventeenth-Century England* (New York: HarperCollins, 2005), 84–6; Lockyer, *Buckingham*, 60.
7. See Bone, chap. 2; Plowden, chaps. 2–3; Whitaker, chaps. 2–5.
8. Brydges's mother, Mary Hopton Brydges, Baroness Chandos, had a house in Stepney, and Brydges mentioned 'his chamber at his Mother's at Stepney' in 1624. His mother died in October 1624, possibly leaving the whole house to her son. *The Gentleman's Magazine: And Historical Chronicle, From January to June, 1826*, v. 139 (London: John Nichols, 1826), 107–10.
9. The articles of accusations and the examinations are in BL Additional 38855, f. 46–8.
10. BL Additional 38855, f. 46–8.
11. BL Additional 38855, f. 46–8.
12. Cyprien de Gamaches, *The Court and Times of Charles the First* (London: Henry Colburn, 1848), 12, 23 April 1625, Joseph Meade to Sir Martin Stuteville; McClure, v. 2, 441–2, 22 June 1622, Chamberlain to Carleton.
13. SP 16/3/62, 9 June 1625, John Williams to Secretary Conway.
14. Paul Slack, *The Impact of Plague in Tudor and Stuart England* (London: Routledge, 1985), 7–9.
15. A. W. Sloan, 'Plague in London under the Early Stuarts', *South African Medical Journal*, v. 48 (April 1974), 882–8; Slack, 207–16, 277–9, 282–303.
16. Sloan, 882–8; Charles Carlton, *Charles I: The Personal Monarch* (New York: Routledge, 1995), 69–70; LJ, v. 3, June through August, 1625.
17. Sloan, 882–8; Carlton, 69–70. Slack argues that there were 26,350 plague burials in London and its liberties in 1625. Slack, 151.
18. Lockyer, *Buckingham*, 414. The portrait of Buckingham now belongs to the Art Gallery of South Australia in Adelaide, and can be viewed on their webpage, <http://www.artgallery.sa.gov.au/agsa/home/Collection/detail.jsp?ecatKey=13098>.
19. Bidwell and Jansson, v. 1, 70.
20. William Paley Baildon, *Les Reports del Cases in Camera Stellata 1593–1609, from the Original MS. Of John Hawarde of the Inner Temple, Esquire, Barrister-at-law* (London, privately printed, 1894), 237–41.
21. Bidwell and Jansson, v. 1, 71, 75–7, 85, 87, 92, 94, 97, 99–101, 119, 122, 138, 143, 145, 156–7, 179, 603, 615, 620–1; LJ (1620–1628), v. 3, 491, 6 Feb. 1626, proxy entered. The journal lists attendance for each day Parliament met, February through June, and John was absent every day.
22. Bidwell and Jansson, v. 2, 60–5, 68, 328–34; v. 3, 99–105, 141–5, 148–52, 414, 445.
23. BL Additional 5834, f. 4; Lockyer, *Buckingham*, 408; Laud, v. 3, 202.

24. SP 16/85/68; Laud, v. 3, 206, 392–5; Birch, *Charles*, v. 1, 296, 30 Nov. 1627, letter from London to Joseph Mead (?). William Laud was Bishop of Bath and Wells at the time, and one of the judges in the case.
25. Laud, v. 3, 206, 392–5; Birch, *Charles I*, v. 1, 296, 30 Nov. 1627, letter from London to Joseph Mead (?).
26. Outhwaite, *The Rise and Fall of the English Ecclesiastical Courts*, 10–11.
27. Seddon, v. 2, 375, 7 Dec. 1627, John Holles, Earl of Clare to John Holles, Lord Haughton.
28. APC, v. 43, 191–2, 19 Dec. 1627.
29. APC, v. 43, 191–2, 19 Dec. 1627.
30. John Fenitt, *Finetti Philoxenis: Some Choice Observations of Sir John Fenitt, Knight and Master of Ceremonies to the Two Last Kings, Touching the Reception and Precedence, and Treatment and Audience, the Punctillos and Contrasts, of Forren Ambassadors in England* (London, 1656), 286–8.
31. *CSP Venice*, v. 20, 565, 20 Jan. 1628, Alvise Contarini, Venetian Ambassador, to the Doge and Senate; Fenitt, 286–8; Birch, *Charles*, v. 1, 312, 12 Jan. 1628, Rev. Joseph Mead to Sir Martin Stuterville; Robert Johnston's eyewitness account in BL Additional 5834, f. 6–7.
32. APC, v. 43, 217–18.
33. *CSP Venice*, v. 20, 565, 20 Jan. 1628, Alvise Contarini, Venetian Ambassador, to the Doge and Senate; Fenitt, 287–8.
34. Seddon, v. 2, 375, 7 Dec. 1627, John Holles, Earl of Clare, to John Holles, Lord Houghton.
35. Birch, *Charles*, v. 1, 312, 12 Jan. 1628, Joseph Mead to Martin Stuteville.
36. BL Additional 5834, f. 6–7.
37. APC, v. 43, 239, 15 Jan. 1628; ibid., 300, 16 Feb. 1628; Birch, *Charles I*, v. 1, 317, 2 Feb. 1628, Joseph Mead to Sir Martin Stuteville.
38. Lockyer, *Buckingham*, 419; Laud, v. 3, 207.
39. Johnson and Jansson Cole, v. 5, 171.
40. Johnson and Jansson Cole, v. 5, 264–5; *LJ*, v. 3, 685, 712–15.
41. Johnson and Jansson Cole, v. 5, 264–6, 293, 311, 314, 353–4, 356, 358–61, 726–7.

Chapter 7

1. Laud, v. 3, 393.
2. *Transactions of the Shropshire Archeological and Natural History Society* (Shrewsbury: Adnitt and Naunton, 1888), v. 11, 261. In 1642, Howard was staying in 'his bed' in Hopesay, recovering from an illness, suggesting he had a house there. *Transactions of the Shropshire*, 2nd series, v. 6, 35–6, 23 Aug. 1642, Frances Newport to Francis Ottley. Norsworthy suggested the Hall in the Forest as their residence, but gave no sources. Norsworthy, 194–5.
3. Bellany, 'The Murder of John Lambe'.
4. Bellany, 'Murder of John Lambe', 63–4.
5. HMC *Salisbury*, v. 22, 244–5; Lockyer, *Buckingham*, 451–9; Whitaker, 100.
6. Edward Hyde, Earl of Clarendon, *The History of the Rebellion and Civil Wars in England* (Oxford: Clarendon Press, 1826), v. 1, 17–18.
7. Undated letters between Katherine, Duchess of Buckingham, and Mary, Countess of Buckingham, HMC *Fourth Report*, 256.
8. ODNB, 'Christopher Villiers', 'George Villiers'; HMC *Fourth Report*, 256.
9. Richard Cust, *Charles I and the Aristocracy, 1625–1642* (New York: Cambridge University Press, 2013), 81. According to Cust, who has carefully studied the court participation of the nobility during the reign of Charles, Purbeck was part of a group of peers who 'kept their distance from the royal court' during the 1630s, in the case of Purbeck, because of his health.

10. SP 16/200/30, 27 Sept. 1631, Charles to Mary, Countess of Buckingham; SP 16/202/28, 26 Oct. 1631, Sir Henry Berkeley to Secretary Dorchester.
11. Laud, v. 3, 393.
12. Bidwell and Jansson, v. 2, 60–1.
13. Arthur Searle, ed., *Barrington Family Letters 1628–1632* (London: Royal Historical Society, 1983), 235–7, April 1632, Sir Thomas Barrington to Lady Barrington; ibid., 238–9, same to same.
14. Valentine Groebner, 'Losing Face, Saving Face: Noses and Honour in the Late Medieval Town', *History Workshop Journal*, v. 40 (1995), 1–15.
15. William Knowler, ed., *The Earl of Stafforde's Letters and Dispatches With an Essay Towards his Life* (London: William Bowyer, 1739), v. 1, 390, 17 March 1635, G. Garrard to Stafford.
16. White, 10; Lyon and Block, 329–30; SP 16/272/125, 165, 26 July 1634, King Charles to Secretary Windebank.
17. From Coke's inventory of 'Household Stuffe at Stoke which never was Sir Xtofer Hatton's', quoted in Drinker Bowen, 526.
18. Norsworthy, 196–7.
19. Seddon, v. 3, 386, 24 July 1628, John Holles, Earl of Clare to the Bishop of Lincoln.
20. Coke's diary, quoted in Drinker Bowen, 532–3.
21. Birch, *Charles I*, v. 2, 93–4, 30 Jan. 1631, Joseph Mead to Martin Stuteville.
22. Quoted in Drinker Bowen, 534.
23. Drinker Bowen, 533, 34, SP 16/278/17, 4 Dec. 1634, Secretary Windebank to Edward Nichols; SP 16/278/56 9, 1634, same to same; SP 16/278/73, 10 Dec. 1634, list of papers removed from Lincoln's Inn.
24. McClure, v. 2, 484, 8 March 1623, Chamberlain to Carleton.
25. Knowler, v. 1, 265–6, 20 June 1634, G. Garrard to Strafford.
26. PROBATE 11/167/125, will of Sir Edward Coke, probated 7 Feb. 1635; SP 16/280/11, undated, filed under 1634, note from Dr Sweit regarding Coke's will, which had been confiscated; SP 16/280/12, undated, filed under 1634. Elizabeth Hatton's petition to King Charles.
27. SP 16/280/13, undated, filed under 1634, petition of Sir Maurice Berkeley to King Charles.
28. PROB 11/167/125, will of Sir Edward Coke. The will calls Crewe 'Randall' instead of 'Ranulphe'. It seems his name was spelled in several different ways.
29. SP 16/280/12, undated, filed under 1634, Elizabeth Hatton's petition to King Charles.
30. SP 16/310/85, undated, Frances, Lady Purbeck to Secretary Windebank.
31. Laud, v. 3, 394; SP 16/313/58, 14 March 1635, warrants; Knowler, v. 1, 390, 17 March 1635, G. Garrard to Stafford.
32. For example, see the description of the long-time imprisonment of the Earl of Northumberland in Betcherman, 1–2, 46–7; and of the orders to Lady Penelope Rich's husband to provide his lady with bedding, linens, hangings, a cook, as well as other servants, APC, v. 31, 167, 176; and Anne Clifford visiting the Countess of Somerset and her little daughter in the Tower in 1619, Clifford, 73.
33. SP 14/183/52, 13 Feb. 1625, Buckingham to Lord Chief Justice.
34. Christopher Durston, *Charles I* (New York: Routledge, 1998), 5, 14; Carleton, *Charles I*, 59, 105, 108, 113–14; Whitaker, 99–116; Bone, 67–93; Plowden, 70–100. Anthony Adolph has suggested that Charles II was potentially Jermyn's child. Anthony Adolph, *The King's Henchman: The Commoner and the Royal who Saved the Monarchy from Cromwell* (London: Gibson Square, 2014), 49–61.
35. Betcherman, 62–5, 88–91.

36. Kevin Sharpe, *The Personal Rule of Charles I* (New Haven: Yale University Press, 1992), 190, 210–12; Carleton, *Charles I*, 59, 62, 135–7; Cust, *Charles*, 150–1; Karen Britland, 'Queen Henrietta Maria's Theatrical Patronage', in Erica Gaffney, ed., *Henrietta Maria: Piety, Politics, and Patronage* (Aldershot: Ashgate, 2008), 57–72; SP 16/442/188, 23 Jan. 1640, Robert Reade to Windebank.
37. McCray, 58–9, 29 Sept. 1618, William Dynely to Sir Richard Beaumont.
38. *ODNB*, 'Christopher Villiers'.
39. Sharpe, 190, 212; Adolph, 67–73; *HMC 12th Report*, v. 2, 40–1, 1633, Henry Jermyn to King Charles; SP 16/238/55, 6 May 1633, Examination of Eleanor Villiers; SP 16/246/48, 12 Sept. 1633, Nicholas to John Pennington.
40. Sharpe, 190, 212; Adolph, 67–73; *HMC 12th Report*, v. 2, 40–1, 1633, Henry Jermyn to King Charles; SP 16/238/55, 6 May 1633, Examination of Eleanor Villiers; SP 16/246/48, 12 Sept. 1633, Nicholas to John Pennington; McCray, v. 1, 175, 9 Jan. 1634, Garrard to Earl of Strafford.
41. On Charles's personality and dislike of challenges, see Durston, 5–6, 8–9; Sharpe, 192–7.
42. *Acts of the Court of High Commission*, in *CSP Domestic, Charles*, (1635), v. 8, 178, 181.
43. *Acts of the Court of High Commission*, in *CSP Domestic, Charles*, (1635), v. 8, 181, 190, 197.
44. Laud, v. 7, 128, 12 May 1635, Laud to Strafford; Knowler, v. 1, 423, 14 May 1635, James Howell to Strafford; ibid., 19 May 1635, G. Garrard to Strafford; ibid., 434, 24 June 1635, Garrard to Strafford.
45. *Acts of the Court of High Commission*, in *CSP Domestic, Charles I*, (1635), v. 8, 197, 202, 205, 227.
46. Knowler, v. 1, 447, 30 July 1635, Garrard to Strafford.

Chapter 8

1. Knowler, v. 1, 447, 30 July 1635, Garrard to Strafford.
2. SP 16/313/117, 8 Feb. 1636.
3. SP 78/100/205, 7 March 1636, John Coke to John Scudamore.
4. SP 16/317/30, 25 March 1636, John Scudamore to John Coke.
5. Wilmer Hunt McCorquodale, 'The Court of Louis XIII: The French Court in an Age of Turmoil, 1610–1643', PhD dissertation, University of Texas at Austin, 1994 (Ann Arbor: UMI, 1994), 148–56, 295; A. Loyd Moote, *Louis XIII, the Just* (Berkeley: University of California Press, 1989), 267–8.
6. *CSP Domestic, Charles I (1635–1636)*, 322, 25 March 1636, John Scudamore to John Coke.
7. R. T. Petersson, *Sir Kenelm Digby, the Ornament of England 1603–1665* (Cambridge, MA: Harvard University Press, 1959), 139–42; E. W. Bligh, *Sir Kenelm Digby and his Venetia* (London: Sampson Low, Marston, 1932), 250; Thomas Longueville, *The Life of Sir Kenelm Digby* (London: Longman, Green, and Co., 1896).
8. Petersson, 143–7.
9. SP 16/344/58, 21/31 Jan. 1636, Sir Kenelm Digby to Edward Conway. It is calendared in 1637, but the context suggests that it was written in 1636. Digby was using New Style dating as the French did.
10. Kenelm Digby, *A Conference with a Lady about Choice of Religion* (Paris, 1638), 29.
11. Quoted in Petersson, 142; Bligh, 251.
12. SP 16/344/58, 21/31 Jan. 1636, Sir Kenelm Digby to Edward Conway.
13. Birch, *Charles I*, v. 2, 242, 13 April 1636, E. R. to Thomas Puckering.
14. Birch, *Charles I*, v. 2, 242, 13 April 1636, E. R. to Thomas Puckering. The French extraordinary ambassador was Henri de la Ferté-Neverre, Marquis de Senecterre (1635–1637). C. H. Firth and

S. C. Lomas, *Notes on the Relations of England and France, 1603–1688: Lists of Ambassadors from England to France, and from France to England* (Oxford: B. H. Blackwell, 1906), 35.

15. Birch, *Charles I*, v. 2, 242, 13 April 1636, E. R. to Thomas Puckering.
16. SP 16/310/85, undated, Frances Purbeck to Francis Windebank. The letter has 1635 noted on it in a later hand, but in all likelihood it is spring 1636, since it mentions her suit to the queen made at that time.
17. SP 16/310/85, Frances Purbeck to Francis Windebank.
18. F. C. Husenbeth, *Notices of the English Colleges and Convents Established on the Continent after the Dissolution of the Religious Houses in England* (Norwich: Bacon and Kinnebrook, 1849), 56–7.
19. Peterson, 141–2.
20. SP 78/101/284, 11 July 1636, John Scudamore to Francis Windebank.
21. SP 16/329/27, 20 July 1636, Theophilus, Earl of Suffolk, to the Privy Council.
22. SP 16/337/161, 22 Dec. 1636, Theophilus, Earl of Suffolk, to the Privy Council.
23. SP 78/102/315, 22 Dec. 1636, John Coke to John Scudamore.
24. Birch, *Charles I*, v. 2, 260, 4 Jan. 1637, E. R. to Mr Puckering.
25. Birch, *Charles I*, v. 2, 268, 17 Jan. 1637, E. R. to Mr Puckering.
26. Bone, 88–92, 100–6; Whitaker, 141–7.
27. Knowler, v. 2, 73, 28 April 1637, Garrard to Stafford.
28. *CPCC*, 1075.
29. SP 78/105/212, 19 March 1638, Augier to unknown.
30. Alan G. R. Smith, *The Emergence of a Nation State: The Commonwealth of England 1529–1660* (London and New York: Longman, 1984), 268–99.
31. *ODNB*, 'Francis Windebank'.
32. The two lawyers were Sir Henry Marten and Sir John Lambe (no relation to the dead doctor and magician). *LJ*, v. 4, 113–14, 21 Dec. 1640.
33. Laud, v. 3, 395.

Chapter 9

1. Lady Purbeck's petition, in *A True State of the Proofs*.
2. Lady Purbeck's petition, in *A True State of the Proofs*.
3. *CJ*, v. 4, 458–60, 10 Jan. 1641.
4. Lady Purbeck's petition, in *A True State of the Proofs*.
5. *LJ*, v. 4, 168–70, 246–7, 275–6, 296, 302–4 (22 Feb., 12 May, 15 June, 20 June, 5 July, 6 July 1641).
6. Outhwaite, *The Rise and Fall of the English Ecclesiastical Courts*, 78; 17 Car. I. cap. 11. *Statutes of the Realm*, v. 112 in Samuel Rawson Gardiner ed., *The Constitutional Documents of the Puritan Revolution, 1625–1660* (Oxford: Clarendon Press, 1906), chap. 35.
7. The lack of clear evidence about Frances's living arrangements has caused earlier writers to misinterpret the course of her life. Longueville argued that a chastened and reformed viscountess returned to her patient and forgiving husband and resumed her married life, after more than a decade and a half of separation and estrangement. Longueville based this assertion on a brief note in the manuscripts collected by the eighteenth-century antiquary William Cole. Cole had found a cache of '14 or 15 loose Papers' written by a Mr Browne Willis in the latter part of the seventeenth century, dealing with the case of Frances because some of Robert's descendants were then trying to resurrect and claim the Viscount Purbeck title. The note that Longueville focused on, however, was not written by Willis, but by someone else, on a small scrap of paper. Among other genealogical

information regarding the Villiers family, the note said that 'Lord Purbeck after 16 years took his wife again, and owned the son'. The writer confused several of the persons involved, including Frances herself, getting her mixed up with her son's wife. While Longueville recognized the many mistakes in the writing, he willingly chose to believe that the part about Frances returning to her husband was correct, even though Willis had neatly noted underneath it: 'Never saw, or owned his wife again, or owned her son, & gave him Nothing in his Will. She died 1645, cohabiting with Sir Robert Howard'. Longueville, *The Curious Case of Lady Purbeck*, 137–9.

8. *LJ*, v. 4, 56–8 (18 April 1640), 45–81 (April–May).

9. SP 16/463/221, 10 Aug. 1640, the king on behalf of John, Viscount Purbeck; SP 16/469/1, 1 Oct. 1640, Secretary Windebank to Purbeck's servant.

10. *LJ*, v. 4, 92, 16 Nov. 1640.

11. *A True State of the Proofs*. These statements may be slanted, though, considering they were preserved and presented as evidence by Robert's descendants, when they were working hard to prove the legitimacy of Robert, and thus their claim to the Purbeck title.

12. SP 16/463/221, 10 Aug. 1640, the king on behalf of John, Viscount Purbeck.

13. PROB 11/200/312, Lady Hatton's will.

14. *Transactions of Shropshire*, s. 2, v. 6, 35–6, 253, 286–7; Causton, *Howard Papers*, 525.

15. He was excused from sitting in 1642 and 1643, and listed as absent in 1644. *LJ*, v. 5, 7–9 (21 April 1642), v. 6, 387–90 (22 Jan. 1644), v. 8, 117–22 (23 Jan. 1646).

16. *LJ*, v. 5, 667–70 (24 March 1643); v. 7, 158–62 (28 Jan. 1645); v. 8, 269–70 (13 April 1646).

17. *LJ*, v. 9, 369–73, 3 Aug. 1647.

18. Quoted in Norsworthy, 244–6.

19. PROB 11/200/312.

20. *CPCC*, 1075.

21. *CJ*, v. 4, 468–71, 9 March 1646; *CPCC*, 857.

22. *LJ*, v. 6, 173–4 (9 Aug 1643); *LJ*, v. 7, 94–6 (12 Dec. 1644).

23. Norsworthy, 248; Causton, 528. Two listings, 29 October 1644 and 8 December 1644. 'At the Committee of the House of Commons for Execucons'.

24. *CJ*, v. 2, 753–5 (6 Sept. 1642); Braddock, 315–16, 326–7. The records of the Oxford Parliament were burned shortly before Oxford fell in 1646.

25. Ann Fanshawe, *The Memoirs of Ann, Lady Fanshawe* (London: J. Lane, 1907), 24–5.

26. Clark, 115, 246.

27. *CPCC*, 1292; *CJ*, v. 6, 566–7, 24 April 1651; *CJ*, v. 7, 131, 12 May 1652.

28. Causton, 528–32; *Transactions of Shropshire*, s. 2, v. 7, 399–400; *ODNB*, 'Edward, Lord Vaux', 'Katherine Howard', 'William Knollys, Earl of Banbury'.

29. *Transactions of Shropshire*, s. 2, v. 7, 392–4. Thanks also to Rev. Anne Ogram, who kindly checked the church in Clun and found the brass plate still there.

30. PROB 6/28/189 1653–4, v. 3, f. 189.

31. *CJ*, v. 8, 258–9, 24 May 1661; *CJ*, v. 8, 263–4, 1 June 1661; *LJ*, v. 11, 550–1 (6 July 1663), 551–2 (7 July 1663); Causton, 528–9.

32. C 6/51/49.

33. PROB 11/177, ff. 218v–19v.

34. PROB 11/274/129.

35. *CPCC*, 1075.

36. PROB 11/200/312.

37. *CPCC*, 1075; Mary Anne Everett Green, ed., *Calendar of Proceedings of the Committee for the Advancement of Money, 1642–1656* (London: H. M. Stationary Office, 1888), v. 2, 667–8.

38. PROB 11/249/637.
39. BL Stowe MS 671, f. 109.
40. BL Stowe MS 671, f. 106, 109, 123.
41. BL Stowe MS 671, f. 107, 122, 123; *HMC Seventh Report*, 110, 117, 126–7.
42. SP 29/28/154, 19 Jan. 1661, Deposition of John Quarley; *CSP Dom Charles II (1661–1662)*, v. 2, 320, Licence for Elizabeth and Robert Villiers to take name Danvers; SP 29/100/161, 27 July 1664, Danvers escape; SP 29/362/137, 10 Nov. 1674, Francis Bastnick to Williamson; *ODNB*, 'Robert Danvers'; Basil Duke Henning, ed., *The History of Parliament: The House of Commons, 1660–1690* (London: Secker & Warburg, 1983), v. 2, 'Robert Danvers alias Villiers (formerly Wright and Howard)'.

Epilogue

1. Bernard Burke, *A Genealogical History of the Dormant, Abeyant, and Extinct Peerages of the English Empire* (London: Harrion, 1866), 559. She continued to call herself Lady Purbeck, even after her second marriage to John Duvall. *LJ*, v. 14, 333–4, 366–7 (7 Nov., 10 Dec. 1689), v. 15, 674–5, 712 (19 Feb., 20 March 1696), v. 16, 481–2 (6 Dec. 1699).
2. *LJ*, v. 12, 672–4 (30 April 1675). Danvers/Villiers had written the petition on 22 April.
3. *A True State of the Proofs*; Sloane MS 2753, f. 39; BL Stowe MS 671, f. 122, 124–32.
4. *A True State of the Proofs*; BL Sloane MS 2753, f. 37–9, BL Stowe MS 671, f. 132–51.
5. *LJ*, v. 12, 678–80, 683–4, 695–7, 699–701 (5, 12, 18, 20 May 1675), v. 13, 15–17 (10 Nov. 1675), 58–60, 63–4 (3, 7 March 1677), 182–3, 192–3, 203–5, 216–17, 221–6, 239, 241–2, 249–250, 251–3, 255–6, 261–4, 274–5, 276–9, 281–3 (14, 22 March, 15 April, 10, 23 May, 5, 7, 15, 18, 20, 26, 27 June, 6, 9, 11 July 1678); SP 29/402/99, 14 March 1678.

Bibliographic Essay

1. Emily Ross, 'The Current of Events: Gossip about the Controversial Marriages of Lady Arbella Stuart and Frances Coke in Jacobean England, 1610–1620', PhD dissertation, University of Otago, Dunedin, New Zealand, 2009; Ross, 'The Case of the Crying Bride: Gossip Letters about the Wedding of Frances Coke'; Ross, 'Whose Letter is it Anyway? An Assessment of Secretarial Involvement in Lady Elizabeth Hatton's Correspondence', *Etudes Epistémè*, no. 21 (2012) [online].
2. Hodgson; Midi Berry, *Nights of the Road* (Self-published, 2015).

SELECT BIBLIOGRAPHY

Manuscript Sources

British Library, London (BL)
    Additional Manuscripts
    Egerton Manuscripts
    Stowe Manuscripts
London Metropolitan Archives (LMA)
Public Record Office, Kew
    Chancery (C)
    Probate (PROB)
    Star Chamber (STAC)
    State Papers (SP)

Printed Primary Sources

Anon. 'Lord Bacon and Sir Edward Coke'. *Athenaeum: Journal of Literature, Science, and the Fine Arts*, 17 May 1862, 661–2.

A True State of the Proofs Offered at the Bar of the House of Lords, by Robert, Son and Heir of Robert, and Grandson of John, late Lord Viscount Purbeck, to Prove the Legitimacy of Robert the Father. London, 1678.

Aubrey, John. *Brief Lives*, ed. Andrew Clark. 2 vols. Oxford: Clarendon Press, 1898.

Baildon, William Paley. *Les Reports del Cases in Camera Stellata 1593–1609, from the Original MS. Of John Hawarde of the Inner Temple, Esquire, Barrister-at-law*. London: privately printed, 1894.

Bidwell, William B. and Maija Jansson, eds. *Proceedings in Parliament 1626*. 4 vols. New Haven: Yale University Press, 1991–6.

Birch, Thomas, ed. *The Court and Times of Charles the First; Illustrated by Authentic and Confidential Letters from Various Public and Private Collections*. 2 vols. London: Henry Colburn, 1848.

Birch, Thomas, ed. *The Court and Times of James the First; Illustrated by Authentic and Confidential Letters from Various Public and Private Collections*. 2 vols. London: Henry Colburn, 1849.

Bray, Gerald, ed. *The Anglican Canons, 1529–1947*. Woodbridge: A Church of England Record Society Publication by Boydell Press, 1998.

Brennan, Michael G., Noel Kinnamon, and Margaret P. Hannay, eds. *The Letters of Rowland Whyte (1595–1608)*. Philadelphia: American Philosophical Society, 2013.

Cabala Sine Scrinia Sacra, Mysteries of State & Government: in Letters of Illustrious Persons and Great Agents; in the Reigns of Henry the Eight, Queen Elizabeth, K: James, and the late King Charles. London: G. Bede and T. Collins, 1654.

Calendar of State Papers, Domestic Series of the Reign of Charles I, Preserved in the State Paper Department and M. Public Record Office (CSP Domestic, Charles I). 23 vols. London: Longman, 1858–72.

Calendar of State Papers, Domestic Series of the Reign of Charles II, Preserved in the State Paper Department and M. Public Record Office (CSP Domestic, Charles II). 28 vols. London: Longman, 1860–1939.

Calendar of State Papers, Domestic Series of the Reign of Elizabeth, Preserved in the State Paper Department and H.M. Public Record Office (CSP Domestic, Elizabeth I). 7 vols. London: Longman, 1858–71.

Calendar of State Papers, Domestic Series of the Reign of James I, Preserved in the State Paper Department and M. Public Record Office (CSP Domestic, James I). 4 vols. London: Longman, 1856–72.

Calendar of State Papers, Domestic Series of the Reign of James II, Preserved in the State Paper Department and M. Public Record Office (CSP Domestic, James II). 3 vols. London: Longman, 1960–72.

Calendar of State Papers and Manuscripts, Relating to English Affairs, Existing in the Archives and Collections of Venice (CSP Venice). 38 vols. London: Her Majesty's Stationery Office, 1900–12.

Castiglione, Baldassare. The Book of the Courtier, trans. Thomas Hoby. London, 1561.

Clarendon, Edward Hyde, Earl. The History of the Rebellion and Civil Wars in England. Vol. 1. Oxford: Clarendon Press, 1826.

Clark, Andrew, ed. Survey of the Antiquities in the City of Oxford Composed in 1661–6 by Anthony Wood. Oxford: Clarendon Press, 1899.

Clifford, D. J. H., ed. The Diaries of Anne Clifford. Stroud: Alan Sutton, 1990.

Dascent, John Roche, E. G. Atkinson, J. V. Lyle, R. F. Monger, and P. A. Penfold. Acts of the Privy Council of England. 46 vols. London: His Majesty's Stationery Office, 1938.

D'Ewes, Simon. A Compleate Journal of the Votes, Speeches and Debates, both of the House of Lords and House of Commons throughout the Whole Reign of Queen Elizabeth, of Glorious Memorie. Wilmington, DE: Scholarly Resources, 1974.

Digby, Kenelm. A Conference with a Lady about Choice of Religion. Paris, 1638.

Fanshawe, Ann. The Memoirs of Ann, Lady Fanshawe. London: J. Lane, 1907.

Fenitt, John. Finetti Philoxenis: Some Choice Observations of Sir John Fenitt, Knight, and Master of Ceremonies to the Two Last Kings, Touching the Reception and Precedence, and Treatment and Audience, the Punctillos and Contrasts, of Forren Ambassadors in England. London, 1656.

Foster, Joseph, ed. London Marriage Licenses 1521–1869. London: Bernard Quaritch, 1887.

Gamaches, Cyprien de. The Court and Times of Charles the First. London: Henry Colburn, 1848.

Gardiner, Samuel Rawson, ed. The Constitutional Documents of the Puritan Revolution, 1625–1660. Oxford: Clarendon Press, 1906.

Green, May Anne Everett, ed. Calendar of Proceedings of the Committee for the Advancement of Money, 1642–1656. 3 vols. London: H. M. Stationery Office, 1888.

Green, Mary Anne Everett, ed. Calendar of Proceedings of the Committee for Compounding 1643–1660 (CPCC). London: Eyre and Spottiswoode, 1890.

Hannay, Margaret and Michael Brennan, eds. Domestic Politics and Family Absence: The Correspondence (1588–1621) of Robert Sidney, First Earl of Leicester, and Barbara Gamage Sidney, Countess of Leicester. Aldershot: Ashgate, 2005.

Historical Manuscript Commission. Calendar of the Most Hon., the Marquis of Salisbury; K. G. Preserved at Hatfield House, Hertfordshire (HMC Salisbury). 24 vols. London: H. M. Stationery Office, 1883–1996.

Historical Manuscript Commission. Fourth Report of the Royal Commission of Historical Manuscripts (HMC Fourth Report). London: Stationery Office, 1874.

Historical Manuscript Commission. Report on the Manuscripts of Lord de L'Isle and Dudley, Preserved at Penshurst Place (HMC Dudley). 6 vols. London: H. M. Stationery Office, 1925–66.

Historical Manuscript Commission. Report on the Manuscripts of the Marquess of Downshire (HMC Downshire). 6 vols. London: H. M. Stationery Office, 1924–96.

Historical Manuscript Commission. *Report on the Manuscripts of the Late Reginald Rawdon Hastings, Esq., of the Manor House of Ashby de la Zouche (HMC Hastings)*. 4 vols. London: H. M. Stationery Office, 1928–47.

Historical Manuscript Commission. *Reports on the Manuscripts of the Duke of Buccleuch and Queensberry, Preserved at Montagu House, Whitehall (HMC Buccleuch)*. 3 vols. London: Eyre and Spottiswoode, 1899.

Historical Manuscript Commission. *Seventh Report of the Royal Commission of Historical Manuscripts (HMC Seventh Report)*. London: Eyre and Spottiswoode, 1879.

Historical Manuscript Commission. *Twelfth Report of the Royal Commission on the Historical Manuscripts (HMC Twelfth Report)*. 3 vols. London, H. M. Stationery Office, 1890.

Howell, T. B. *A Complete Collection of State Trials and Proceedings for High Treason and Other Crimes and Misdemeanors from the Earliest Period to the Year 1783*. Vol. 2. London: T. C. Hansard, 1816.

Hyde, Edward, Earl of Clarendon. *The History of the Rebellion and Civil Wars in England*. Oxford: Oxford University Press, 1843.

Johnson, Robert C. and Maija Jansson Cole, eds. *Proceedings in Parliament 1628*. 5 vols. New Haven: Yale University Press, 1977–83.

Johnston, Robert. *Historia Rerum Britannicarum*. Amsterdam, 1655.

Journal of the House of Commons (CJ). Vols. 3–19. London: H. M. Stationery Office, 1767–1830.

Journal of the House of Lords (LJ). Vols. 1–16. London: H. M. Stationery Office, 1802–13.

Knowler, William, ed. *The Earl of Stafforde's Letters and Dispatches, With an Essay Towards his Life*. 2 vols. London: W. Bowyer, 1739.

Knox, John. *The First Blast of the Trumpet Against the Monstrous Regiment of Women* (1558). New York: Da Capo Press, 1972.

Laud, William. *The Works of the Most Revered Father in God, William Laud D.D., sometime Archbishop of Canterbury*. 7 vols. Oxford: John Henry Press, 1853–7.

Lee, Maurice, ed. *Dudley Carleton to John Chamberlain 1603–1624: Jacobean Letters*. New Brunswick: Rutgers University Press, 1972.

McClure, Norman Egbert, ed. *The Letters of John Chamberlain*. 2 vols. Philadelphia: American Philosophical Society, 1939.

McCray, W. D., ed. *Beaumont Papers: Letters Relating to the Family of Beaumont, of Whitley, Yorkshire, from the Fifteenth to the Seventeenth Centuries*. London: Nichols and Sons, 1884.

Madden, Frederick, Bulkeley Bandinel, and John Gough Nichols, eds. *Collectanea Topographica et Genealogica*. London: J. B. Nichols, 1840.

Newdigate-Newdegate, Lady, ed. *Gossip From a Muniment Room, Being Passages in the Lives of Anne and Mary Fytton 1574–1618*. London: David Nutt in the Strand, 1898.

Ridley, Sir Thomas. *A View of the Civile and Ecclesiastical Law: and Wherein the Practice is Streitened and May Be Relieved Within This Land*. 4th ed. Oxford, 1676.

Sawyer, Ralph. *Memorials of Affairs of State in the Reign of Q. Elizabeth and K. James I*. 3 vols. London: Printed for W. B. by T. Ward, 1775.

Searle, Arthur, ed. *Barrington Family Letters 1628–1632*. London: Royal Historical Society, 1983.

Seddon, P. R., ed. *Letters of John Holles, 1587–1637*. 3 vols. Nottingham: Thoroton Society, 1975.

Smyth, John. *The Berkeley Manuscripts: The Lives of the Berkeleys, Lords of the Manor, Honour and Castle of Berkeley in the County of Gloucester, from 1066–1618*, ed. Sir John Maclean. Vol. 1. Gloucester: John Bellows, 1883.

Stephens, Robert, ed. *Letters of Sir Francis Bacon, Baron of Verulam, Viscount St. Alban, and Lord High Chancellor of England. Written during the Reign of King James the First*. London: Benjamin Tooke, 1702.

Strype, John, ed. *The Life and Acts of John Whitgift*. 3 vols. Oxford: Clarendon Press, 1822.

Swinburne, Henry. *A Treatise of Spousals or Marriage Contracts*. London: Printed by S. Roycroft for Robert Clavell, 1686.

Wilson, Arthur. *The History of Great Britain, being the Life and Reign of King James I*. London, 1653.

Yorke, Philip, Earl of Hardwicke, ed. *Letters to and from Sir Dudley Carleton during his Embassy in Holland*. London, 1775.

Secondary Sources

Abbott, Mary. *Family Ties: English Families 1540–1920*. New York: Routledge, 1993.

Adair, Richard. *Courtship, Illegitimacy and Marriage in Early Modern England*. Manchester: Manchester University Press, 1996.

Adolph, Anthony. *The King's Henchman: The Commoner and the Royal who Saved the Monarchy from Cromwell*. London: Gibson Square, 2014.

Ankarloo, Bengt, Stuart Clark, and William Monter. *Witchcraft and Magic in Europe: The Period of the Witch Trials*. Philadelphia: University of Philadelphia Press, 2002.

Banks, George. *The Story of Corfe Castle*. London: John Murray, 1853.

Barroll, Leeds. *Anna of Denmark, Queen of England: A Cultural Biography*. Philadelphia: University of Pennsylvania Press, 2001.

Bayle, Pierre. *A General Dictionary Historical and Critical*, ed. and trans. John Peter Bernard, Thomas Birch, John Lockman, et al. 16 vols. London: James Bettenham, 1736.

Bellany, Alastair. 'The Murder of John Lambe: Crowd Violence, Court Scandal and Popular Politics in Early Seventeenth-Century England'. *Past & Present*, v. 200 (August 2008), 38–76.

Bellany, Alastair. *The Politics of Court Scandal in Early Modern England*. New York: Cambridge University Press, 2002.

Bellany, Alastair and Thomas Cogswell. *The Murder of King James*. New Haven: Yale University Press, 2015.

Bergeron, David M. *King James and Letters of Homoerotic Desire*. Iowa City: University of Iowa Press, 1999.

Bergeron, David M. *Royal Family, Royal Lovers: King James of England and Scotland*. Columbia: University of Missouri Press, 1991.

Berry, Midi. *Nights of the Road*. Self-published, 2015.

Betcherman, Lita-Rose. *Court Lady and Country Wife: Two Noble Sisters in Seventeenth-Century England*. New York: HarperCollins, 2005.

Blackstone, William. *Commentaries on the Laws of England: A Facsimile of the First Edition of 1765–1769*. Chicago: University of Chicago Press, 1979.

Bligh, E. W. *Sir Kenelm Digby and his Venetia*. London: Sampson Low, Marston, 1932.

Bone, Quentin. *Henrietta Maria, Queen of the Cavaliers*. Urbana: University of Illinois Press, 1972.

Bowen, Catherine Drinker. *The Lion and the Throne: The Life and Times of Sir Edward Coke (1552–1634)*. Boston: Little, Brown and Company, 1956.

Boxer, Marilyn and Jean Quataert, eds. *Connecting Spheres: European Women in a Globalizing World, 1500 to the Present*. New York: Oxford University Press, 2000.

Boyer, Allen. *Sir Edward Coke and the Elizabethan Age*. Stanford: Stanford University Press, 2003.

Braddick, Michael. *God's Fury, England's Fire: A New History of the English Civil Wars*. New York: Allen Lane, 2008.

Brundage, James. *Law, Sex and Christian Society in Medieval Europe*. Chicago: University of Chicago Press, 1987.

Burke, Bernard. *A Genealogical History of the Dormant, Abeyant, and Extinct Peerages of the English Empire*. London: Harrion, 1866.

Burns, Richard. *Ecclesiastical Law*. London: Stahan and Woodfall, 1788.

Campbell, John. *The Lives of the Chief Justices of England*. 4 vols. London: Murray, 1849.

Cardwell, Edward, ed. *The Reformation of the Ecclesiastical Laws as Attempted in the Reigns of King Henry VIII, King Edward VI, and Queen Elizabeth*. Oxford: Oxford University Press, 1850.

Carlton, Charles. *Charles I: The Personal Monarch*. New York: Routledge, 1995.

Causton, H. Kent Staple. *The Howard Papers, with a Biographical Pedigree and Criticism*. London: Henry Kent Causton and Son, 1862.

Classen, Albrecht, ed. *Childhood in the Middle Ages and the Renaissance: The Results of a Paradigm Shift in the History of Mentality*. Berlin: Walter de Gryuter, 2005.

Crawford, Patricia. *Blood, Bodies and Families in Early Modern England*. Edinburgh: Pearson, 2004.

Cruikshank, Eveline. *The Stuart Courts*. Thrupp: Sutton Publishing, 2000.

Cumming, Valerie. *A Visual History of Costume: The Seventeenth Century*. New York: Drama Books Publishers, 1984.

Cunningham, Hugh. *Children and Childhood in Western Society Since 1500*. New York: Longman, 1995.

Cust, Richard. *Charles I and the Aristocracy, 1625–1642*. New York: Cambridge University Press, 2013.

Donahue, Charles. *Law, Marriage and Society in the Later Middle Ages: Arguments About Marriage in Five Courts*. New York: Cambridge University Press, 2007.

Durston, Christopher. *Charles I*. New York: Routledge, 1998.

Erickson, Amy Louise. 'Common Law, Common Practice: The Use of Marriage Settlements in Early Modern England'. *Economic History Review*, v. 43 (1990), 21–39.

Evans, Jennifer. 'Gentle Purges corrected with hot Spices, whether they work or not, do vehemently provoke Venery: Menstrual Provocation and Procreation in Early Modern England'. *Social History of Medicine*, v. 25 (2012), 2–19.

Firth, C. H. and S. C. Lomas. *Notes on the Relations of England and France, 1603–1688: Lists of Ambassadors from England to France, and from France to England*. Oxford: B. H. Blackwell, 1906.

Foka, Anna and Jonas Liliequist, eds. *Laughter, Humor, and the (Un)making of Gender: Historical and Cultural Perspectives*. New York: Palgrave Macmillan, 2015.

Foyster, Elizabeth. *Meanings of Manhood in Early Modern England*. New York: Oxford University Press, 2003.

Gaffney, Erica, ed. *Henrietta Maria: Piety, Politics, and Patronage*. Aldershot: Ashgate, 2008.

Gater, G. H. and E. P. Wheeler, eds. *Survey of London: volume 18: St Martin-in-the-Fields II: The Strand*. London: London County Council, 1937.

The Gentleman's Magazine: And Historical Chronicle, From January to June, 1826, v. 139. London: John Nichols, 1826.

Goldring, Elizabeth, Faith Eales, Elizabeth Clarke, and Jayne Elisabeth Archer, eds. *John Nichols's The Progresses and Public Processions of Queen Elizabeth I: A New Edition of the Early Modern Sources*. 5 vols. Oxford: Oxford University Press, 2014.

'The Great Bed of Ware'. Accessed 1 July 2014, <http://www.greatbedofware.org.uk/>.

'The Great Bed of Ware'. Victoria and Albert Museum. Accessed 1 July 2014, <http://www.vam.ac.uk/content/articles/t/the-great-bed-of-ware/>.

Groebner, Valentine. 'Losing Face, Saving Face: Noses and Honour in the Late Medieval Town'. *History Workshop Journal*, v. 40 (1995), 1–15.

Hannay, Margaret. *Mary Sidney, Lady Wroth*. Aldershot: Ashgate, 2010.

Haw, Reginald. *The State of Matrimony: An Investigation of the Relationship between Ecclesiastical and Civil Marriage in England after the Reformation with a Consideration of the Laws relating thereto*. London: SPCK, 1952.

Henning, Basil Duke, ed. *The History of Parliament: The House of Commons, 1660–1690*. 3 vols. London: Secker & Warburg, 1983.

Herrup, Cynthia. *A House in Gross Disorder: Sex, Law and the Second Earl of Castlehaven*. New York: Oxford University Press, 1999.

Hodgson, Natalie. *Fateful Beauty: The Story of Frances Coke, 1602–1642*. London: Eye Books, 2006.

Husenbeth, F. C. *Notices of the English Colleges and Convents Established on the Continent after the Dissolution of the Religious Houses in England*. Norwich: Bacon and Kinnebrook, 1849.

Ingram, Martin. *Church Courts, Sex, and Marriage in England, 1570–1640*. Cambridge: Cambridge University Press, 1987.

Jardine, Lisa and Alan Stewart. *Hostage to Fortune: The Troubled Life of Francis Bacon*. London: Victor Gollancz, 1999.

Kassell, Lauren. *Medicine and Magic in Elizabethan London: Simon Forman, Astrologer, Alchemist, and Physician*. Oxford: Clarendon Press, 2005.

Kilday, Anne Marie. *A History of Infanticide in Britain c.1600 to the Present*. New York: Palgrave Macmillan, 2015.

King, Walter. 'Punishment for Bastardy in Early Seventeenth-Century England'. *Albion*, v. 10 (1978), 130–51.

Kleinman, Ruth. *Anne of Austria, Queen of France*. Columbus: Ohio State University Press, 1985.

Laslett, Peter. *The World We Have Lost, Further Explored*, 3rd ed. London: Routledge, 2000.

Laslett, Peter, Karla Oosterveen, and Richard Smith, eds. *Bastardy and its Comparative History*. Cambridge, MA: Harvard University Press, 1980.

Lee, Maurice. *Great Britain's Solomon: King James VI and I in His Three Kingdoms*. Urbana: University of Illinois Press, 1990.

Lewis, Hilda. *Call Lady Purbeck*. New York: St. Martin's Press, 1961.

Lindley, David. *Court Masques: Jacobean and Caroline Entertainments, 1605–1640*. Oxford: Clarendon Press, 1995.

Lindley, David. *The Trials of Frances Howard: Fact and Fiction at the Court of King James*. New York: Routledge, 1993.

Lockyer, Roger. *Buckingham: The Life and Political Career of George Villiers, First Duke of Buckingham 1592–1628*. New York: Longman, 1981.

Lockyer, Roger. *James IV and I*. New York: Longman, 1998.

Longueville, Thomas. *The Curious Case of Lady Purbeck: A Scandal of the XVIIth Century*. London: Longman, Green, and Co., 1909.

Longueville, Thomas. *The Life of Sir Kenelm Digby*. London: Longman, Green, and Co., 1896.

Loyd, David. *State-worthies, or the Statesmen and Favourites of England, from the Reformation to the Revolution*. Vol. 2. London: J. Robson, 1766.

Lyon, Hastings and Leon Block. *Edward Coke: Oracle of the Law*. New York: Houghton Mifflin, 1929.

McCarthy, Conor. *Marriage in Medieval England: Law, Literature, and Practice*. Rochester, NY: Boydell Press, 2004.

McClaren, Angus. *Reproductive Rituals: The Perception of Fertility in England from the Sixteenth Century to the Nineteenth Century*. New York: Methuen, 1984.

McCorquodale, Wilmer Hunt. 'The Court of Louis XIII: The French Court in an Age of Turmoil, 1610–1643'. PhD dissertation, University of Texas at Austin, 1994. Ann Arbor: UMI, 1994.

Macfarlane, Alan. *Marriage and Love in England: Modes of Reproduction 1300–1840*. Oxford: Blackwell, 1986.

McManus, Clare. *Women on the Renaissance Stage: Anna of Denmark and Female Masquing in the Stuart Court (1590–1619)*. New York: Manchester University Press, 2002.

Matthew, Henry and Brian Harrison, gen. eds. *Oxford Dictionary of National Biography (ODNB)*. 60 vols. Oxford: Oxford University Press, 2004.

Miller, Naomi J. and Naomi Yavneh, eds. *Gender and Early Modern Constructions of Childhood*. Aldershot: Ashgate, 2011.

Miller, Naomi J. and Naomi Yavneh, eds. *Maternal Measures: Figuring Caregiving in the Early Modern Period*. Aldershot: Ashgate, 2000.

Moote, A. Loyd. *Louis XIII, the Just*. Berkeley: University of California Press, 1989.

Nichols, J. B. *The Progresses, Processions, and Magnificent Festivities of King James the First*. 4 vols. London: J. B. Nichols, 1828.

Nichols, J. B. *The Progresses and Public Processions of Queen Elizabeth*. 3 vols. London: J. B. Nichols, 1823.

Norsworthy, Laura. *The Lady of Bleeding Heart Yard: Lady Elizabeth Hatton, 1578–1646*. New York: Harcourt Brace and Co., 1936.

O'Hara, Diana. *Courtship and Constraints: Rethinking Early Modern Marriage in Tudor England*. New York: Manchester University Press, 2000.

Outhwaite, R. B. *Clandestine Marriage in England, 1500–1850*. London: Hambledon Press, 1995.

Outhwaite, R. B. *The Rise and Fall of the English Ecclesiastical Courts, 1500–1860*. Cambridge: Cambridge University Press, 2006.

Page, William, ed. *A History of the County of Buckingham*. Vols. 3 and 4. London: Victoria County History, 1925.

Parker, John Lawson. *The Life and Times of William Laud, Lord Archbishop of Canterbury*. 2 vols. London: C. J. G and F. Rivington, 1829.

Peachy, Stuart. *The Book of Pies, 1580–1660, volume I: Pastry and Meat Pies*. Bristol: Historical Management Associates, 1995.

Peck, Linda. *Court Patronage and Corruption in Early Stuart England*. Boston: Unwin Hyman, 1990.

Pedersen, Frederick. *Marriage Disputes in Medieval England*. London: Hambledon Press, 2000.

Pennington, Donald and Keith Thomas, eds. *Puritans and Revolutionaries: Essays in Seventeenth-Century History Presented to Christopher Hill*. Oxford: Clarendon Press, 1978.

Petersson, R. T. *Sir Kenelm Digby, the Ornament of England 1603–1665*. Cambridge, MA: Harvard University Press, 1959.

Plowden, Alison. *Henrietta Maria, Charles I's Indomitable Queen*. Phoenix Mill: Sutton Publishing, 2001.

Pollock, Linda. 'Childbearing and Female Bonding in Early Modern England'. *Social History*, v. 22 (1997), 286–306.

Purkiss, Diane. *The English Civil War: Papists, Gentlewomen, Soldiers, and Witchfinders in the Birth of Modern Britain*. New York: Basic Books, 2006.

Quaife, G. R. *Wanton Wenches and Wayward Wives: Peasants and Illicit Sex in Early Seventeenth-Century England*. New Brunswick: Rutgers University Press, 1979.

Reynolds, Anna. *In Fine Style: The Art of Tudor and Stuart Fashion*. London: Royal Collection Trust, 2013.

Rickman, Johanna. *Love, Lust, and License in Early Modern England: Illicit Sex and the Nobility*. Aldershot: Ashgate, 2008.

Roper, Lyndal. *Witch Craze: Terror and Fantasy in Baroque Germany*. New Haven: Yale University Press, 2004.

Ross, Emily. 'The Case of the Crying Bride: Gossip Letters about the Wedding of Frances Coke'. *Comitatus: A Journal of Medieval & Renaissance Studies*, v. 40 (2009), 231–47.

Ross, Emily. 'The Current of Events: Gossip about the Controversial Marriages of Lady Arbella Stuart and Frances Coke in Jacobean England, 1610–1620'. PhD dissertation, University of Otago, Dunedin, New Zealand, 2009.

Ross, Emily. 'Whose Letter is it Anyway? An Assessment of Secretarial Involvement in Lady Elizabeth Hatton's Correspondence'. *Etudes Epistémè*, no. 21 (2012) [online].

Rowse, A. L. *Simon Forman: Sex and Society in Shakespeare's Age*. London: Weidenfeld & Nicolson, 1974.

Rowse, A. L. *Sir Walter Raleigh: His Family and Private Life*. New York: Harper, 1962.

Sharp, Kevin. *The Personal Rule of Charles I*. New Haven: Yale University Press, 1992.

Sim, Alison. *Food and Feast in Tudor England*. New York: St. Martin's Press, 1997.

Slack, Paul. *The Impact of Plague in Tudor and Stuart England*. London: Routledge, 1985.

Sloan, A. W. 'Plague in London under the Early Stuarts'. *South African Medical Journal*, v. 48 (April 1974), 882–8.

Smith, Alan G. R. *The Emergence of a Nation State: The Commonwealth of England 1529–1660*. London and New York: Longman, 1984.

Somerset, Anne. *Unnatural Murder: Poison at the Court of King James*. London: Weidenfeld & Nicolson, 1997.

Stewart, Alan. *The Cradle King: A Life of James VI and I*. London: Chatto & Windus, 2003.

Stretton, Tim. *Women Waging Law in Elizabethan England*. New York: Cambridge University Press, 1998.

Thirsk, Joan. *Food in Early Modern England: Phases, Fads, and Fashions 1500–1760*. New York: Continuum Books, 2006.

Thomas, Keith. 'The Puritans and Adultery: The Act of 1650 Reconsidered'. In Donald Pennington and Keith Thomas, eds., *Puritans and Revolutionaries: Essays in Seventeenth-Century History Presented to Christopher Hill*. Oxford: Clarendon Press, 1978, 257–82.

Thrush, Andrew and John P. Ferris. *The History of Parliament: The House of Commons 1604–1629*. 6 vols. Cambridge: Cambridge University Press, 2010.

Traister, Barbara Howard. *The Notorious Astrological Physician of London: Works and Days of Simon Forman*. Chicago: University of Chicago Press, 2001.

Transactions of the Shropshire Archeological and Natural History Society. 12 vols. Shrewsbury: Adnitt and Naunton, 1888–1930.

Usher, Roland. *The Rise and Fall of the Court of High Commission*. Oxford: Clarendon Press, 1913.

Vincent, Susan. *Dressing the Elite: Clothes in Early Modern England*. New York: Berg, 2003.

Whitaker, Katie. *A Royal Passion: The Turbulent Marriage of King Charles I of England and Henrietta Maria of France*. London: Norton, 2010.

White, Stephen. *Sir Edward Coke and the Grievances of the Commonwealth*. Manchester: Manchester University Press, 1979.

Wilson, Adrian. *Ritual and Conflict: The Social Relations of Childbirth in Early Modern England*. Aldershot: Ashgate, 2013.

Woolrych, Humphrey. *The Life of the Right Honourable Sir Edward Coke, Knt., Lord Chief Justice of the King's Bench*. South Hackensack: Rothman Reprints, 1972 (orig. 1826).

Wrigley, E. A., R. S. Davies, J. E. Oeppen, and R. S. Schofield. *English Population History from Family Reconstitution 1580–1837*. New York: Cambridge University Press, 1997.

Young, Michael. *James VI and I and the History of Homosexuality*. Basingstoke: Macmillan, 2000.

PICTURE CREDITS

1.1 Corfe Castle ruins, Isle of Purbeck, Dorset. Oxford University Press.

2.1 Hampton Court Palace, Hampton Court. Oxford University Press.

2.2 King James I of England and VI of Scotland. Daniel Mytens, 1621. National Portrait Gallery, London.

3.1 The Villiers family. William Greatbach, after George Perfect Harding (mid-nineteenth century), after original seventeenth-century painting. National Portrait Gallery, London.

3.2 Frances Coke Villiers, Viscountess Purbeck. Michiel van Miereveldt, c.1623. Ashdown House, Lambourn, UK. National Trust.

3.3 Ashdown House, Lambourn. Photo: Stocker1970/Shutterstock.

4.1 York Watergate, Victoria Embankment Garden, London. Photo: Chris Dorney/Shutterstock.

5.1 Lambeth Palace, London. Photo: Pete Spiro/Shutterstock.

6.1 Map of London, c.1600. Johanna Luthman and Alok Nath.

7.1 Rural landscape in Clun, Shropshire. Photo: Andrew Roland/Shutterstock.

7.2 Map of England and northern France. Johanna Luthman and Alok Nath.

7.3 Sir Edward Coke. John Payne, after unknown artist, 1628–9. National Portrait Gallery, London.

7.4 William Laud, Archbishop of Canterbury. After Anthony van Dyck, c.1635. National Portrait Gallery, London.

7.5 King Charles I, Queen Henrietta Maria, and their children, the future King Charles II and Princess Mary. Engraving by Bernard Baron (1741), after Antony van Dyck, 1632. National Portrait Gallery, London.

9.1 St Mary the Virgin, University Church in Oxford. Photo: Richard Semik/Shutterstock.

INDEX

Note: Figures are indicated by an italic *f* following the page number.